Unwrapping The Mysteries Of Asperger's

The Search for Truth and Discovery of Solutions - Guide For Girls and Women with Asperger's Syndrome

Kristi Hubbard

Foreword by Liane Holliday Willey

AuthorHouse™
1663 Liberty Drive
Bloomington, IN 47403
www.authorhouse.com
Phone: 1-800-839-8640

©2010 Kristi Hubbard. All rights reserved.

No part of this book may be reproduced, stored in a retrieval system, or transmitted by any means without the written permission of the author.

First published by AuthorHouse 3/31/2010

ISBN: 978-1-4490-9490-4 (e)
ISBN: 978-1-4490-9489-8 (sc)
ISBN: 978-1-4490-9488-1 (hc)

Library of Congress Control Number: 2010923980

Printed in the United States of America
Bloomington, Indiana

This book is printed on acid-free paper.

Foreword by Liane Holliday Willey

Editorial assistance provided by Brooke Rawlins

Type: Psychology/Autism; Reference/Personal and Practical Guides; Social Science/Women's Studies; Biography & Autobiography/General

This book is written as a source of information and insight. The information should not be used as a substitute for the advice of a qualified clinician, psychologist or medical professional. All efforts have been made to ensure the accuracy of the information presented as the date published. The author disclaims responsibility for any negative effect from the use or application of the information contained.

Note: Names of some of the people mentioned in this book have been changed to protect their identity.

Contents

Dedication vii
Foreword ix
Introduction xiii
What really is Asperger's, and How is it Similar to Autism? 1
Girls vs. Boys with Asperger's 21
Clues From Early Childhood 47
School Career as a Professional Student 65
The Real World, College and Autism 99
Learning How to Effectively Participate in a Family 111
Perception, Thinking, Recognizing Patterns and More 127
Overcoming Sensory Issues and Social Difficulties 159
The Search for Purpose and Absolute Truth 187
Solutions for Girls and Women 207
Insight for Caregivers and Teachers 249
Understanding and preventing autism 259

Dedication

My dear loved ones: my intelligent dad, my caring mom, my loving husband, my precious children, and my best friends. I love you.

Foreword

Kristi Hubbard's new book **Unwrapping The Mysteries of Aspergers: The Search for Truth and Discovery of Solutions, Guide for Girls and Women with Asperger's Syndrome** gives me the feeling I'm sitting with an old friend, having a cup of hot chocolate while we discuss matters important to our heart. Her enthusiasm behind her discovery of her Asperger's syndrome - what it is, what it means to society, how it touches people so differently and most interesting, how women in the AS community stand in their own little island - is catching and warming.

Woven around her first person experiences and scholarly references, is insight on many of the questions and concerns females with AS surely experience at some point in their life. I like that. It makes reading the book not just a lovely time spent with a friend, but also a teaching tool women and their supporters, can put to good use.

Kristi engages her readers with open-ended questions that tug for not just an answer, but rather, a dialogue that will lead to the clearing up of misunderstandings and the putting away of preconceived stereotypes. Kristi makes one think, explore and analyze the notion of AS making it clear there should be a cozy spot in this world for people on the spectrum to rest and be nurtured and respected and encouraged.

As engaging as the book is, in many ways it reminds me of a master's thesis. As an academic myself, I enjoy that style. It is not condescending. It is educational while remaining a slice of life. Teachers, I believe, will be particularly drawn to this book for that reason as much as any other. It's set up in a way that makes it possible to cherry pick this section or that, allowing the reader to concentrate on the academic research cited, or the discussion points illuminated, or the first person stories shared. That's cool. It makes the book a read everyone can enjoy on a number of levels.

When you read this book, prepare yourself to be moved by my favorite parts - the letters from Kristi's loved ones. If only everyone had these kinds of letters to cuddle with when times are low or feelings are hurt! They are letters that prove, no matter how different a soul might be, the goodness inside a person is the stuff that really matters.

While most of the book is a catalyst for positive discussion, it is about AS and by default that means there simply has to be some poignant moments, some tug at the heart sad passages. I for one, find the sad stuff surrounding AS stories to be difficult to read, but in some ways more important than the surface meaning would suggest. You see, for people with AS life can appear to be almost normal, almost without peril. But at the core, there will always be a hungry pit waiting for the social faux pas, the career mistake or the relationship struggle to hurl the Aspie downward. Kristi would have been remiss had she not included her hardships. Read them and ask yourself if you can be part of the future that helps people to avoid similar struggles, simply because they were an Aspie - a person with a different mindset than most others.

Get this book and put it on your coffee table. It will provide a stress-free way for others to be introduced to AS, the world of AS for women, and the realization that AS is not something to be neither afraid of nor ashamed of. Put a stack of sticky notes by the book and let people mark their favorite passages. Ask them to write thoughts about those passages on their notes. Then share those notes with each other. That's what this book will move you to do - to talk, to grow and to learn together.

Liane Holliday Willey

Liane Holliday Willey, EdD, is the author of the international best selling books, **Pretending to be Normal: Living with Asperger's Syndrome; Asperger Syndrome in the Family: Redefining Normal;** and **Asperger**

Syndrome in Adolescence: Living With the Ups, the Downs and Things in Between (ed). In addition, Liane has contributed to many other books and journals and is also the senior editor of the magajournal *Autism Spectrum Quarterly.* Many newspapers have featured Liane and her work, and she has been on many national and international radio shows. Liane, having Asperger's, is a writer, editor, consultant, motivational speaker, freelance author, mother and wife.

Introduction

There was a group of girls, age 13, and I was one of them. I felt like I was looking at them through the opposite end of a pair of binoculars. They seemed so far away and so out of reach. We were all sitting on the floor of the school gym in a big clump. They were all talking, laughing and having fun. Why wasn't I talking, laughing and having fun with them? Why did they all hush up, turn and stare at me when I said something? I was not able to interpret what they were thinking by the bizarre looks on their faces. Why couldn't I join in their happy discussions? They all talked about make-up, shoes and name-brand clothes and seemed to be so passionate about hairstyles, fashion and painting their nails. I didn't enjoy those things. Was there something wrong with me? Why was I so different from them?

One morning during my first semester of graduate school, one of my classmates handed me a sheet of paper. "I heard you worked with children who had autism and thought you may be interested in this," she said. I saw the heading "Characteristics of Asperger's Syndrome." I had heard the word "Asperger's" just a couple of years before. From my understanding Asperger's simply meant, "mild autism." I was currently working with a child who had autism whose older brother was diagnosed with Asperger's syndrome. His brother seemed pretty "normal" to me. When I met this child, he was in a typical classroom. He conversed well with his friends and with me. I had assumed that because of these factors, he had overcome his "mild autism." Apparently, I was wrong. I did not know what "mild autism" was. And at that point in my education I also neglected to understand that autism was a large spectrum of differences expressed in many ways by a multitude of individuals.

I began reading through the list of Asperger's characteristics and suddenly felt I could no longer breath. The world stopped momentarily – or at least my world. Taking things literally, difficulty understanding sarcasm, difficulty with small talk, obsessed with facts and rules – the list continued on as my eyes quickly scanned the long list of Asperger's idiosyncrasies. Certain lights being bothersome, specific sounds perceived as irritating, dislike certain textures, difficulty in social situations, preference for friendships with older and younger people - the list went on and on - filled with familiarity. Tendency to be a loner, preference to communicate through written form rather than face-to-face, difficulty with reading body language, visual learner… I paused and placed the paper aside. How is it that I can relate to this list? I picked up the list and began scrutinizing. Tuning things out of non-interest, easily stressed, only able to focus on one thing at a time, appearance of sometimes being in own world, bluntness, difficulty expressing empathy, preference for non-fiction rather than fiction, easily distracted and startled. I read through that list over and over as I realized that I, myself, had most of those characteristics. Surely I didn't have Asperger's syndrome! Me, have "mild autism," no way!

I later brought the paper home to show to my husband hoping that my silly perception had gotten the best of me. "This list describes you," he blurted out. For the next several days and nights, my husband's words and that dreaded list played over and over in my head like someone was in charge of a remote control; constantly pressing rewind and play, rewind and play, rewind and play. I had thousands of flashbacks of my childhood and adolescence of when "Asperger's" explained it. All those other girls, talking and laughing, talking and laughing. I didn't understand them; they didn't understand me. I was the black sheep. Who is that weird girl I saw in the mirror? What about all those times I asked my parents to stop chewing so loudly? People getting mad at me for being rude and unsympathetic. "You don't pay attention, you are not listening.…" There is a problem, I have to get a book, where is a book to help me solve that problem!? I have to have the facts, what are the statistics? NO! The flag is red, everybody get out of the ocean, and it's a rule! Sitting on strangers' laps. Those awful socks and terrible blue jeans. "You are so weird!" Please turn off that light! I have to write a letter, I just can't say it face to face. Silly and oblivious. I am going to jump out of my skin, I can't sit still, emotions are strangling me, I am drowning in something I don't know what!

"Oh, so that explains it." I have Asperger's Syndrome. FINALLY, there was an explanation of why I had been so different and have had such difficulty with social situations and making friends my entire life. My Dad. My Dad has it too! He doesn't even know what it is. I have to tell him.

I had many questions and I wanted answers. I wanted to know what autism really was, what caused it, how it was related to Asperger's and how to prevent it. As a truth and knowledge seeker, I read everything I could find. I want to share what I have found.

Despite my new realization, I made the decision to keep my having Asperger's a secret. After all, it wasn't even diagnosed to people until 1994. That weird word was unknown to all my friends and family. I liked attention, but not that particular kind of attention. I didn't want anyone to worry about me, since it was considered a "disorder."

I did not feel the need to go pay a clinician to give me an official diagnosis. I was 23 years old. What good would it do for me to pay money to someone to say, "you have Asperger's" at my age I thought? Just thinking about calling a clinician to make an appointment caused great anxiety. The thought of driving to the office, getting out of the car and walking into the building caused my heart rate to speed up.

Years later, after having this knowledge built up inside of me I attended a conference by Tony Attwood, the world's most known Asperger expert. He briefly spoke on the subject of girls with Asperger's going unnoticed because boys express their characteristics more obviously. That man influenced me to write a book. A book for girls who have Asperger's Syndrome or think they might have it. So, here I am writing this book with the hopes of helping other girls and women who have felt lost and different. I want to provide all those girls with a summary of years of research and years of experimenting with solutions to common problems. I also desire this book to be helpful for family members and teachers or anyone else dealing with the complexities of Asperger's.

There seems to be a debate on whether or not people who self-diagnosis have the "real Asperger's." There are 27 definitions (December 2009) from different people of Asperger's in the urban dictionary with the option that other people can vote if they agree or not. Looking at them, there are so many different perspectives and so many different opinions on Asperger's syndrome! It appears that some people diagnosed with Asperger's get angry with those who self-diagnosis. Why in the world would someone who doesn't truly have the characteristics of Asperger's self-diagnosis themselves? It is not like having Asperger's syndrome is the most popular thing. Michael Carley, the executive director of The Global and Regional Asperger's Syndrome Partnership, in his book *Asperger's from the Inside Out* mentions that people who self-diagnose are correct 99% of the time.

There has not yet been created a scale or categories of autism or Asperger's. However, I need to be able to communicate in some way the different places on the spectrum. Lets say the autism spectrum consisted of a scale of 1-20, number 1 being very mild and 20 being very severe. Numbers 1-9 would be Asperger's syndrome, while 10-20 would be autism. Number 1 would be extremely mild while 20 would be extremely severe. Since 1999, I have worked with children utilizing the principles of behavior analysis on all different places on the spectrum. A person's place on the spectrum changes over time. Depending on many factors including family involvement, life structure, health, environment, age etc, a person's place on the spectrum can increase or decrease. Considering all the characteristics and understanding that they are all manifested with a wide range of severity, I would estimate my current extent of having Asperger's to be a five. I believe my place on the spectrum went from a two in preschool to an eight in sixth grade, then down to a six the last year of high school and to a steady five as an adult.

I believe that Asperger's is more common than what most people assume because there is so much diversity in how different people express their characteristics. The most recent report I read on the rate of Asperger's said one out of 76 school aged children had Asperger's (Doyle, 2009). Dr. Tony Attwood mentioned at the conference that girls and women may express their characteristics differently than boys, or learn to hide them, and therefore may go unnoticed. Many girls may appear bashful or shy.

People with Asperger's appreciate being able to know what is about to come so I am going to describe what is in this book. I begin this book describing what Asperger's is, how it is related to autism and the autism spectrum, summarizing what the top experts say on Asperger's, and discuss and comment on those descriptions. In the second chapter I discuss the differences between girl's and boys with Asperger's, summarizing available research and what top experts say on the subject, as well as summarizing research done on typical boys and girls to better understand differences of children with Asperger's, and include my personal experience with working with girls and boys on the autism spectrum.

The following chapter discusses early childhood clues; signs in family members and my personal experience as a little child. In the next chapter, I describe my silent journey through school sharing experiences that reflect my Asperger's characteristics and how my life changed after being exposed to an environmental toxic insult. My mother and three life best friends write letters describing their experiences and perceptions of me while growing up. Although they agree I was weird and out of my comfort zone in social situations, they had no idea I was struggling with Asperger's characteristics. I was able to hide most of them. I share my experience with college and facing the real world, getting married and learning how to be a wife, having children and learning how to be a mother. My husband writes a letter on what it is like being married to a girl with Asperger's.

I discuss specific characteristics of Asperger's and share solutions including solving problems verses showing empathy, difficulty converting meaning into expressive language, repetitive thinking, auditory processing verses visual processing, bluntness verses authenticity, intense interests and focus, literal perception, way of thinking and memory, being resourceful and trying to understand typical behavior, keeping friendships and loyalty, recognizing friendships and acquaintances, small talk, anxiety, obsession with knowledge and facts, sudden changes in schedule, asking repetitive questions, difficulty following movies, the necessity of having to figure out a cause from an effect, recognizing patterns that can be seen and unseen and whether or not to join the social mainstream. Dealing with and tolerating sensory issues and overcoming social difficulties are discussed with solutions provided.

I talk about my intensive search for the purpose of life, what is truly important, what is the absolute truth and how to get to know who God really is by recognizing patterns in the Bible and what is the purpose of life. I offer advice and solutions to common struggles girls with Asperger's face including: academics and education, peer pressure, growing up, concerns with the body, making and keeping friends, deciding on whether or not to join the social cliques, disappointment of not meeting expectations or pleasing others, intense emotions, frustrating experiences, discerning who can be trusted, structuring time, choosing a career, boys and dating, attending baby showers and bridal showers, marriage, sex, pregnancy, motherhood, money management, health and food, time management, self accountability, overcoming life's problems, when a loved one dies, character development and quality of life, and whether or not to tell people you have Asperger's. I also share insight for teachers and parents so they can support and help their girls through some of their struggles, and to understand that girl's don't necessarily need to be precisely changed to be exactly like everybody else, but need understanding, support and knowledge that they can make the choice whether or not to join in on the typical mainstream or be happier as they embrace their differences with the acceptance of those who love them or some of both.

I end this book summarizing years of research with the explanation of a clearer picture of what autism really is and how putting together the pieces of the puzzle so many researchers have found creates a better understanding. Utilizing methods and analyzing observable clues as well as genetic clues, I was able to prevent my own children from developing the severe expression of autism. I share my story. It is extremely important for girls with Asperger's to know that they can possibly prevent their children from developing autism. I share information and clues to look for and methods to take to decrease the chances of a child from developing autism.

Throughout this book and at the end of relevant chapters, I suggest and recommend readings for further knowledge and understanding on specific issues and topics. I believe there are so many girls like me who have learned to cover up and hide their struggles. Girls can learn how to overcome these struggles, they can learn strategies, coping skills, social skills and most importantly they can learn to accept themselves and even appreciate themselves being different while leaning on their strengths. Join me in my journey with Asperger's, finding out why I was so different, my search for truth and discovery of solutions.

References

Carley, M.J. (2008). *Asperger's From the Inside Out. A Supportive and Practical Guide for Anyone with Asperger's Syndrome.* Penguin Group (USA), Inc.

Doyle. S. (2009). *Festival to Sound New Autism Note.* Huntsville Times Local News. Wednesday, November 4, 2009, Page A3.

CHAPTER ONE

What really is Asperger's, and How is it Similar to Autism?

"We each have our own way of living in the world, together we are like a symphony. Some are the melody, some are the rhythm, and some are the harmony. It all blends together, we are like a symphony, and each part is crucial. We all contribute to the song of life." ...Sondra Williams

There has been difficulty of where to classify the name "Asperger's Syndrome." The word "Asperger's" can mean many different things to different people. Currently, most experts agree that Asperger's is a part of the autism spectrum because of the many similar characteristics. Some experts perceive it to be the same as "high functioning autism," while others think of it as a step above high functioning autism. Some see it to be a completely different condition than autism. A group of researchers from Yale University suggest that the neuropsychological profiles of children with high functioning autism are different than those with Asperger's syndrome and intervention strategies should be of a different nature (Klin, Volkmar, Sparrow, Cicchetti & Rourke 1995). However, research from other scientists have not identified specific profiles showing that the two groups are different from each other based on neuropsychological testing although there is the difference that Asperger's having a higher IQ due to higher verbal abilities (Manjiviona & Prior 1999). In Dr. Tony Attwood's (2003) paper, "Is There a Difference Between Asperger's Syndrome and High Functioning Autism?," Attwood concludes that research and clinical experience suggest there is no clear evidence they are different because there are more similarities than differences. Some professionals use the terms "high functioning autism" and "Asperger's" interchangeably while others believe there are differences between the terms "autism" and "Asperger's." According to the DSMV-IV, autism and Asperger's are two different conditions but they are both considered pervasive developmental disorders.

Although many of the characteristics are the same in Asperger's and autism, the severity and number of the characteristics are much more in autism than Asperger's. Other main differences between autism and Asperger's, is that there typically is not a language delay in people with Asperger's or a delay in the development of self help skills. People with Asperger's tend to be more aware of the social world and give effort to fit in but find it difficult. Most people with Asperger's can live a fairly typical life, go to college, get married and have children but some people with severe autism may not be able to live on their own. Children with autism are typically diagnosed between the ages of 18 months to three years old. Most children with Asperger's syndrome are diagnosed later in their childhood or adulthood, with an average age of 11 years old (Howlin and Asgharian 1999).

It is not practical to give a good single definition of Asperger's because people with it have different characteristics with a different level of severity. People express and respond to their characteristics differently based on gender, personality, temperament, birth order, number and gender of siblings, environment and family structure. For thorough understanding of what Asperger's really is, I am going to describe how it became, what it is and who has it. I am also going to summarize and comment on some of the top experts descriptions and list the most common characteristics. It is very important to keep in mind that not all people with Asperger's have all the characteristics while the characteristics individuals experience range from mild to severe.

Asperger's: Where did the name come from, what is it and who has it?

The name "Asperger's" came from a man named Hans Asperger from Austria. In 1944 he published a paper from an investigation of more than 400 children who portrayed certain behaviors that deviated from typical. In

1994, Asperger's syndrome became part of the Diagnostic Statistical Manual of Mental Disorders. About the same time in 1943 Leo Kanner, who was a child psychologist in Boston, recognized an unusual pattern of behavior in many children he saw and named the condition 'early infantile autism.' Autism had been added to the Diagnostic Statistical Manual in 1952. The term "autism" means to "escape from reality."

Most people with Asperger's appear as different to typical people. People who have Asperger's will admit that they find the rules of social behavior difficult and that they know they are different from others. However, the social difficulties are only a problem in a social environment where everyone is expected to act social. Most of them try really hard to fit in and may claim they are pretending to be like everybody else. They may have feelings that they don't fit in but don't know why. They may have difficulty understanding sarcasm and tend to interpret conversations literally. They express different social characteristics and have logical ways of thinking and a unique perception. They have difficulty understanding small talk and may not participate in "chit chat." They may have less concern for personal hygiene and clothing styles- preferring to dress comfortably rather than stylish. People with Asperger's may be perceived as disrespectful and rude with little awareness of hurting other people's feelings and have limited nonverbal communication. As they mature, they become aware of their inability to understand social cues, develop a fear of making a social mistake, and they may begin to fear social situations. They may not understand or "read between the lines" when people are hinting and would much rather be told directly what to do. People with Asperger's tend to process social information slower than typical people and may become exhausted with the incredible effort needed to process social information. Many people with Asperger's have high IQ's. People with Asperger's syndrome can be taught, or these individuals can figure out on their own, to decode social cues intellectually, rather than instinctively. Because some people cannot verbalize what they understand instinctively, this can be frustrating (Harmon, 2003-2009; online Dictionaries and Encyclopedias).

Well-known people that have been thought to have Asperger's are Albert Einstein, Isaac Newton, Benjamin Franklin, Napoleon Bonaparte, George Washington, John Quincy Adams, Andrew Jackson, Andrew Johnson, Abraham Lincoln, James Garfield, Teddy Roosevelt, William Taft, Harry Truman, Catherine the Great, Lous IV, Cleopatra, Wilhem II, Alexander

Foreword by Liane Holliday Willey

the Great, Leonardo da Vinci, Vincent van Gogh, Beethoven, Elvis, Jeremy Bentham, Socrates, Henry Ford, Bill Gates, Robin Williams, Tom Hanks, Marilyn Monroe, Clark Gable, Virginia Wolf, Shakespeare, Goethe, Isaac Asimov and Charles Dickinson (Fattig, 2007). Other people thought to have Asperger's syndrome are Al Gore, Andy Kaufman, Andy Warhol, Bob Dylan, Carl Jung, Mark Twain, Michael Jackson, Mozart, Nikola Tesla, Thomas Jefferson, Vincent Van Gogh and Woody Allen (Duncan, 2009).

Expert's description of Asperger's

Dr. Tony Attwood, who is a clinical psychologist working with people on the autism spectrum for over 30 years, gives his perspective:

"From my clinical experience I consider that children and adults with Asperger's Syndrome have a different, not defective, way of thinking. The person usually has a strong desire to seek knowledge, truth and perfection with a different set of priorities than would be expected with other people. There is also a different perception of situations and sensory experiences. The overriding priority may be to solve a problem rather than satisfy the social or emotional needs of others. The person values being creative rather than co-operative. The person with Asperger's syndrome may perceive errors that are not apparent to others, giving considerable attention to detail, rather than noticing the "big picture." The person is usually renowned for being direct, speaking their mind and being honest and determined and having a strong sense of social justice. The person may actively seek and enjoy solitude, be a loyal friend and have a distinct sense of humor. However, the person with Asperger's Syndrome can have difficulty with the management and expression of emotions. Children and adults with Asperger's syndrome may have levels of anxiety, sadness or anger that indicate a secondary mood disorder. There may also be problems expressing the degree of love and affection expected by others. Fortunately, we now have successful psychological treatment programs to help manage and express emotions."

Simon Baron-Cohen, director of the Autism Research Center at the University of Cambridege, has summarized Asperger's Syndrome in 10 characteristics: finding social situations confusing, viewing small talk as difficult, disliking imaginative story-writing at school, ability to efficiently pick up details and facts, finding it difficult to work out what other people are thinking and feeling, ability to focus on certain things for very long periods, are rude even when they didn't intend to be, have unusually strong and narrow interests, do certain things in an inflexible, repetitive way and have always had difficulty making friends. Baron-Cohen implies that teachers should be educated about Asperger's syndrome and for society to recognize and appreciate the difference (Health Care Industry, 2001).

Wendy Lawson (2003), a writer and a woman with Asperger's, states that people with Asperger's have the characteristic of monotropism, unlike those individuals who possess polytropism. Monotropism is only being able to focus on one thing at a time. This can be difficult when it comes to socializing in groups, but it can be positive in terms of concentrating on one thing at a time. Polytropism is being able to tend to several things at once, such as being able to make multiple connections using the combination of visual, auditory and spatial senses.

Liane Holliday Willey's (1999) perspective form her book *Pretending to Be Normal*:

"Like other people, those with Asperger's are often creative, intelligent, interesting, productive and learned in countless ways. They are often kind, warm, gracious, loving, funny and enjoyable. And like everyone, AS people have their share of hardship, their share of disappointment and dismay. It can be harrowing to see life through surreal lenses that warp and tangle and convolute the most simplest of activities, that neurologically typical consider ordinary, things like shopping, driving, studying, keeping a job, paying bills and visiting friends…

No matter the hardships, I do not wish for a cure to Asperger's Syndrome. What I wish for, is a cure for the common ill that pervades too many lives; the ill that makes people compare themselves to a normal that is measured in terms of perfect and absolute standards, most of which are impossible for anyone to reach…"

Liane Holliday Willey (2001) in *Asperger Syndrome in the Family* encourages a focus on the good characteristics of a person with Asperger's. She says "It doesn't overshadow the fact that there are real issues aspies must learn to deal with, but at the same time, it nudges one to figure out that AS is not the end." Her list "Twenty First-Rate Ways to Describe Aspies:

"Aspies Are: very loyal, open and honest, guardians of those less able, detail oriented, uninterested in social politics, often witty and entertaining, capable of developing very strong splinter skills, storage banks for facts and figures, tenacious researchers and thinkers, logical, enthusiastic about their passionate interests, able to create beautiful images in their mind's eye, finely tuned in to their sensory systems, ethical and principled, dependable, good at word games and word play, inquisitive, rule followers, unambiguous, average to above average in intelligence."

Dr. John Ortiz (2004), founder of the Asperger Syndrome Institute, has a very interesting view of the conditions on the autism spectrum. He states in his article, "The Spectrum of Distraction: Autism, OCD, Asperger's and ADD," that all four of these conditions are the same illness but contracted at different ages, and the age of onset will determine what will distract the person. Therefore, response to the symptoms reveal the age of the onset of the illness and that the symptoms are also a "compulsive" replay of what was at one time a typical response to human life. Ortiz defines autism to be "a social impairment, wherein a person suffers from a pervasive category of socially disconnecting distractions." The principle symptom is the "the profound inability to connect to socially normal people" and the principle behavior is "compulsively focusing on things other than personal relationships at the expense of personal relationships." He states that using this definition, all four of the conditions are a variety of autism, and all people suffer some degree of autism. Dr. Ortiz believes that if people can see the autistic traits in themselves, they can better help the more severely autistic.

Discussion

I feel it important to comment on Dr. Ortiz's perspective on the "age of onset." I have worked with children who have experienced the onset of autistic symptoms at different ages. One little boy I worked using techniques of behavior analysis was six years old when he had been diagnosed with

ODD (obsessive defiant disorder) and PDD (pervasive developmental disorder) and later received a diagnosis of Asperger's at the age of eight. His mom reported to me that the boy's father has characteristics of Asperger's, and she, in fear of her son developing autism, delayed her son's vaccines until he was five years old. According to his mom, shortly after his third routine of vaccines, the boy began to hallucinate. He developed difficulty with controlling his impulsive behavior with sudden bursts of tantrums, and he began to slip into his own world, fixating on objects. Other children I have worked with have parents reporting similar stories about "a regression and sudden change in my child's behavior." Some parents report a gradual change in their child's behavior and development.

I, myself, began experiencing major changes in thinking, feeling and perception shortly after receiving a measles vaccine when I was 10 years old. Although I had experienced mild characteristics of Asperger's before age 10, I began experiencing a higher number of characteristics with much more severity. It is likely that if I had been exposed to that same environmental toxic insult, with my immune system the way it was, at a much earlier age, I may have developed autism. I wonder if there is a difference between an original "Asperger's," such as those who have a genius IQ and have difficulty relating to people of average intelligence because of their high intellect and the type of Asperger's that may have been induced from an environmental insult. Perhaps they are both the same, only manifested in different ways. Of course, research would need to be done to examine this.

When I hear a child has autism, I don't have a clear picture of how that particular child is considering the diversity in individuals. So I have to ask questions and do a developmental assessment to get a better understanding of where the child is on the spectrum. How old is the child? Is the child verbal? If so, how much? Can the child understand language? If so, how much? Does the child make eye contact? How much time does the child engage in self-stimulation behaviors? What self-stimulation behaviors does the child engage in? What does the child eat? Does the child speak to peers? How much? Can the child read? Does the child comprehend what he/she reads? To what extent? What is the child good at? What are the child's primary interests? Does the child have trouble paying attention to things outside his/her interest? How well does the child display joint attention? On what level does the child solve math problems or problem solve? Does the child learn better by hearing, seeing, doing or a combination? Does the child have special areas of strength such as problem solving, hyperlexia, memorizing, numbers or musical talent? What sensory problems does the child have? Does the child have siblings, and if so, what ages? Does the child have medical problems such as frequent ear infections, rashes or yeast? Does the child's parents have any medical issues? And a very important question to ask is "Is the child a boy or a girl?" Girls on the spectrum tend to manifest their characteristics in different ways than boys. Of course, this should be expected. Boys and girls are different.

Experts who are revising the diagnostic statistical manual have proposed to eliminate the "Asperger's" and PDD-NOS from the manual and these conditions will be included as an "autism spectrum disorder." This might be a problem because the spectrum is so wide ranging from very severe with very low IQ to extremely high functioning with very high IQ. If this happens, many people on the high end of the spectrum will be missed, as they wouldn't get an evaluation for an autism spectrum condition. Also, a child's place on the spectrum changes over time. A big challenge for the diagnostic manual team on autism is how to measure severity in a condition that often causes a very uneven profile of abilities and disabilities (Wallis, 2009). I believe that what people need is a better distinction, different categories or subtypes of autism spectrum conditions, not putting them all together as a single diagnosis. In a poll from About.com:Autism "Should Asperger syndrome and PDD-NOS be removed as diagnoses from the DSM?," 48 percent of people surveyed voted absolutely not because Asperger's and PDD-NOS are distinct disorders; 17 percent voted no because the terms serve a purpose and should be left alone; 6 percent voted probably not; 8 percent voted maybe; 8 percent voted probably because if experts can't agree on their meaning, then why leave them; and 9 percent voted absolutely because they are too vague and confusing. This survey comprised of 304 votes. In another poll, "Should Asperger syndrome be included on the autism spectrum," 59 percent voted absolutely yes; 12 percent voted probably; 6 percent voted unsure; 14 percent voted probably not; and 6 percent voted absolutely not. This survey comprised of 379 votes (About.com:Autism, November 27th, 2009).

Currently, the terms "Asperger's," "autism" and "high-functioning autism" are all considered by professionals to be on the autism spectrum. Autism spectrum characteristics seem to have multi-dimensional attributes because of the observable behavioral excesses and deficits as well as the biomedical excesses and deficits involved. People on the autism spectrum are very different in terms of the number and severity of their characteristics. Their IQ ranges from very low to very gifted. However, the IQ of people with Asperger's ranges from average to very gifted. They also have their own methods of expressing, coping and dealing with their characteristics.

Autism spectrum conditions are not mental disorders. However, I think a mental disorder can possibly result from having Asperger's or autism (a physical chemical imbalance of neurotransmitters and hormones). The diagnostic manual describes autism as being and autistic disorder. Instead of using the word "disorder" in reference to Asperger's or autism, I prefer using the term "condition." In addition, instead of using the word "normal" I prefer to use the word "typical" because my understanding of the word "normal" doesn't describe anyone. Also, for many professionals and doctors, the viewpoint on autism and related conditions has shifted from a "behavioral disorder" to a "medical condition" over the past decade. Although it may be more difficult for some people on the spectrum, it is very possible for them to utilize their strengths and talents, have joyful relationships, families, and live happy and productive lives. It is a matter of searching and finding the treasure of knowledge and truth.

"Asperger's Syndrome Characteristics"

Below is a list of Asperger's Syndrome characteristics that Roger Meyer's (2003-2008) put together extracting information from medical diagnostic criteria, descriptions offered by medical and counseling professionals, articles by educators and from employment biographies of approximately a dozen independent-living, medically or self-diagnosed adults over the age of 25. While every person manifests some these characteristics, what distinguishes adults with Asperger's is their consistency of appearance, their intensity, and the number of them appearing simultaneously. Some characteristics do not apply to everyone with Asperger's and those consulting this list should not feel compelled to find all the characteristics.

Foreword by Liane Holliday Willey

Social Characteristics

- Difficulty in accepting criticism or correction
- Difficulty in offering correction or criticism without appearing harsh, pedantic or insensitive
- Difficulty in perceiving and applying unwritten social rules or protocols
- "Immature" manners
- Failure to distinguish between private and public personal care habits: i.e., brushing, public attention to skin problems, nose picking, teeth picking, ear canal cleaning, clothing arrangement
- Naïve trust in others
- Shyness
- Low or no conversational participation in group meetings or conferences
- Constant anxiety about performance and acceptance, despite recognition and commendation
- Scrupulous honesty, often expressed in an apparently disarming or inappropriate manner or setting
- Bluntness in emotional expression
- "Flat affect"
- Discomfort manipulating or "playing games" with others
- Unmodulated reaction in being manipulated, patronized, or "handled" by others
- Low to medium level of paranoia
- Low to no apparent sense of humor; bizarre sense of humor (often stemming from a "private" internal thread of humor being inserted in public conversation without preparation or warming others up to the reason for the "punchline")
- Difficulty with reciprocal displays of pleasantries and greetings
- Problems expressing empathy or comfort to/with others: sadness, condolence, congratulations, etc.
- Pouting,, ruminating, fixating on bad experiences with people or events for an inordinate length of time
- Difficulty with adopting a social mask to obscure real feelings, moods, reactions
- Using social masks inappropriately (you are "xv" while everyone else is ????)
- Abrupt and strong expression of likes and dislikes
- Rigid adherence to rules and social conventions where flexibility is desirable
- Apparent absence of relaxation, recreational, or "time out" activities
- "Serious" all the time
- Known for single-mindedness
- Flash temper
- Tantrums
- Excessive talk
- Difficulty in forming friendships and intimate relationships; difficulty in distinguishing between acquaintance and friendship
- Social isolation and intense concern for privacy
- Limited clothing preference; discomfort with formal attire or uniforms
- Preference for bland or bare environments in living arrangements
- Difficulty judging others' personal space - Limited by intensely pursued interests
- Often perceived as "being in their own world"

Physical Manifestations

- Strong sensory sensitivities: touch and tactile sensations, sounds, lighting and colors, odors, taste
- Clumsiness
- Balance difficulties
- Difficulty in judging distances, height, depth
- Difficulty in recognizing others' faces (prosopagnosia)
- Stims (self-stimulatory behavior serving to reduce anxiety, stress, or to express pleasure)
- Self-injurious or disfiguring behaviors
- Nail-biting
- Unusual gait, stance, posture
- Gross or fine motor coordination problems
- Depression
- Anxiety
- Sleep difficulties
- Verbosity
- Difficulty expressing anger (excessive or "bottled up")
- Low apparent sexual interest
- Flat or monotone vocal expression; limited range of inflection
- Difficulty with initiating or maintaining eye contact
- Elevated voice volume during periods of stress and frustration
- Strong food preferences and aversions
- Unusual and rigidly adhered to eating behaviors
- Bad or unusual personal hygiene

Shared Diagnostic Conditions

- Learning Disability
- Attention Deficit Disorder (ADD)
- Obsessive Compulsive Disorder (OCD)
- Central Auditory Processing Disorder (CAPD)
- Hyperlexia
- Depression
- Anxiety
- Non-verbal Learning Disorder (NVLD)
- Hypertension
- Semantic Pragmatic Language Disorder
- Tourette's Syndrome
- Dysthymia

Foreword by Liane Holliday Willey

Cognitive Characteristics

- Susceptibility to distraction
- Difficulty in expressing emotions
- Resistance to or failure to respond to talk therapy
- Mental shutdown response to conflicting demands and multi-tasking
- Generalized confusion during periods of stress
- Low understanding of the reciprocal rules of conversation: interrupting, dominating, minimum participation, difficult in shifting topics, problem with initiating or terminating conversation, subject preservation
- Insensitivity to the non-verbal cues of others (stance, posture, facial expressions)
- Preservation best characterized by the term "bulldog tenacity"
- Literal interpretation of instructions (failure to read between the lines)
- Interpreting words and phrases literally (problem with colloquialisms, cliches, neologism, turns of phrase, common humorous expressions)
- Preference for visually oriented instruction and training
- Dependence on step-by-step learning procedures (disorientation occurs when a step is assumed, deleted, or otherwise overlooked in instruction)
- Difficulty in generalizing
- Preference for repetitive, often simple routines
- Difficulty in understanding rules for games of social entertainment
- Missing or misconstruing others' agendas, priorities, preferences
- Impulsiveness
- Compelling need to finish one task completely before starting another
- Rigid adherence to rules and routines
- Difficulty in interpreting meaning to others' activities; difficulty in drawing relationships between an activity or event
- Exquisite attention to detail, principally visual, or details which can be visualized ("Thinking in Pictures") or cognitive details (often those learned by rote)
- Concrete thinking
- Distractibility due to focus on external or internal sensations, thoughts, and/or sensory input (appearing to be in a world of one's own or day-dreaming)
- Difficulty in assessing relative importance of details (an aspect o the trees/forest problem)
- Poor judgment of when a task is finished (often attributable to perfectionism or an apparent unwillingness to follow differential standards for quality)
- Difficulty in imagining others' thoughts in a similar or identical event or circumstance that are different from one's own ("Theory of Mind" issues)
- Difficulty with organizing and sequencing (planning and execution; successful performance of tasks in a logical, functional order)
- Difficulty in assessing cause and effect relationships (behaviors and consequences)
- Relaxation techniques and developing recreational "release" interest may require formal instruction
- Rage, tantrum, shutdown, self-isolating reactions appearing "out of nowhere"
- Substantial hidden self-anger, anger towards others, and resentment
- Difficulty in estimating time to complete tasks
- Difficulty in learning self-monitoring techniques
- Disinclination to produce expected results in an orthodox manner
- Psychometric testing shows great deviance between verbal and performance results
- Extreme reaction to changes in routine, surroundings, people
- Stilted, pedantic conversational style ("The Professor")

Work Characteristics

- Difficulty with "teamwork"
- Deliberate withholding of peak performance due to belief that one's best efforts may remain unrecognized, unrewarded, or appropriated by others
- Intense pride in expertise or performance, often perceived by others as "flouting behavior"
- Sarcasm, negativism, criticism
- Difficulty in accepting compliments, often responding with quizzical or self-deprecatory language
- Tendency to "lose it" during sensory overload, multitask demands, or when contradictory and confusing priorities have been set
- Difficult in starting project
- Discomfort with competition, out of scale reactions to losing
- Low motivation to perform tasks of no immediate personal interest
- Oversight or forgetting of tasks without formal reminders such as lists or schedules - Great concern about order and appearance of personal work area
- Slow performance
- Perfectionism
- Difficult with unstructured time
- Reluctance to ask for help or seek comfort - Excessive questions
- Low sensitivity to risks in the environment to self and/or others
- Difficulty with writing and reports
- Reliance on internal speech process to "talk" oneself through a task or procedure
- Stress, frustration and anger reaction to interruptions
- Difficulty in negotiating either in conflict situations or as a self-advocate
- Very low level of assertiveness
- Reluctance to accept positions of authority or supervision
- Strong desire to coach or mentor newcomers
- Difficulty in handling relationships with authority figures
- Often viewed as vulnerable or less able to resist harassment and badgering by others
- Punctual and conscientious
- Avoids socializing, "hanging out," or small talk on and off the job

Diagnostic Criteria

I have included both the current diagnostic criteria for Asperger's and autism for a better understanding how it is diagnosed and to better distinguish between the two conditions. If a child has the characteristics of autism or Asperger's but does not meet the criteria in the diagnostic manual then he/she is usually diagnosed with PDD-NOS (Pervasive Developmental Disorder – Not Otherwise Specified).

Diagnostic Criteria for Asperger's Disorder (American Psychological Association, 1994)

A. Qualitative impairment in social interaction, as manifested by at least two of the following:

>(1) marked impairment in the use of multiple nonverbal behaviors such as eye-to-eye gaze, facial expression, body postures, and gestures to regulate social interaction
>
>(2) failure to develop peer relationships appropriate to developmental level
>
>(3) a lack of spontaneous seeking to share enjoyment, interests, or achievements with other people (e.g., by a lack of showing, bringing, or pointing out objects of interest to other people)
>
>(4) lack of social or emotional reciprocity

B. Restricted repetitive and stereotyped patterns of behavior, interests, and activities, as manifested by at least one of the following:

>(1) encompassing preoccupation with one or more stereotyped and restricted patterns of interest that is abnormal either in intensity or focus
>
>(2) apparently inflexible adherence to specific, nonfunctional routines or rituals
>
>(3) stereotyped and repetitive motor mannerisms (e.g., hand or finger flapping or twisting, or complex whole-body movements)
>
>(4) persistent preoccupation with parts of objects

C. The disturbance causes clinically significant impairment in social, occupational, or other important areas of functioning.

D. There is no clinically significant general delay in language (e.g., single words used by age 2 years, communicative phrases used by age 3 years).

E. There is no clinically significant delay in cognitive development or in the development of age-appropriate self-help skills, adaptive behavior (other than in social interaction), and curiosity about the environment in childhood.

F. Criteria are not met for another specific Pervasive Developmental Disorder or Schizophrenia

Diagnostic criteria for Autistic Disorder (American Psychological Association, 1994)

A. A total of six (or more) items from (1), (2), and (3), with at least two from (1), and one each from (2) and (3):

(1) qualitative impairment in social interaction, as manifested by at least two of the following:

(a) marked impairment in the use of multiple nonverbal behaviors such as eye-to-eye gaze, facial expression, body postures, and gestures to regulate social interaction

(b) failure to develop peer relationships appropriate to developmental level

(c) a lack of spontaneous seeking to share enjoyment, interests, or achievements with other people (e.g., by a lack of showing, bringing, or pointing out objects of interest)

(d) lack of social or emotional reciprocity

(2) qualitative impairments in communication as manifested by at least one of the following:

(a) delay in, or total lack of, the development of spoken language (not accompanied by an attempt to compensate through alternative modes of communication such as gesture or mime)

(b) in individuals with adequate speech, marked impairment in the ability to initiate or sustain a conversation with others

(c) stereotyped and repetitive use of language or idiosyncratic language

(d) lack of varied, spontaneous make-believe play or social imitative play appropriate to developmental level

(3) restricted repetitive and stereotyped patterns of behavior, interests, and activities, as manifested by at least one of the following:

(a) encompassing preoccupation with one or more stereotyped and restricted patterns of interest that is abnormal either in intensity or focus

(b) apparently inflexible adherence to specific, nonfunctional routines or rituals

(c) stereotyped and repetitive motor mannerisms (e.g., hand or finger flapping or twisting, or complex whole-body movements)

(d) persistent preoccupation with parts of objects

B. Delays or abnormal functioning in at least one of the following areas, with onset prior to age 3 years: (1) social interaction, (2) language as used in social communication, or (3) symbolic or imaginative play.

C. The disturbance is not better accounted for by Rett's Disorder or Childhood Disintegrative Disorder.

Suggested readings

- *The Complete Guide to Asperger's Syndrome* by Tony Attwood (2008)
- *The OASIS Guide to Asperger Syndrome: Completely Revised and Updated: Advice, Support, Insight, and Inspiration* by Patricia Romanowski Bashe, Barbara L. Kirby, Simon Baron-Cohen, and Tony Attwood (2005)
- *The Myriad Gifts of Asperger's Syndrome* by John Ortiz (2008)

- *Can I Tell You About Asperger Syndrome? A Guide for Friends and Family* by Jude Welton, Jane Telford, and Elizabeth Newson (2003)
- *Misdiagnosis And Dual Diagnoses Of Gifted Children And Adults: ADHD, Bipolar, OCD, Asperger's, Depression, And Other Disorders* by James T. Webb, Edward R. Amend, Nadia E. Webb, and Jean Goerss (2005)

References

About.com:Autism (2009). Poll Results. Should Asperger Syndrome be included in the Autism Spectrum? Retrieved November 27th, 2009. http://autism.about.com/gi/pages/poll.htm?linkback=http%3A%2F%2Fautism.about.com%2Fb%2F2009%2F11%2F08%2Fshould-asperger-syndrome-be-considered-an-autism-spectrum-disorder.htm&poll_id=7697857725&poll=4

About.com:Autism (2009). Poll Results. Should Asperger Syndrome and PDD-NOS be removed as a diagnosis from the DSM? Retrieved November 27th, 2009. http://autism.about.com/gi/pages/poll.htm?poll_id=7258201247&linkback=http://autism.about.com/b/2009/11/03/should-the-diagnoses-asperger-syndrome-and-pdd-nos-be-removed-from-the-diagnostic-manual.htm

American Psychiatric Association (1994). *Diagnostic and statistical manual (4th ed.).* Washington, DC: Author.

Attwood, Tony. (2003). *Is There a Difference Between Asperger's Syndrome and High Functioning Autism?* Retrieved October 12th, 2009. www.sacramentoasis.com/docs/8-22-03/as_&_hfa.pdf.

Attwood, Tony. (2007-2008). *What is Asperger's syndrome?* Retrieved October 14th, http://www.tonyattwood.com.au/ad.html.

Duncan. (2009). Famous People with Asperger's Syndrome. In the Light. Retrieved October 23rd, 2009. http://www.inthelight.co.nz/spirit/aspergerpeople.htm

Fattig, Michelle. (2007). Famous People with Asperger's Syndrome. Disabled World. Retrieved October 23rd, 2009. http://www.disabled-world.com/artman/publish/article_2086.shtml

Gillson, Sharon. (2000). *Characteristic Behaviors of Autism.* Retreived October 12th, 2009. http://www.suite101.com/article.cfm/autism/46554.

Health Care Industry (2001). Opinion interview with Simon Baron-Cohen. *New Scientist, 170* (April 14), 42.

Harmon, Jane. (2003-2009). *What is Asperger's Syndrome?* Retrieved October, 18th, 2009, from http://www.wisegeek.com/what-is-aspergers-syndrome.htm.

Howlin P. and Asgharian A. (1999). *The diagnosis of autism and Asperger syndrome: findings from a survey of 770 families.* Developmental Medicine and Child Neurology, 41, 834-839.

Klin A., Volkmar F.R., , Sparrow S.S., , Cicchetti D. V., and Rourke B.P. (1995). *Validity and neuropsychological characterization of Asperger Syndrome: Convergence with Nonverbal Learning Disabilities Syndrome.* Journal of Child psychology and Psychiatry 36, 1127-40. Retrieved October 14th, 2009. http://www.maapservices.org/Publications/Volkmar_Article.asp.

Lawson, W. (2003). *Build your own life: A self help guide for individuals with Aspergers syndrome* (pp21-24). Great Britain: Athenaeum Press.

Manjiviona, J. and Prior M. (1999). Neuropsychological profiles of children with Asperger syndrome and autism. Autism 3, 327-356.

Meyer, Roger N. (2003-2008). *Aspires: Climbing the Mountain Together.* Retreived

October 14th, 2009. www.aspiresrelationships.com/articles_as_characteristics.htm.

Ortiz, John (2004). *The Spectrum of Distraction: Autism, OCD, Asperger's, ADD*. Retrieved October 16th, 2009. http://theemergencesite.com/Tech/TechIssues-Autism-OCD-Aspergers-ADD.htm.

Wallis, C. (2009). A Powerful Identity, a Vanishing Diagnosis. The New York Times, Health. Retrieved November 8th, 2009. http://www.nytimes.com/2009/11/03/health/03asperger.html?_r=2

Willey, L.H. (1999). Pretending to be Normal. Living with Asperger's Syndrome. Jessica Kingsley Publishers, London.

Willey, L.H. (2001). Asperger Syndrome in the Family. Redefining Normal. Jessica Kingsley Publishers, London.

CHAPTER TWO

Girls vs. Boys with Asperger's

Although boys are four times more likely to be diagnosed than girls, current attention has experts thinking that more girls may have Asperger's than originally predicted. Because girls may have different symptoms or express their characteristics differently than boys do, some girls with Asperger's syndrome may not become diagnosed. This chapter summarizes what some of the top Asperger's Syndrome experts and researchers have to say about girls with the condition. Reasons are also discussed as to why many girls may go unnoticed or undiagnosed, as well as existing research examining the differences between girls and boys on the autism spectrum is explained. Other discussions in this chapter include the exploration of research analyzing the differences in typical boys and girls to better understand differences in children with Asperger's, my personal experience with girls and boys on the spectrum and the options of creating more programs for girls with Asperger's. A discussion section finalizes this chapter on boys verses girls with the condition.

Amanda Hill (2009), the social affairs correspondent for the *Observer*, states that Dr. Judith Gould, a chartered consultant clinical psychologist with more than 35 years experience in autism spectrum disorders and director of the National Autistic Society's Lorna Wing center for Autism and co-founder of the Center for Social and Communication Disorders, has accused the medical world of missing and overlooking girls with the condition. These medical experts, according to Gould, may be condemning the girls to lives of such misery that some resort to extreme self harm and even eating disorders. It is estimated that 20 percent of girls with anorexia have Asperger's. Gould believes that significantly more girls have Asperger's than anticipated, estimating the ratio to be 2.5 boys to every girl.

It may not be that girls have different characteristics of Asperger's than boys; it is more likely that girls cope with and manifest their characteristics differently than boys. This makes sense considering there are so many differences in the behaviors of typical girls and boys. Tony Attwood (2006) states, "It appears that many girls with Asperger's Syndrome have the same profile of abilities as boys, but a subtler, or less severe, expression of the characteristics." Therefore, girls have difficulties in social situations as boys do but their difficulties may not be recognized because of how they express those difficulties. Girls with Aspergers feel different, and they just don't know why. They have a desire to fit in but they just don't know how and may feel shame, embarrassment and frustration. Girls with Asperger's may keep their struggles to themselves and try to compensate for their deficiencies by carefully observing others and pretending to be like them. Girls with Asperger's may use their intelligence to hide their social struggles.

There is limited research examining the differences between girls and boys with Asperger's, however, this should not prevent girls from getting the attention and support they need. Gould said: "We're failing girls at the moment. We are doing many thousands of them a great disservice. They are either not being picked up in the first place, but if they ask for help they are being turned away. Even if they are referred for diagnosis, they are commonly rejected" (Hill, 2009). Many girls with Asperger's may not find out they have it until their difference creates a disastrous or near-disastrous situation (Myers, 2006).

In Hill's article "Doctor's are Failing to Spot Asperger's in Girls" (2009), Jane Asher, the society's president, says that other people's misconceptions of women with Asperger's makes their particular battles and struggles even more difficult. Girls are not being identified because there is the stereotyped perspective of what Asperger's is based entirely on how boys present the characteristics. Hill (2009) quotes Tony Attwood in the article.

"Girls slip through the diagnostic net, said Attwood, because they are so good at camouflaging or masking their symptoms. Boys tend to externalise their problems, while girls learn that, if they're good, their differences will not be noticed, he said. Boys go into attack mode when frustrated, while girls suffer in silence and become passive-aggressive. Girls learn to appease and apologise. They learn to observe people from a distance and imitate them. It is only if you look closely and ask the right questions, you see the terror in their eyes and see that their reactions are a learnt script. Girls also escape diagnosis, said Attwood, because they are more social than boys with the condition. Their symptoms can also be missed because it is the intensity of their interests that is unusual, and not the oddity of what they do. The impairments to their social life or interests tend not to stand out in the same way as boys' do, he said."

Asperger experts have just recently began paying attention to girls with Asperger's and little scientific research has been done. What they do say is very important. However, examining what research has been done, along with analyzing personal experiences, why girls may go undiagnosed and research on typical boys and girls, there can be a much better understanding of girls with Asperger's.

Reasons why girls with Asperger's may go unnoticed

Are boys four times as likely than girls to be diagnosed with Asperger's because they are four times more likely to develop it, or because of the different socialization processes girls encounter (Harmon, 2003-2009)? Although it may be true that boys are more likely to develop Asperger's than girls, far more girls have Asperger's than thought because of the different socialization processes they encounter, their different methods of coping with these processes and because of the basic methods in the ways boys and girls express themselves. Girls and boys are different. Women are different than men. Typical girls are different from typical boys. Before diving into the research examining the differences between typical girls and boys, lets first explore this question. What are reasons why girls with Asperger's go unnoticed? Consider the following points below.

- Girls with Asperger's are more likely than boys with Asperger's to be supported and included by their natural peer group – other girls. Boy peer groups are more intolerant of others being different. Girls are better than boys at observing and imitating others in order to hide their struggles with social situations (Attwood, 2006). Typical girls may be more willing to help girls on the spectrum to fit in while typical boys may ignore boys on the spectrum. Typical girls ability to empathize better than typical boys would cause them to be more nurturing and help girls with Asperger's when they are upset.

- Psychologists may not give a diagnosis unless the appearance of the behavioral characteristics is very clear and observable.
- Girls may be missed in their early school years because of the perception of them having more passive personalities or being shy, innocent or bashful.
- Parents and teachers may perceive girls to be coping well, therefore, do not seek a diagnostic assessment.
- Girls may not disrupt the classroom as boys do and therefore teachers don't pay attention to them (Wagner, 2006). Aggressive and disruptive behavior is much more noticeable than quiet and shy behavior. In a classroom with 25 or more kids and just a couple of teachers of course the teacher's attention will be directed to the more disruptive children as well as the children who are very participative.
- Girls may keep their feelings of frustration, confusion or embarrassment quiet while boys act out on those kinds of feelings. Therefore, the behavior of boys is more obvious than girls (Catherine Faherty, 2002).
- Although girls may have many of the characteristics of Asperger's, the severity of them for some girls may be less severe than boys.
- The criteria for diagnosing Asperger's is the same for boys and girls.
- Girls with Asperger's seem to have less motor impairment, a broader range of obsessive interests, and a stronger desire to connect with others, despite their social impairment (Interlandi, 2008).
- Because the observable symptoms are milder, parents are more reluctant to bring their daughter in for a diagnosis (The Confluence, 2009).

Are there any research examining differences between girls and boys on the autism spectrum? Yes, a little.

- Boys with autism have more serious social and communication problems earlier in life, while girls show more social and communication problems during adolescence (McLennan, Lord, & Schopler, 1993).
- Boys with autism tend to engage in disruptive behavior for purposes of gaining desired objects, escaping demands and escaping undesirable sensory stimulation. Girls engage in disruptive behavior for gaining caregiver attention or avoiding nonspecific demands from the caregiver (Reese et al. 2005).
- Shane Nichols, Gina Moravcik and Samara Tetenbaum (2009) give a summary of differences in clinical presentations between boys and girls with autism spectrum conditions in *Girls Growing up on the Autism Spectrum*. Their summary:

"Boys tend to have higher overall Intelligent Quotients than girls with autism spectrum conditions; boys engage in more restricted and repetitive play; girls have better pretend play skills; girls have stronger communication skills based on diagnostic instruments; boys have identifiable social impairments earlier than girls; boys are more easily distracted with more difficulty focusing; disruptive behavior in boys have different purposes than girls; girls with mild characteristics may not be included in research; girls tend to receive lower total scores on developmental instruments."

These are all very good reasons and points to examine why girls with Asperger's are different than boys with Asperger's. Further understanding will be revealed after examining the research done on typical girls and boys. Findings from the research presented below will help anyone to better understand the differences between girls and boys with Asperger's.

Foreword by Liane Holliday Willey

Examining differences in typical boys and girls to understand differences in boys and girls with Asperger's

Why do typical little girls, on average, tend to like playing with baby dolls and stuffed animals while typical little boys tend to be attracted to trains and trucks? Why do women, on average, tend to pursue careers in social work, teaching and nursing while men tend to look for careers like computers and engineering? Girls and boys are different. They have different instincts, different hormones, different interests and different intelligence.

According to Simon Baron-Cohen (2003) there are two identifiable types of intelligence relating to boys and girls: empathizing and systemizing. They are two very different kinds of processes and having one over the other does not mean having more overall intelligence. Empathizing is for making sense of someone's behavior, and systemizing is for predicting outcomes. Empathizing is the ability to identify other people's emotions and thoughts, and being able to respond to them with appropriate emotions. Good empathizers can take the perspective of another person, understand their feelings and respond to those feelings with the appropriate emotional response. This can be perceived as having "theory of mind," or being able to read another's mind, something children with autism develop much later in life than average (Davis, 1994). Empathizing can be seen as a trait, and females, on average, spontaneously empathize more than males (Baron-Cohen, 2003). Systemizing is the analyzing, exploring, and constructing; being able to intuitively figure out how things work; being able to make things work. This is done to understand and predict the system to visualize and invent a new one. Good systemizers have an exact eye for detail with an orderly mind (Baron-Cohen, Wheelwright, Griffin, Lawson & Hill, 2002). The reward of systemizing is in the discovering the causes of things because this discovery gives you control over the world. Boys, on average, are better at systemizing than girls (Baron-Cohen, 2003).

There is scientific research studying the differences between boys and girls

- Young girls show more concern for fairness and develop 'theory of mind' earlier in life than boys (Baron-Cohen, O'Riordan, Jones, Stone, & Plaisted, 1999).
- Boys have more trouble learning how to share (Crombie & Desjardins,1993).
- Boys tend to establish dominance hierarchies better than girls and spend time monitoring and maintaining the hierarchy, which is based on acting tough whereas girls develop social hierarchies (Strayer, 1980).
- Girls and women show more concern and behaviors of comforting than boys and men (Hoffman, 1977).
- Women are more sensitive to facial expressions and judging emotion and nonverbal communication on the *Profile of Nonverbal Sensitivity* (Hall, 1984).
- Women are more accurate on the *Reading the Mind in the Eyes* test that Sally Wheelwright and Baron-Cohen (2001) created by being able to identify the emotion just by looking at a picture of eyes.
- Girls and women value intimacy more than boys and men from the *Friendship and Relationship questionnaire* (FQ) developed by Wheelwright and Baron-Cohen (1998).
- Girls already in the group tend to be more attentive to a newcomer, and boys tend to ignore a newcomer's attempt to join in (Maccoby, 1998).
- More girls tend to enjoy more one-to-one interaction; value best friends and get emotional if excluded; spend more time cementing the closeness of relationships; female agenda is more centered on another person's emotional states (Maccoby, 1998).
- Men tend to spend more time demonstrating their knowledge, skill, and status; women tend to praise each other's looks (Cambell, 1995).
- In parenting styles, Mothers are more likely to hold infants in a face to face position, follow through the child's choice of topic in play, and communicate in more of a way the child can understand (Mannle & Tomasello, 1987).

- In eye contact and face perception, female infants look longer at people's faces while boys look longer at a mobile (Connellan, Baron-Sohen, Wheelwright, Ba'tki & Ahluwalia, 2001).
- Women score higher on average than men on *The Empathy Quotient* (EQ) developed by Baron-Cohen, et al. (2003).
- Males score higher on average than females on *The Systemizing Quotient* (SQ) developed by Baron-Cohen, et al. (2003).
- Young boys are more interested in playing with vehicles, guns, swords and mechanical toys because they are more interested in constructional systems than girls (Lutchmays & Baron-Cohen, 2002).
- Men tend to choose professions such as math, physics, and engineering and score on average 50 points higher on the SAT math section than women (Benditt, 1994).
- The competitors at the International Mathematical Olympiad are mostly males (Stanley, 1990).
- Men are better at detecting particular features and detect movements better than women (Geary, 1998).
- Boys are better and faster at constructing a three-dimensional object from a front view of a picture (Kimura, 1999).
- Men are more accurate at throwing darts at a target, better at frisbee throwing, and intercepting balls that were flung from a launcher, and are better at estimating when a moving object moving towards them with reach them (Watson & Kimura, 1991; Nicholson & Kimura, 1996).
- Boys are more interested in collecting things and focusing on exact differences in the components of their collections (Berlin, Boster, & O'Neill, 1981).

If the same research studies listed above were done on girls and boys with Asperger's, the results are likely to be the same. Many researchers are currently pursuing the question, "What causes sex differences in ASDs?" It is very possible that what causes sex differences between typical girls and boys also cause the sex differences between girls and boys with Asperger's. Sex differences are very real.

Although Baron-Cohen (2003) suggests that people on the autism spectrum have an exaggerated pattern of systemizing, he does not make any inferences or suggestions about girls verses boys with Asperger's. However, he does offer the suggestion that the place on the autism spectrum may be measured. Simon Baron-Cohen created *The Emapthy Quotient* (EQ), *The Systemizing Quotient* (SQ) and *The Autism Quotient* (AQ) to see where a person is on the spectrum of empathy, systemizing and autism. According to Baron-Cohen, people on the autism spectrum tend to score low on the EQ and high on both the SQ and AQ. Baron-Cohen sees autism as an imbalance between two types of intelligence: empathizing and systemizing. Research shows from Baron-Cohen's EQ, SQ, and AQ, autistic people are extreme systemizes and do it in an unusual way. On the AQ, Baron-Cohen states that mathematicians scored the highest of all and were closely followed by engineers, computer scientists, and physicists. Of course, there are always individual differences. Some people may score high on all three quotients, and some may score low on all three. The EQ, SQ, and AQ may help people, adults in particular, estimate where they place on the spectrum. It would be fascinating to do research on examining the differences between girls and boys with Asperger's using the three quotients Simon Baron-Cohen has created to get an even better understanding of the differences between girls and boys with Asperger's. However, because a person's place on the spectrum may change with time and over contexts, these quotients may not be fully reliable. But it would be interesting for an adult with Asperger's to take it every few years to see how their scores change.

Making inferences on the above research with assuming typical girls are better empathizers than boys, and boys are better systematizers than girls, it is likely girls with Asperger's, on average, are better empathizers than boys with Aspergers. However, they are probably not as good as typical girls with Asperger's at empathizing. Or perhaps girls with Asperger's may be able to empathize but do it in an unusual way, or they may fail to recognize situations where an empathetic response is typical. They may not be able to always perceive when it is the best time to show an appropriate empathetic response. They may be able to see another person's perspective, but instead of showing the typical socially appropriate empathetic response, they may tend to offer advice or a solution to the problem another person is having. This might be because girls with Asperger's may be better systematizers than typical girls. Using the quotients Simon Baron-Cohen created, these theories can be tested.

Because there are so many differences in typical boys and girls, it makes sense that there would be individual differences in girls and boys with Asperger's. Exploring and understanding differences in typical boys and girls helps us understand differences between boys and girls with Asperger's! Girls with Asperger's face certain issues that are unique to them.

Personal experience with girls and boys on the autism spectrum

When I first began working with children who had autism in 1999, I had worked with several boys with moderate to severe autism before I began with my first little girl. Referring to the 20-point scale of the autism spectrum I discussed in the introduction (1-9 Aspergers, 10-20 autism) I estimate my first few boys to be on the spectrum of between 15 and 20. Therefore, based on the boys I had been working with, I had formed my perception of what autism was. I had not even heard the words "Asperger's" or "autism spectrum" at that time. Taking my perception of what autism was, it was only after about 15 minutes on my first visit with the three-year-old little girl that I had determined she was not autistic. She easily made eye contact, she complied to everything I asked of her from her set of programs and she imitated everything I did. We played with Legos, and she listened attentively while I read her a book. She sat on my lap and it was easy to make her laugh without the toys in the bag I brought. Surely this child didn't have autism I thought. She did have some echolalia, but at the time I thought that was normal for a three year-old-child. After my visit with her, I told her mom I didn't think she was autistic. Her mom informed me that she did indeed have autism because she knew how to recognize the symptoms based upon her work with children with developmental delays before having children of her own. Would her mom had been able to recognize there was something different about her daughter if it weren't for her previous experience with children on the spectrum? I think many new therapists, new professionals and parents may assume their child doesn't have autism because of either lack of understanding, knowledge and/or relying on their perception of what autism is based on the boys.

I continued to visit this little girl for two hours at a time several times a week, and as I got to know her as a person better, and had the opportunity to observe her in a typical classroom, I began to see that she was not exactly like typical children. She was very sensitive to certain sensory stimuli such as sounds and textures. This little girl would also become upset and cry when the schedule suddenly changed and when something from her toy sets were missing. Looking back on when I first began with this girl, I estimate she was on the spectrum of about 11 within the 20-point scale. After a year of working with her, I began to take her places including the library, the mall, the duckpond and to church. I felt a strong connection with her and felt I understood many of the problems she was dealing with. I remember shadowing her at her preschool one day. We walked into the lunchroom and she began shaking and insisting on leaving the lunchroom due to her ears hurting. There was a loud cleaning machine that the custodian was using to clean the floors on the other side of the lunchroom. Her teacher assumed that she was just scared of the machine and that it was important for her to work through her fear and go back into the lunchroom. However, I knew that the girl perceived the machine to be too loud and hurt her ears so I kindly asked the machine be turned off during lunchtime since there were also so many kids in the lunchroom.

When this girl was nine years old, she received the diagnosis of giftedness, and a year later was said to have Asperger's instead of autism. She had very involved parents and many different types of therapies including ABA therapy, speech therapy, sensory integration and vision therapy. I now estimate her to be on the the spectrum, from the 20-point scale, of a seven and look for her place on the spectrum to continue moving down as she continues to make remarkable progress by using her giftedness to overcome struggles.

In addition to working with more boys, I began working with other little girls and they too didn't express their symptoms as clearly and boldly as the boys did. Their affection and ability to play with toys and puppets caused me to think that girls with autism were much less severe than boys. Except for a few girls, one who was later diagnosed with Rett's syndrome, another who had severe food allergies, and another who later found out she had cerebal palsy, most girls I worked with were much easier in terms of behavior management than the boys, even the very youngest of age two and the oldest of age 14. I also noticed that the girls were more determined to learn and determined to overcome their struggles than the boys. I believe this determination helps them and many other girls on the spectrum overcome many of the struggles they faced and meet academic standards. Girls enjoy coloring and writing much more than the boys. In fact, some of the boys I have worked with absolutely hated to color, therefore, I had to compete with their hate of coloring using the best positive reinforcement for that particular child in order to teach them how to color and teach them to like coloring since coloring is something frequently done in early school years. After working with many children from places all over the spectrum, I do believe that girls can have the same characteristics, and some of them to the same number and degree as boys, but they have the tendency to express those sympoms differently and cover up many of their characteristics with their typical "girlish" behaviors such as playing with dolls, interest in animals, being more quiet, bashful, shy and affectionate.

During my first few years of working with children with autism, I learned that not all children with autism were the same, in fact, each one of them was very different in terms of language, social skills, communication skills, cognition, problem solving, mathematical ability, reading ability, reading comprehension, self stimulation behaviors, obsessive compulsive behaviors, disruptive behaviors, aggressive behaviors and self injurious behaviors. I was happy to learn about the "autism spectrum" and "Asperger's" after making that inference. I think it is very important for parents, professionals and anyone else involved in the field of autism to understand that every child on the autism spectrum is on a different place. Not one child is like another and girls are not like boys. Therefore every program for each child will not be exactly the same. Programs should be created strictly on an individual basis.

Over the years, I learned to be able to analyze the children's behaviors and determine just why those behaviors were occuring and how to help them learn better replacement behaviors to get their needs met. I have a tendency to look for patterns to solve problems. I learned that there were patterns to all behaviors and they all had a specific causes. There is a pattern to the level of autism a child has with considering genetics, parent's characteristics, medical issues, degree of heavy metals in the blood, what type of metals there are, history of pregnancy, childbirth, food cravings, allergies, immune system functioning, living environment, mood, structure and exposure to other specific toxins. Every cause has an effect. Every effect has a cause. The pieces of the puzzle can be gathered, analyzed and put together for a clearer picture.

Creating more programs for girls with Asperger's

Currently, there are very few centers advertised that offer specific services for girls with autism spectrum conditions and their families. Shana Nichols, Gina Moravcik and Semara Tetenbaum, authors of *Girls Growing up on the Autism Spectrum* have a highly successful program in Denver, Colorado that includes friendship skills development for teen girls with autism spectrum conditions, group therapy, community outings, parent support and networking, individual sessions, consultations and trainings. Perhaps existing centers for autism spectrum conditions can include and follow their protocol for providing services for girls with Asperger's. Different states provide different services, so it is good to contact the state autism society for more information regarding specific services for girls.

In order for programs to better help girls with Aspergers, complete understanding of them is necessary. A good way to better understand girls with Asperger's is to listen to them. It is important to hear from women who have Asperger's. In order to get a very thorough understanding of how women express and cope with their Asperger characteristics, it is good to hear their personal stories of their experiences while growing up. Several books have been written by women such as: Temple Grandin's *Thinking in Pictures: My Life with Autism*, Liane Holiday-Willey *Pretending to be Normal*, Donna William's *Nobody Nowhere* and Wendy Lawson's *Life Behind Glass. A Personal Account of Autism Spectrum Disorder*. While each woman has a different place on the spectrum, they each have their own experience to share dealing with the characteristic's of Asperger's. With more women on the autism spectrum writing about their personal experiences, there will be more understanding for parents and professionals to understanding girls with Asperger's, and the levels of severity, which therefore will lead better diagnosing and better programs. If you are a girl with Asperger's or think you might have Asperger's, please provide answers to the following questions and send them to flower@nehp.net.

Questions for girls and women with Asperger's

1. When did you make the realization that you were different?
2. Was it difficult to accept that you were different?
3. If you were diagnosed, when were you diagnosed? If not diagnosed by a clinician, when did you self-diagnose?
4. What kind of support would you best benefit from?
5. How do you feel about your life?
6. Do you have any problems with anxiety, depression or obsessive compulsiveness?
7. What are your sensory issues?
8. What were your main Asperger characteristics during your school years?
9. What are your main Asperger characteristics during adulthood?
10. Are you married/single? If not married, do you want to get married?
11. Did you go to college, if so, what did you major in? What is your highest level of education?
12. Do you have children, if so, how many? Do any of your children have characteristics of Asperger's or autism?
13. What would you say to the world in order for other people to better understand you?

I was able to contact several girls on the Internet who feel they have Asperger's and they provided me with their answers to the above questions.

Amanda Bailey, age 17 from Belgium

1) I realised I was different when I was about 11 years old. I talked about my interests, at that time it was mainly the universe, and I couldn't understand why the other kids thought I was odd, why they didn't listen, and why they didnt find it interesting too.

2) When I was younger it could be difficult to be different, I clearly observed that I had less friends than people around me. But it wasn'tt the fact that I had less friends, I really didnt care, just that it indicated that maybe there was something not right about me, and I couldn't tell what.

3) I self-diagnosed in the spring of 2009. I was 17 and wanted to figure out what was wrong with me. I'm planning on going to see a clinician when I turn 18 because I dont want to involve my mum. I think its best if she just think I am a extremely difficult teenager.

4) I think I will need some phycological help. If a pattern breaks, I will often burst into tears for no reason (could be a bus comming 2 min late, or that I didn't wake up at nine on a saturday if I had planned it – even though I don't have to get up by a specific reason).

5) I feel that my life has been devoted to finding the truth. And I am determined that it can be found by combining maths, physics, philosophy and art. So this is how I spend all my time possible, and I do not intent to waste it. I think my life is very rich!

6) I suffer from depression if anybody takes what I am obsessed by away from me. Mostly its maths, and it can be one of my classmates taking my math notebook from me, and I freak out (I know all this is silly, but I cant help it, and in these situations I feel ashamed).

7) I dont think I have any sensory issues, at least not so serious that I have noticed/or is a problem for me.

8) I'm extremely antisocial and devoted to my work. The teachers settled that I was only a problem child, because I had difficulties expressing myself (about feelings etc and therefore reacted aggressive, this actually got me expelled when I was 11, they didn't know what to do with me (I never actually hurt anyone physically, but they claimed I could do so).

9) I will not be an adult for another three months, but at this point I prefer to avoid small talk, still determined to find some truth, enjoy advanced words, often repeat sentences I like (and I do this all the time), I have got certain routines, and I want complete order (a perfectionist). I'm very sensitive to human touch, mostly I dont like it, and even sometimes I feel like washing my self afterwards. And I have difficulties relating to the real world, feel best in my own world of abstract mathematics.

10) My love of my life is currently in the army, but we have talked about being engaged, so yes I do plan to get married.

11) I havn't attended college yet.

12) I havn't any children yet.

13) I would say that people shouldn't mind us as much as some of them do. And they should leave us alone, and respect that we don't find joy in simply just getting drunk. They should be aware of the condition, instead of mocking with the word "nerd". As well as they should mind my moments of rage over nothing, just, ignore it. In the same time, they should respect my limits of touching - not feel offended by it. And just accept, that we aren't all alike, but we would never do anything on purpose to hurt any of them.

Kerry Thompson, age 25, from London

1. I've known since a young age that I was different. I was never like my peers and didn't fit in well at school. As a result I was bullied throughout most of my school life.

2. It has been difficult at times, especially during all the years when I didn't know about Asperger's. It is hard trying to grow up in a world that doesn't feel right. Sometimes I feel proud about who I am and would not want to change myself, and at other times I just wish I could be a bit more normal or able to do simple things that other people take for granted.

3. I haven't been officially diagnosed yet, but I am seeking a diagnosis. When I first found out about Asperger's I went to my GP and said that's what I thought I had but he said there is no way I can have it and that was that. I have since found out that doctors do not have a lot of knowledge about the condition and are often reluctant to diagnose. I have no doubt I have it and people very close to me agree so I will try again with a different doctor soon.

4. Definitely social skills training. Being told what to do in certain situations, what not to do, strategies to deal with conflict etc. I saw a psychologist for

anxiety and mentioned I thought I had Aspergers, but he didn't understand how to help at all. He always talked about emotions and feelings and he just didn't get the fact that I don't understand emotions and feelings. I felt like banging my head against the wall in every session. It needs to be easier to get support for aspergers. It is so difficult and for people who find it hard to express their feelings it is difficult in the first place to even disclose that they are having difficulties.

5. I wouldn't change my life for anything, I just wish it was easier. Because you can't physically see I have something wrong with me people treat me like they would treat other people and often this causes me a lot of anxiety, but it never gets fixed because I can't communicate my distress. I have lost friends because they think bad things about me, but it's just because they don't understand my issues, and this upsets me more than anything.

6. I have big problems with anxiety, and now this has also led to me having quite bad IBS. This has added even more embarrassment and uncomfortableness to my life. I used to suffer a lot from depression, but it's not so bad now. I go through patches of having mood swings though, one minute I can be on top of the world and the next second very depressed. I suffered from OCD badly when I was younger and rituals would take up hours of every day. It has got better over time though. It gets worse when I am anxious though.

7. I have so many sensory issues it really gets in the way of life. I can't stand hearing people eat and small noises other people barely notice really bother me. Also loud, sudden noises often reduce me to tears. I am a very picky eater and people comment on it a lot, which really bothers me. I can't stand a lot of smells and doing the cleaning can be a real bother. I have had to go and lie in a dark room sobbing many times during cleaning the house. It's all the smells I can't deal with. Touch is also an issue, I hate being touched lightly and often knock my boyfriend away when he tries to touch me, which he sees as me being disinterested but really I just can't stand the way he is touching me. But I'm unable to communicate this so we are both left feeling miserable.

8. Saying and doing inappropriate things, OCD, interests different to my peers, social anxieties.

9. Sensory issues, lack of showing emotions, social anxieties, needing routines and control.

10. I'm in a long term relationship. He knows I'm not like most other people, but he says that's why he likes me. He doesn't know I have aspergers yet, but I am trying to tell him my difficulties. Usually I email him when talking about my difficulties as I find this means of communication easiest.

11. I have a teaching degree and have been a teacher for nearly five years. I love working with children, because I find them so much less confusing than adults. Teaching suits me because I love being very organised and making lists and things like that and we have lots of routines and a timetable. It does cause me stress when unpredictable things happen, but I can usually cope with it. I do find teaching hard though because of the staff and parents. Communicating with adults is very hard for me, and I think I put on a good show and make myself seem natural, but it is hard work for me. I often get home from work and have to sleep because I am so exhausted, my boyfriend doesn't understand why yet, he just thinks I'm lazy.

12. I have no children, but I really want some. I think I will be a good mum, but I worry if I will cope.

13. Really I want to write a user manual for myself, but clearly that's not going to happen. I think the best things to say are: 1) if I'm being stubborn or controlling it is most likely I'm anxious so instead of trying to get your own way try and figure out why I am anxious, 2) say exactly how you feel and what you want, don't assume I will understand your NT riddles, 3) if I won't make eye contact with you, it means I'm uncomfortable, if it's a conversation that can be done via email or something similar that would probably be better.

I also received answers from a boy with Asperger's. Compare his answers to the girls.

Jaimes Dallymore, age 30, United Kingdom

1. There was a definite change when I started secondary school.

2. Yes, I misbehaved a lot (making silly noises in class) and was statemented aged 14 and it was recommended by the educational psychologist that I go to a boarding school.

3. I was diagnosed in August 2002 when I was 23.

4. Hmm this question is tricky... as some 'support' I've been given particularly with regards to trying to find and keep a suitable job has become more of a hindrance at times.

5. Fairly content. At least a lot more than I used to be.

6. Yes, I've had issues with all three and have had a few 'breakdowns' in the last five years, which required hospitalization. For the best part of the last three years though I've been fairly stable. I had a big issue with OCD as a teenager (having to write everything I thought and heard down) but since my last breakdown I feel that I'm over the worst.

7. Not sure how to answer this... same as above I suppose.

8. Talking incessantly about one topic at times, being the classroom clown, not recognizing when enough was enough etc.

9. Finding it hard to concentrate on one thing for too long at a time (especially a mundane task). This is why keeping work has been tough. If it's something I enjoy and find a challenge on the other hand I can do it for hours.

10. I'm single and I'm not sure I want to get married, at least not yet.

11. I studied at university for two years but quit due to having a breakdown.

12. No.

13. Let me do my own thing and do what keeps me well, as I'm a bit of a free spirit.

Foreword by Liane Holliday Willey

What I find interesting is that Jaimes being a boy responded to his feelings of being different by "misbehaving" and "being the class clown." He was given a diagnosis. Amanda and Kerry, both girls, grew up unnoticed but are sure they have Asperger's. Kerry had even tried to seek a diagnosis but did not receive one. "I have since found out that doctors do not have a lot of knowledge about the condition and are often reluctant to diagnose." Anyone very familiar with Asperger's Syndrome can tell from her answers that she has it. There is still the need to spread awareness. I wonder how many girls out there are still trying to figure out why they are so different. With the spread of Asperger's awareness, they will soon find out.

Discussion

Our society has been creating standards and teaching techniques based on the needs with boys who have Asperger's. So many girls have struggled with Asperger's, yet teachers and parents may not be aware. Girls are a different population with Asperger's with specific struggles and specific needs. They need recognition and support while teachers and parents can learn to identify and appreciate them. Examining existing research on boys and girls on the autism spectrum, and examining the research done on typical boys and girls helps us all better understand girls with Asperger's. In addition, hearing personal stories from girls with Asperger's will help better understand individual differences, perspectives and needs.

Although therapies such as applied behavior analysis, speech therapy, sensory integration therapy, vision therapy, and music therapy are very beneficial to all children, girls may need specific help with issues that they face. These girls can benefit from social therapy, group therapy, individual cognitive therapy, academic adjustments, learning how to tolerate and cope with sensory sensitivities, learning how to cope with intense emotions, and importantly learn they are not alone in what they experience. Girls don't need professionals and teachers specifically to change them and make them be like everybody else. Girls with Asperger's need to be accepted, understood and given appropriate solutions to the issues they face. Some of them will need help with decoding the social rules and given the decision for themselves whether or not they want to be in the typical peer mainstream or if they are happy with themselves. There is so much learning girls with Asperger's can do that will help them have wonderful, successful, joyful, productive and happy lives. Teachers and parents can learn how to support their girls.

In the next few chapters, I share clues and experiences of my own life with Asperger's moving from an estimated two on the scale mentioned in the introduction, then up to an eight in middle school, down to a six by the last year of high school and to a five after getting married. In addition and throughout I include my perceptions and conclusions from analyzing the children with autism spectrum conditions I have worked with since 1999. I offer understanding, relation, solutions and advice.

Suggested Readings

- *Asperger's and Girls* featuring Tony Attwood and Temple Grandin (2006)
- *Pretending to be Normal* by Liane Holiday Willey (1999)
- *Thinking in Pictures* by Temple Grandin (1995)
- *Life Behind Glass. A Personal Account of Autism Spectrum Disorder* by Wendy Lawson (2003)
- *Nobody Nowhere: The Remarkable Autobiography of an Autistic Girl* by Donna Williams (1992)
- *Women From Another Planet?: Our Lives in the Universe of Autism* by Jean Miller (2003)
- *The Essential Difference: The Truth about the Male and Female Brain* by Simon Baron Cohen (2003)
- *Asperger's - If You Only Knew: A Family's Struggle with Asperger's Syndrome* by Sophia Summers (2007)
- *Finding a Different Kind of Normal: Misadventures With Asperger Syndrome* by Jeanette Purkis (2006)
- *Born on the Wrong Planet* by Erika Hammerschmidt (2008)
- *Congratulations! It's Asperger Syndrome* by Jen Birch (2003)

References

Attwood, Tony. (2006). *The Pattern of Abilities and Development of Girls with Asperger's Syndrome.* Asperger's and Girls. Future Horizons, Inc.

Benditt, L. (1994). Women in science. Comparisons across cultures. *Science, 263*, 1391-1496.

Berlin, B., Boster, J.S. & O'Neill, J.P. (1981). The perceptual basis of ethnobiological classification: evidence from Aguaruna Jfvaro ornithology. *Journal of Ethnobiology, 1*, 95-108.

Blanc, R. Le. (2009, September 8). *The Symptoms of Asperger's Syndrome in Interactions Between Persons.* Retrieved October 18, 2009, from http://ezinearticles.com/?The-Symptoms-of-Aspergers-Syndrome-in-Interactions-Between-Persons&id=2889502

Baron-Cohen, S. (2003). *The Essential Difference: The Truth about the Male and Female Brain.* New York: Basic Books.

Baron-Cohen, S. & Wheelwright, S. (1998, *in press*). The friendship and relationship questionnaire(FQ): An investigation of adults with Asperger syndrome or high-functioning autism, and normal sex differences. *Journal of Autism and Developmental Disorders.*

Baron-Cohen, S., O'Riordan, M., Jones, R., Stone, V., & Plaisted, K. (1999).

Recognition of faux pas by normally developing children and children with Aspergers Syndrome or high functioning autism. *Journal of Autism and Developmental Disorders, 29*, 407-418.

Baron-Cohen, S., Wheelwright, S., Griffin, R., Lawson, J., & Hill, J. (2002). The exact mind: empathizing and systemizing in autism spectrum conditions, in U. Goswami (ed.), *Handbook of Cognitive Development.* Oxford, Blackwell.

Campbell, A. (1995). A few good men: evolutionary psychology and female adolescent aggression. *Ethiology and Sociobiology, 16,* 99-123.

Connellan, J., Baron-Sohen, S., Wheelwright, S., Ba'tki, A. & Ahluwalia, J. (2001). Sex differences in human neonatal social perception. *Infant Behavior and Development, 23,* 113-118.

Crombie, G. & Desjardins, M.J. (1993). Predictors of gender, the relative importance of children's play, games and personality characteristics? New Orleans, conference paper, Society for research in Child Development (SRCD).

Darula, B. (2009, August 17). *Is There Proof That Boys Have More Symptoms of Autism Than Girls? What Do the Experts Say?.* Retrieved October 18, 2009, from http://ezinearticles.com/?Is-There-Proof-That-Boys-Have-More-Symptoms-of-Autism-Than-Girls?-What-Do-the-Experts-Say?&id=2772920

Davis, C. & Fox. J. (2001). Functional behavioral assessment and students with autism. *Focus on Autism & Other Developmental Disabilities, 16,* 202-205.

Faherty, Catherine. (2002). *Asperger's Syndrome in Women: A different Set of Challenges?* Autism-Asperger's Digest. Arlington, TX: Future Horizons.

Geary, D. (1998). *Male, Female.* Washington DC, American Psychological Association.

Hall, J. (1984). *Nonverbal sex differences: communication accuracy and expressive style.* Baltimore, Johns Hopkins University Press.

Hill, Amanda. (2009). *Doctor's are failing to spot Asperger's in girls.* Retreived October 18th, 2009 at http://www.guardian.co.uk/lifeandstyle/2009/apr/12/autism-aspergers-girls.

Hoffman, M.L. (1977). Sex differences in empathy and related behaviors. *Psychological Bulletin, 84,* 712-722.

Interlandi, J. (2008). More than Just 'Quirky'. The Mind, Life, Health; Newsweek. November 13, 2008. Retrieved November 23rd, 2009. http://www.newsweek.com/id/168868

Kimura, D. (1999). *Sex and Cognition.* Cambridge, Mass., MIT Press.

Lutchmaya, S., Baron-Cohen, S. & Raggatt, P. (2002). Foetal testosterone and vocabulary size in 18 and 24 month old infants. *Infant Behavior and Development, 24(4),* 418-424.

Maccoby, E. E. (1998). *The Two Sexes: Growing Up Apart, Coming Together.* Cambridge, Massachusetts: Harvard University Press.

Mannle, S. & Tomasello, M. (1987). Fathers, siblings, and the bridge hypothesis in K.A. Nelson and A van Kleek (eds.). *Children's Language,* Hillside, N.J., Erlbaum.

McLennan, J.D., Lord, C. and Schopler, E. (1993). Sex differences in higher functioning people with autism. Journal of Autism and Developmental Disorders 23, 217-227.

Myers, Jennifer M. (2006) Foreword to Asperger's and Girls. Future Horizons, Inc.

Nichols, S., Moravcik, G.M., Tetenbaum, S.P. (2009). Girls Growing up on the Autism Spectrum : What Parents and Professionals should know about the Pre-teen and Teenage Years. Jessica Kingsley Publishers, London.

Stanley, J.C. (1990). We need to know why women falter in math. *The Chronicle of Higher Education.*

Strayer, F.F. (1980). Child etiology and the study of preschool social relations in H.C.

Foot, A.J. Chapman and J.R. Smith (eds.), *Friendship and Social Relations In Children.* New York, John Wiley and Sons Inc. The Confluence (2009). Asperger's in Girls: A Lonely Childhood Undiagnosed. Retrieved November 23rd, 2009. http://riverdaughter.wordpress.com/2009/04/22/aspergers-in-girls-a-lonely-childhood-undiagnosed/

Reese, R., Richman, D., Belmont, L., and Morse, P. (2005). Functional characteristics of disruptive behavior in developmental disables children with and without autism. Journal of Autism and Developmental Disorders 35, 419-428.

Wagner, Shelia. (2006). *Educating the Female Student with Asperger's.* Future Horizons, Inc.

Watson, N.V. & Kimura, D. (1991). Nontrivial sex differences in throwing and intercepting: relation to psychometrically-defined spatial functions. *Personality and Individual Differences, 12,* 375-385.

CHAPTER 3

Clues From Early Childhood

Researchers agree that autism spectrum conditions have a genetic component. I think there may be observable behaviors or signs in young children that may lead to a better prediction of the condition. With these signs, a reaction to an environmental insult such as a heavy metal and other environmental toxin, which can trigger the increase in number and intensity of the characteristics, may be predicted. I think it is possible to prevent or at least decrease the chances or severity of the sudden or gradual onset of the increase in these characteristics that would place a person on the autism spectrum. There are many factors to look for in family members, characteristics to observe in infancy and early childhood. In this chapter, I describe observable clues in infancy and early childhood. I include a list of questions, or a checklist of possible indicators to look for in babies and preschoolers. I also share events in this chapter of my recollections from my early childhood years in terms of specific events and health issues. Lastly, signs from a parent – my own dad - are discussed, along with a closing discussion.

Things to look for in babies and preschoolers

When you were a baby and young child, did you have any of these characteristics below? The following questions are designed to identify possible characteristics in infants and young children. These characteristics could possibly be clues that the child may be a part of the milder end of autism spectrum. A regression to a more severe part of the spectrum may take place with an environmental insult. Clues do not necessarily reflect only autism or Asperger's, but also similar conditions such as ADHD, ADD, OCD, ODD and even giftedness.

Infants

- Did the infant have a difficult birth with temporary lack of oxygen?
- Does the infant have a poor immune system, often times experiencing infections such as ear or upper-respiratory infections?
- Does the infant require frequent use of antibiotics?
- Does the infant have skin rashes such as eczema and/or yeast or fungal rashes?
- Does the infant appear sensitive to loud noises? Does the infant shake or flinch with hearing typical everyday noises such as a bag rattling or the air-conditioner turning on?
- Does the infant demand to be held a particular way with specific movement, such as being bounced in an upright position, but gets fussy with any other movement like swaying or even remaining still?
- Does the infant have difficulty relaxing and sleeping?
- Is it difficult to calm the infant by cuddling or stroking?
- Does the infant have a parent who has an autoimmune condition such as rheumatoid arthritis, diabetes, thyroid disease or fibromyalgia?
- Does the infant have a parent or close relative with many characteristics of Asperger's?
- Does the infant have a parent or close family member who is involved in engineering, physics, math or computer science?

Young children

- Does the child stare into space at times and appear in his/her own world?
- Does the child avoid playing with other children of the same age?
- Does the child appear to dislike large crowds?
- Does the child either over-react to pain or under-react to pain?
- Does the child have difficulty recognizing basic emotions in people or pictures?
- Does the child have intense interests while ignoring everything else?
- Is the child a picky eater?
- Does the child eat things that are not edible such as crayons, soap or glue?
- Does the child have allergies?
- Does the child crave dairy products?
- Does the child crave wheat products such as pasta, crackers and bread?
- Does the child suffer from constipation or diarrhea?
- Does the child speak of having very vivid dreams and insist on describing every detail of those dreams?
- Does the child have an unusual tone of speaking?
- Does the child have difficulty making eye contact?
- Does the child speak with very precise detail?
- Does the child have difficulty learning information of non-interest?
- Does the child have a good long-term memory, such as being able to remember a minor detail in the past that most people would have forgotten?
- Does the child either lack imaginary play (don't do it at all) or do it in excess (do it almost constantly)?
- Does the child seem to constantly ask questions about topics of fascination?
- Does the child become very upset by changes in a schedule?
- Does the child suddenly tantrum for no apparent reason?
- Does the child have difficulty sitting still while squirming, bouncing and jumping most of the time?

- Does the child insist on doing things certain ways and reject suggestions to doing them other ways?
- Does the child sometimes or much of the time walk on his/her toes?
- Does the child sometimes appear to be clumsy?
- Does the child either have an intense fear of or an intense liking to water?
- Does the child hold his/her ears with specific noises?
- Does the child complain about socks hurting, clothes feeling too tight, or very sensitive to what shoes he/she wears?
- Does the child get motion sickness when participating in activities, such as swinging too long or riding in a car on curvy roads?
- Does the child engage in behaviors for long periods of time, such as running back and forth, flapping his/her arms, starring at spinning objects or taking off and putting on the lids to pens or markers?
- Does the child appear to have a low attention span, such as being unable able to focus on anything of non-interest?
- Does the child appear to be intelligent for his/her age?
- Does the child make an effort to predict things, or does the child frequently ask questions about what is coming next on the schedule?
- Does the child enjoy lining up toys or grouping them in some way?
- Does the child enjoy collecting things?
- Does the child laugh at things that don't seem funny?

These questions were developed from my years of experience providing therapy for children on the autism spectrum, my own situation, experience from observing my own children and from extensive research from autism experts and specific medical professionals while analyzing patterns in cause and effect. Answering yes to many of them does not mean a child definitely has Asperger's. The answers to the questions are just clues to be aware. If many of the questions received a "yes" answer, methods can be taken to improve immune system functioning and methods can be used to prevent exposure to environmental toxins to decrease the chances of a child regressing into autism or a more severe place on the spectrum.

My early childhood

I do not believe that I had enough characteristics as a little child to be considered as having "Asperger's Syndrome." I did have many characteristics that I perceive now to be good clues. It became more obvious once I started school and became even more obvious when I was eleven years old and up.

I remember feeling very happy as a little kid and my pictures all have me smiling from ear to ear. The joyfulness that I had as a preschooler gradually diminished throughout my school years. I wonder how many children lose their joyfulness during the school years when they began to realize they are different than the other kids. It was a shocking realization. I was so happy and I thought everybody else was just like me. When I discovered that I was a square peg and most everybody else was a round peg, I was confused, embarrassed and temporarily determined to become a round peg too. But it wasn't until I finally accepted that I was a square peg that allowed myself to feel joy once again.

My parents did not keep a record of my milestones or first words but my mom said she remembers that I did not learn my colors until age three because she couldn't get me to pay attention long enough in order to teach me. I referred to all colors as "color." She said I had no interest in watching TV. Since I didn't have any brothers or sisters, it was common for me to play alone. I greatly enjoyed playing with blocks, tinker toys and my hammer and peg toy. I also enjoyed grouping things together by size or by color. I began collecting things such as baby pinecones and stuffed animals and found a great deal of pleasure adding to my collections. I would arrange and rearrange them over and over. By the time I was 15, I had large collections of ceramic cats, foreign money, old US coins, shells, rocks, hats, snow globes, squishy balls and candy. By the time I was 17, I began to get really irritated at the clutter my collections brought about and decided to get rid of most of them. This relieved a great deal of unwanted clutter in my brain.

I remember when I was three and four years old looking for matches around the house to eat. I remember searching in the drawers in the kitchen and in my parent's rooms for boxes of matches. When I found one, I remember I would eat the match head off every match in a packet. I got great satisfaction out of this. Matches were made with mostly phosphorus sesquisulfide and potassium. I wonder if my body was lacking a mineral. I have seen many children with autism eat things that were not food such as crayons, erasers, pencils and paper. One child I worked with ate items including lotion, toothpaste, soap, foam, cotton and even chewed on the blinds in his bedroom. I believe these children were lacking essential vitamins and minerals.

When I was about three years old, I remember having an intense interest in umbrellas and when asked what I wanted for Christmas or birthday I would answer "umbrella!" I liked the way they looked when they were open; it gave me comfort and made me feel protected. My mom said all kids love umbrellas and it was normal for me to want to play with them. I also had an intense interest in kittens and cats. I remember feeling all happy and gooey inside when I saw a kitten. The feelings of joy were wonderful when I got to hold one. My dad got me my first cat when I was three, and I remember holding, petting and playing with my cat. I put that cat inside of things so it wouldn't get away. My mom said she found the cat in the kitchen trashcan one day. By the time I was 13, my room was covered in cat posters, and I had a very large collection of ceramic cats. I didn't care much for puppies or other animals. I became greatly interested in barnyard animals when I was 11. After I found out I had Asperger's I told my husband that I thought cats have Asperger's because they flinch when suddenly touched. Cats are independent, dislike crowds and are very particular who they like.

My mom enrolled me in dance lessons when I was three. On the first lesson, there was another girl named Casey who stood next to me and smiled. Wow, she had pigtails just like me, she had dark brown hair just like me and she was wearing the exact same pink leotard that I was. I smiled back at her and followed her to the corner where the mats were, and we began tumbling around. Despite the dance instructor's constant requests that we pay attention, Casey and I did not obey. We laughed and played, and we were therefore separated. I was ultimately moved to another class due to my misbehavior. But that was not the end to the friendship between Casey and myself. We later became best friends when we found ourselves in each other's first grade class at school.

I hated Barbie dolls. I once tried playing with the dolls because my mom really wanted me to but it was not fun at all. What do you do with a bunch of little women made out of plastic? I later found out that other girls liked to play with Barbie dolls but I just couldn't get myself to like them even when I tried. Although I hated Barbies, I greatly loved baby dolls. I loved to pretend I was a mommy, and my baby doll was a real baby. I loved to change their clothes, pretend to feed them, change their diapers, push them around in a stroller, sing them a lullaby and put them to bed. I remember carrying my baby doll with me when we went places like to the store and out to eat. When I would see other mothers with their real babies I would feel so important because to me, I had a real baby to. This is typical behavior of a little girl, and I believe there might be some kind instinct for little girls to be attracted to babies.

I remember my socks hurting my feet and I couldn't stand wearing them. I also hated shoes and preferred to go barefooted. When my Mom insisted I wear them, I begged her to cut out the seams. I hated jeans or any tight clothing; they were very uncomfortable.

My dad bought a video camera when I was three so I retrieved the videos while writing this chapter. Most of the videos of me were with my parents and not with other kids, except my older cousins and I copied everything thing they did. I remember loving it when my older cousins came over. There was one in particular who was four years older than me that I loved being with. In the videos, I am playing with her constantly. As I grew older I found that I also loved playing with children much younger than me. My next-door neighbor was four years younger than me, and we spent a lot of time together. I remember frequently playing "school" with her and "house" with her as I would be the teacher, she the student or I would be the mother and her the daughter. When I was with older children I took the role as a follower, and when I was with younger children I took the role as the leader. I had a very hard time playing with children of my own age. I didn't know which role to take. As an adult, most of my friends are either much older or much younger than I am, except my few best friends I grew up with going to school.

My observations of ages three to five on the home videos, I was mostly a very loud, high energetic and happy child. I was always smiling, laughing and jumping around. Most people told me I was very hyper all throughout my childhood. Almost all of the home videos were taken vacations such as the beach and the mountains. Looking at the videos, I looked like a typical little girl with mostly typical behavior for a young child. However, I didn't grow out of many of my childish behaviors like other kids did at the time they did. I couldn't understand why my peers wanted to change, because I was happy being the same active, silly person.

Interesting moments in the videos:

- Many instances when my Dad would ask me a question, he would have to ask me several times before I would notice or respond. There were videos of me looking at something or playing in the sand when my Dad would ask me a question and I would completely ignore him. While this might be a little bit typical for small children, it is not for older children and adults. I have always struggled with paying attention. People today in my life today tell me they are talking to me but I don't seem to be aware of it – I really was not aware. People have told me that I seem to be "spaced out" or "in my own world."
- When I was three at Disney World, one of the people dressed up in a Chip and Dale costume came over to me and touched my face, I then looked away with an irritated look on my face and wouldn't look back. My mom now recalls that I didn't like to be suddenly touched.
- When I was three, I was sitting on the bench at the races eating raw oysters like they were candy. I remember loving the squishy slimy feeling as I ate them. Oysters are an excellent source of zinc. Zinc is a mineral most people on the autism spectrum, when tested, lack.
- When my parents and I went to visit my grandmother and other relatives when I was four, I went around growling at people and all the ceramic or stuffed animals, and then laughed hysterically. I also frequently lifted up my skirt. None of the adults corrected me or told me to stopped growling. My mom reports that I always acted like that so she didn't think anything of it.

- At the beach I would run up and down the beach screaming and hollering with my arms up and my hands flapped over flopping myself in and out of the sand and water. My mom said that all kids with high energy run up and down the beach screaming. I did this in my early teens as well. Cute for a little kid, but not so cute for an older kid.
- I swam in the ocean very well for such a young girl, anticipated big waves and loved being knocked over by them. I remember how much I loved the feeling of water on my face while I was swimming. My mom tells me I was able to jump off the diving board and swim to the side by myself by age three. I loved water.
- In the videos, I would frequently give my mom backwards hugs while smiling and laughing. She always spoke of me as very affectionate when I was a young child. Many children on the spectrum prefer backwards hugs.
- Most of the time the camera was on me, I was smiling and making funny faces.
- There were hardly any video of me being still; I was always jumping, running, swimming, hiking, riding my trike etc…

Health

I remember having a lot of ear infections and my mom would iron little handkerchiefs for me to put on my ear. The heat from the handkerchief was pleasant to my aching ear. I was prescribed antibiotics for all the ear infections. I also had strep throat very frequently and I remember crying whenever my throat began to hurt because I knew I was going to have to get another shot of penicillin. I don't know how many ear infections I had, but I do clearly remember the terrible pain. My mom reports that I had several ear infections each year and had strep throat about every other month.

After I began school, I also had frequent sinus infections. I also tended to run fevers that were not explained by a virus or bacteria, and they would usually last a day. The ear infections discontinued when I was around nine but the sinus infections and fevers for no apparent reason continued throughout life. I really think the fevers were either a result from multiple food allergies bombarding my immune system or from high stress. To this day I will run a low-grade fever during extremely stressful events.

I began having very frequent nosebleeds when I was three. I remember having them in the middle of the night and having to get up and stay up until they stopped. During the fall and spring, I would have up to five nosebleeds a day. Finally when I was a teenager I went to the doctor when I was wasn't able to get them to stop within an hour after starting and the doctor burned the bloodvessels in my nose. This hurt so badly, but I was glad that the frequency of the nosebleeds decreased to about one a month. I still have them.

I had bad allergies as a child, suffering from a stuffy and runny nose all the time. I remember taking a lot of allergy medicine. I still have allergies, especially in the fall and spring and when I am in musty and moldy places but don't take much allergy medicine because it doesn't seem to help. And I can't stand the way it makes me feel.

All of these health issues point to a problem in immune system functioning. If I were exposed to a toxin, my immune system would not be able to handle it properly. When I became exposed to toxins later in life, such as mercury and all of the other harmful ingredients in vaccines, this marked the time when characteristics of Asperger's really began to emerge and pervade my entire life.

This pattern shows itself in children diagnosed on the autism spectrum. I am unable to think of a family I have worked with who had a child with autism that didn't have immune system problems with ear infections and need for antibiotics. Most of the children I have worked with also had yeast and food allergies. Many parents didn't even know that their children had so many allergies until they had blood tests administered.

My Dad – clues from a parent

My dad was a wonderful dad. He was compassionate and gentle and would get upset if he saw a hurt animal or homeless person. Wild squirrels would eat out of his hands and once he made friends with a wild dove who visited him every day. He said when he was a boy he could never get the guts to shoot and animal when he went hunting. My dad was a deep thinker, very private person and very sensitive although he put on this macho act for everyone. Although he was an excellent engineer and very systematic in his thinking, he wrote hundreds of poems and essays on the meaning of life, and also very silly humorous poems. He was the protector of his family and made sure all of our needs were met, including making sure the refrigerator and cabinets were always full and the doors always locked.

My dad was very punctual, and he did what he said he was going to do at the time he said he would do it. He played softball with me in the backyard, took me on motorcycle rides, took us to the beach and the mountains. I liked the security of being able to trust his plans. I loved him because he was my dad and his behavior was all I knew of a dad. As I grew older I recognized that he was a little different from my friends' dads. They were not as punctual and did not have any cute little quirks that my dad had. They had a lot of friends but my dad had a few. The good thing is that my dad didn't spend all of his time with his friends and instead, he spent much of his time with his family. My dad liked to be silly, goofy and tell jokes. But on the other extreme he was very quiet, serious and logical. I remember the long talks we used to have on the back porch. He would tell me about his childhood and talk about other people. He didn't understand other people nor could he relate to them. He enjoyed having "intellectual" conversations and would get angry with my mom for not participating. He enjoyed philosophy, having debates and arguing. Even if he agreed with you on a topic he would pretend to disagree for the enjoyment of having an argument.

My Dad would frequently ask me questions like "What do you know for sure?" "What does it mean to be successful?" My responses were always different but here is a typical conversation we would have.

Dad: "Kristi, what do you know for sure?"

Me: "I know for sure that the grass is green."

Dad: "But how do you know it is green and not some other color?"

Me: "Because it looks like it is green Dad."

Dad: "But how do you know that what you see is green. Somebody else may see it as a different color but they label it as green because that is what they see?"

Me: "I will never know that for sure, I can't get in somebody else's body to see through their eyes."

Dad: "So you don't know for sure the grass is green then?"

Me: "Well Dad, I know for sure that my perception of the grass is green"

Dad: "But the problem in the world is that there are too many perceptions, take religion for example, how do you know which perception is right?"

Me: "The one that God says is right is the one that is right."

Dad: "How can you determine which one is right with so many people thinking that what they believe is right."

Me: "The Bible says what it says, I can't help it if people misinterpret it."

Dad: "But you are like everybody else, you think that what you perceive is what is the truth, there can't be multiple truths?"

Me: "hmmmm, well, hmmmmmmmm, Dad, most religions agree that God is the creator……..but, hmmmmmmmmmmm, well, the Bible says Jesus is the only way to Heaven, that is what it says and that is what I believe."

Dad: "How do you know the Bible is the truth?"

Me: "How do you not know the Bible is the truth?

Dad: "What makes you think it is true?"

Me: "All the predictions in the Bible came true and it was written by men who were inspired by God and the Holy Spirit."

Dad: "How do you know that for sure?"

Me: "Because history proves it. What about faith? What do you know for sure Dad?"

Dad: "Jesus is they way, he is my only hope although I do not fully understand."

Me: "I don't understand either, but I don't think God wants us to fully understand, he just wants us to trust Him, right?"

Dad: "How do you know for sure?"

Me: "How do you know for sure?"

I took an IQ test when I was in college and scored a 124. I knew my dad would score high on an IQ test but when I challenged him to the IQ test when he was 62, he said he didn't want to take it because he probably wouldn't score as high as he did before joining the army. I asked him what he scored and he said "140." Wow, I didn't know that! My dad a genius! I said "Do you know that a score of 140 means that you are highly gifted and nearly a genius?" He said he knew. He had never mentioned this before. I wonder why? It makes sense, because he wasn't able to relate to other people although he wanted to, and he became very frustrated when other people couldn't relate to him. He would sometimes get so angry when my mom and I couldn't understand or relate to his ideas. He was the principle engineer for Boing designing the space station. I have his resumes, all his awards and his college degree. I find them to be remarkably impressive according to the American view of what success is regarding a career. A lot of people with Asperger's are good engineers. Many of the children I have worked with on the autism spectrum have close family members who are engineers. Research shows that autism occurs significantly more often in families of the fields of physics, engineering and mathematics (Baron-Cohen, et. al, 1998).

When I found out I had Asperger's and realized that he did too, I told my dad all about Asperger's and the characteristics. I asked him if he thought he had it. He nodded his head yes. I asked him if he thought I had it and he again, nodded his head yes. I left it at that. He didn't seem interested in talking about it.

My dad also struggled with alcoholism. When he wasn't drinking he was mostly quiet, serious and logical. When he was under the influence of a little alcohol, he was very silly and goofy and fun. He frequently liked to pretend he was a toe eater and put ketchup on my feet pretending to eat my toes. He was funny and made me laugh. He liked to tell jokes and when we had guests over he would tell them jokes. My friends would tell me that I was so lucky to have a dad like I did and that he was such a cool dad. When he was under the influence of a lot of alcohol, I stayed in my room with the door locked.

My dad couldn't stand the sound of the vacuum cleaner or the lawn mower. He required my mom to do it all when he was at work. He also couldn't stand to be touched at times. I remember him flinching a lot when I touched him unexpectedly. All children and people I know with Asperger's or autism seem to have sensory issues. My dad also had terrible allergies, I mean horrible. He would have these sneeze attacks that would last like 30 minutes, sneeze after sneeze with his eyes pouring with water. In the fall and spring he had these attacks almost everyday. After I learned more about food allergies, Asperger's and autism I thought my dad was probably allergic to some foods. People crave what they are allergic to and my dad craved alcohol. What is in alcohol? Yeast. He probably had a problem with yeast build up in his body and he struggled with fungus growing on his feet and legs. When he first began drinking, he experienced a social relief because he was more relaxed and was accepted by other people. In fact when he had parties, he drank alcohol, but he was always the life of the party. Being able to fit and relate to other people is extremely reinforcing and after a while, he became physically addicted to alcohol.

One day when I was 18, I got so mad at him and told him off. I hate to see wasted potential and he was the most intelligent person I knew so I yelled at him for wasting his life on alcohol and told him with his intelligence he could do so much. He began to cry. He said he wanted to stop alcohol, it controlled him, he wished he never took the first drink, that his body hurt so badly when he went a long time without it. He did have severe withdrawals when he went over eight hours without it. He began sweating intensely and shaking uncontrollably. I was so worried and felt so scared for him that I would give him the alcohol when that happened. When I was 21, I read a book to help me prepare to get him in a facility to help him get off the alcohol that would give him other medicines to help with the withdrawals. When I had my plan all ready, my Mom told him what I was doing. He suddenly gave up hard liquor and drink only wine. He was much quieter after that and easy to be around. So I didn't think it necessary to follow through with getting him to the facility. He really didn't want to go and he gave up hard liquor for the rest of his life.

My dad died at age 67. He had given up hard liquor for six years. His health was bad but he absolutely refused to go to the doctor. He was the most stubborn man I have ever known. He did, however, go the doctor in his late 50s and received a diagnosis of Parkinson's disease. Research suggests that Parkinson's disease can be caused by certain toxins and oxidative stress that damages the substantia nigra in the brain and is associated with dopamine and other neurotransmitter dysfunction (Haines, 2005). There is research suggesting that mercury, and the dental amalgam contributes to the development of Parkinson's disease (Miller, 2003). My dentist was also diagnosed with Parkinson's disease and had to retire early. I didn't know at the time that dentists have an array of health problems, which research suggests results from being frequently exposed to mercury. A couple years later my dad had terrible skin cancer on his chest so he went to the doctor and had it surgically fixed. Two months before he died, he became extremely sick and couldn't eat but still refused to go to the doctor despite my and my mother's efforts to get him to go. Based on his symptoms I assume he had cancer or cirrhoses of the liver. My dad's death had been an absolute tragedy to me and I miss him so much. I wasn't able to read his poems or writings until two years after his death. Now, I read them frequently because it is like having a conversation with him as his writings reflect his personality, temperament and opinions. My dad was not a religious man but he claimed that Jesus was the savior and the way to Heaven. He wrote numerous beautiful poems on Jesus. I treasure them so much are read them frequently. I am so proud of my dad. He was a wonderful dad.

Discussion: Clues of genetic predisposition to environmental trigger

Are their chances that a particular child will develop and autism spectrum condition? When a parent has many characteristics of Asperger's, their children will have a higher risk. My dad had Asperger's, although we didn't find out until I found out that I had it. There is a name for the group of characteristics we embrace. Nobody even knew that there was a name for it until 1994 when it was added to the diagnostic manual and even then most clinicians were not accustomed to diagnosing it. I think the spread of autism awareness and Asperger's awareness can help parents identify it in themselves to know if their children may be at greater risk. Many of the children who have autism I have worked with have a parent with many Asperger's characteristics. I don't think they are even aware of it.

Children are insulted with environmental toxins and poor nutrition at a much earlier age today then they were 20 or 30 years ago, so there may not be enough time in infancy or early childhood to observe if there are subtle observable characteristics or clues. When environmental insults such as toxins enter the body while the immune system is already at hard work can cause the immune system to dysfunction. The toxins are then free to do damage to the brain and body.

All people have some characteristics of Asperger's, but it is the number and the intensity that will place a person on the spectrum. When I was a kid, I appeared to be a typical little girl to people, but there were a few behaviors that may have been clues that a later environmental insult to the immune system could trigger and increase in number and intensity of the characteristics. Disliking being touched, sensitive to socks and shoes, hysterical laughing, difficulty being still, backwards hugging, running back and forth with arms up and hands flipped and frequent infections may be some clues. But it is also important to keep in mind that some people with Asperger's may not appear or feel different until they are in social situations. For many, Asperger's is not diagnosed until the time when all children perceive social status to be highly important and the characteristics of Asperger's become much more obvious. And for many girls, they learn to blend in or pretend they are fitting in even when they are not. It is the individual girl who knows if she is having such struggles, because to the observer she may just a little quieter than the other kids.

My own children have many of the clues presented in this chapter and I believe I was able to prevent them from developing classic autism and will share that story at the end of the last chapter as it ties in better with that chapter better than this one. Children I have seen diagnosed with "autism" are much different than those diagnosed with "high functioning autism" or "Asperger's Syndrome." Children with autism may not have any language and have developmental delays pervading all or most areas of development. Their age of onset was much earlier in life so they were more affected. More clues of Asperger's will become apparent in social situations and groups of children and follow in the elementary school years and become clearer in the middle school years and high school years.

References

Baron-Cohen, S., Bolton, P., Wheelwright, S., Scahill, V., Short, L., Mead, G. & Smith (1998). Autism occurs more often in families of physicists, engineers, and mathematicians. Autism, 1998, 2, 296-301.

Haines, S. D. (2005). Parkinson's Disease: What Causes it? WebMD. Better information, better health. Retrieved November 14th, 2009. http://www.webmd.com/parkinsons-disease/parkinsons-causes

Miller, K., Ochudlo, S., Opala, G., Smolicha, W., Siuda, J. (2003). Parkinsonism in chronic occupational metallic mercury intoxication. Neurol Neurochir Pol. 2003;37 Suppl 5:31-8.

CHAPTER 4

School Career as a Professional Student

Once a child begins school, it can be easier to compare behavior to the other kids. This can be a good thing and a bad thing. It can be good to be able to detect signs about individual differences that may reflect the need for early intervention and specific types of therapies. It can be bad because many parents and teachers feel the need to do what it takes to make a child that doesn't seem typical to be exactly like the other children.

Another thing to consider is that children who are very quiet do not get much attention in classroom settings and will probably be overlooked. In this chapter I share events from my perspective throughout my school. None of my teachers or my parents knew how I perceived things or how I felt. Most people assumed I was just shy. Of course, nobody knew the term "Asperger's" when I was a child. With awareness, more teachers and parents can be able to observe clues from infancy throughout the school years. I didn't come to the awareness that I was different from the other girls until I was almost a teenager. At the end of this chapter, my Mother and best friends share their perspective of me growing up. Their perspective illustrates how well I covered up my feelings and difficulties.

Foreword by Liane Holliday Willey

Kindergarten – happy with one friend

On the first day of kindergarten I remember trying to make myself cry because I thought children were supposed to cry on the first day of school. I was sitting on the carpet with my head in my hands trying to make tears when a little girl sat by me and said, "It's ok, you don't have to cry," so I stopped and asked her "do you want to be my friend?" I find it interesting that my crying, or pretending to cry, attracted her to me. We remained friends the entire year. Since I had a friend, I didn't feel the need to have another. I am not able to remember any of the other children in the class; her name is the only name I remember, Shela. I was happy with just one friend. I remember trying to make sure that we always stood together in line. We always sat together at lunch and played together on the playground.

One day outside on the playground, she insisted that we play "no boys allowed fort" with some other girls. I didn't like that idea and insisted that we played see-saw because I knew that was a two-girl event. Shela went to play with the group of girls; however, I stayed on one end of the seesaw waiting for her until it was time to go in. She went in without me, and I remember feeling so lonely and betrayed. I remember trying to compete for her attention and get her to play with just me. I think I was successful much of the time.

I don't remember much about academics in kindergarten. I remember mostly playing with Playdoh, coloring, drawing, gluing and cutting things. One day during free playtime, I made a castle using all the large wooden blocks. The teacher came over to me and said, "Wow, did you build that all by yourself?" I nodded and then she said "Well, lets leave it here so your mommy can see it when she comes to get you." During clean up time, some of the other kids tried to take the castle down, and I insisted that they didn't but they continued to destroy my castle. They wouldn't listen to me and so I finally screamed with anger "MRS. SHELDON SAID I COULD SHOW IT TO MY MOMMY!" and the teacher immediately came over and told the other kids to leave it alone. Then she gave me extra time to rebuild it. I was so thrilled that my mom was going to see it I couldn't think about anything else that day. Knowing that my parents were proud of me was always extremely important.

First grade – it's ok to have two friends

First grade was very difficult for me because I wasn't learning how to read at the pace the other children were. I was in the lowest reading group and remember just how hard reading was. I didn't want to learn how to read. It was frustrating and stressful. On our report cards we received an E for excellent, an S for satisfactory or a U for unsatisfactory. I got mostly S's and a couple U's throughout the year. We didn't get number grades until I was in 4th grade.

The first day of first grade was good because Casey was in my class. We both remembered each other from the three years earlier in the first few weeks of dance! We both also had a great interest for cats. So we became best friends. Her mother visited the class often and I always went to her mother to ask if Casey could come to my house to play. It wasn't long before our mothers were best friends as well. We grew up together, went camping together, and we used to rent a local hotel with a swimming pool several times each summer so we could swim all day. Now, Casey wasn't anything like me, in fact, we were exact opposites. This became more apparent as we grew up but because of our strong foundation at an early age we remained great friends. She was a social genius, and I was a social phobic. At times with groups of girls, she would bridge the gap between me and other girls. She also didn't mind my quirks and actually thought they were funny and participated in them – such as making animal noises. I thought making animal noises, especially the sheep and cow, were the most hilarious sounds in the world! We would make animal noises and fall over laughing. This may be cute for young children, but for teenagers, not so cute.

Not long after first grade began, another girl named Jenny began sitting with us at lunch and so I decided it was ok to have two friends, but no more because two was just enough. Later on in the year another girl named Kimberly tried to be our friend but I didn't let her because I thought two friends were enough. I didn't think about the possibility of having multiple friends. I didn't realize at the time that I hurt Kimberly's feelings. I must have ignored or tuned out the other kids in my class because I have little memory of them.

Foreword by Liane Holliday Willey

What I remember of first grade was that I didn't like having to sit in the desk for long periods of time and greatly looked forward to PE, lunch and even bathroom breaks. I dreaded going to sit in reading group so much and when I got there I couldn't pay attention even if I tried. The other kids were reading and I wasn't so this caused a lot of anxiety, which I think prevented me from being able to focus. I also remember trying to avoid getting in trouble. I hated to get my name on the board and the reason why most kids got their names on the board was due to talking. I made effort not to talk during class time and daydreamed about lunch, PE and bathroom breaks so I could be with Casey and Jenny.

Second grade – fear of being a bad girl

I began learning how to read in second grade but remained in the lowest reading group. I remember my mother making sight word flashcards and working with me at home. I concentrated on reading the words and making the right sounds so hard that I didn't make the connection that the words had meaning. I was terrible in reading comprehension. I could not pay attention to what I was reading! And I couldn't tell when a sentence began or ended. I remember the struggle so well but also remember the determination I had that I was not going to give up. I spent the whole year remaining quiet in fear of getting my name on the board. I had very little interaction with the teacher; I was quiet and tried to be good so she had no reason to talk to me.

However, I did have one friend in my class named Sally. I sat by her at lunch and we played together on the playground. Although I liked her friendship, I didn't think she was a "good girl." She got into trouble frequently and wanted to break the rules and she got her name on the board with checks. One day while we were playing on the school playground, I let her talk me into going into the forest, which was against the rules. The teacher caught us and made us write, "I will not leave the playground" 20 times.

One day Sally came to school crying and told me that her mother died. I stared at her, speechless, intense emotion filled my body and I literally felt paralyzed. I didn't know what to do or what to say. She stopped crying when the teacher began class. Then suddenly the fear hit me like the speed of light. Because I perceived Sally to be a "bad girl," I thought that my mother would die if I were a "bad girl" too. This became a terrible problem for several months. I was so extremely scared that if I did something bad that my mom would die. I would think of all the bad things I had done and dwell on them over and over. This is when I discovered the word "guilt." I heard the word guilt on the TV one day and asked my mom what it meant and she said "you feel guilty when you feel bad about something you did wrong." On a scale from one to 10, my level of guilt was a 10. I repeatedly told my mom all the bad things I could remember, such as going into the forest against the school rules, secretly eating extra children's vitamins when she wasn't looking and getting cookies from the cabinet without asking. She then told me that it was okay, that I wasn't a bad girl.

There was a little boy that lived across the street from me that I enjoyed playing with sometimes who was almost a year younger than me. One day he asked me if he could stick his penis in me. I said "NO, that is for married people only." He was only six years old but he tried to persuade me and I resisted until he stopped asking. But the incident left me feeling incredibly guilty and bad. I felt so dirty about the experience and worried that I was such a bad girl, even though I didn't allow him to touch me. I became worried that I might be pregnant (I was only seven years old). Every day when I got home from school I wanted to hug my mother for long periods of time and I wanted her to rock me. I wanted to be held by my mother all the time, and I didn't want her out of my sight. I told her all about my friend from school who did bad things and her Mother died and I was afraid that she would die if I were a bad girl. The fear and anxiety that my mother might die was body piercing and left me paralyzed at times.

School was terrible. I just went through the motions of everything but my mind was on making sure I was a good girl. This went on for several months until my mom and I ran into my friend Sally at K-mart one day and Sally introduced me to her MOTHER! WHAT?! Her mother didn't die after all. The next day at school I asked her why she told me her Mother died and she said "Oh I was just mad at my mom that day." I was very angry with her for lying to me, but also relieved that her mother was still alive, despite that she did bad things. My fear and anxiety about my mom dying decreased after that and I got on with life. I did forgive my friend for lying to me because I still wanted to sit by her at lunch and play with her on the playground. However, I didn't allow myself to trust her or become best friends with her.

Third grade – multiple emotions

Third grade was not much different than second grade. I had little or no interaction with the teacher and tried to be good. I decided that I wanted to learn how to read. Reading came along very slowly, but I managed to make it to the top reading group by the end of the year. Although I could read the words I still had trouble comprehending meaning. I enjoyed math and didn't feel any struggle in that area. My friend Jenny from first grade was in my class and I was so happy because I really liked being her friend. We stayed together the whole year, sat together at lunch, played on the playground and she came over to play at my house sometimes. She was very slow in academics, both reading and math and frequently asked me for help, especially the math. I loved to help her.

One day Jenny asked me about a math problem we were supposed to be doing on our own and the teacher got on to her for talking and she began to cry loudly. The teacher sent her to the corner for disrupting the class and she cried even louder and then screaming out "I WANT MY MOMMY" over and over. So, the teacher took her out of the classroom. All the other kids immediately began laughing. I looked at them with disbelief and shock, and then suddenly felt so sad for my friend and so mad at the other kids for laughing I burst into tears. I was so embarrassed for crying that I buried my face in my arms on my desk. A few of the other kids noticed and asked me what was the matter. I ignored them; I was shaking and felt like I was losing control over my body and losing control over everything. Too much emotion all at once! The teacher came in by herself and took me out to the hallway. She asked me why I was crying; I couldn't stop crying to say anything and then she hugged me until I calmed down a little. She asked me again and I told her "the other kids were laughing at Jenny." The teacher talked to me about my friend and told me that she had problems at home with her mom and dad getting a divorce. She encouraged me to go to the bathroom to talk to and be with Jenny alone. So I went to the bathroom and she was there and we just cried together. I felt so sorry for her that her parents were getting a divorce. We stood there staring at each other while we ended our crying until I told her "I am sorry what happened" and she said "me too." I really loved my friend. She was MY friend and I was going to be HER friend. I didn't want anyone to laugh at her.

I remember one day in third grade, the teacher told us to write our list of spelling words in alphabetical order. I had no idea what "alphabetical order" meant. I noticed that the other children were writing away so I thought I could try to figure it out. I looked at my list of words and examined them carefully. There had to be some kind of "order" to these words. I noticed that the words had a different number of letters except a few had the same number. There were 20 words. So I put them in order by writing the word with the least number of letters first and the word with the most letters last. The words that had the same number of letters I wrote all of them on the same line. There! I figured out how to put a list of words in alphabetical order. I was so proud. When the teacher handed us back our papers, there was a big X right next to each of my words and a big U with a sad face at the top of my paper. WHAT!? How could that be? I looked over at my classmate's paper and she had an E with a happy face. I asked my classmate if I could see her paper and she gave it to me. I examined it carefully and saw that there was no order to the number of letters in the words. I asked her how she did it and she said that she looked at the alphabet on the wall and wrote the words that had the first letter that came first on the wall. I examined her paper again. oh I get it….alphabetical order. She said the teacher told us how to do it before she gave the assignment. Guess I wasn't paying attention. How did I not pay attention to the word alphabetical? I don't remember paying attention in school.

Fourth Grade – a life-changing year

I had a very strict teacher in fourth grade. She would not tolerate any foolishness or silly behavior. She was known as the strictest teacher in fourth grade. Our class was so well behaved and won several pizza parties that year. Fourth grade was the first year that I received number grades – that reflected a letter grade from A to F. My first six weeks I made a couple F's, a couple D's and the rest C's. I didn't understand at first why I had done so poorly. I didn't know what the numbers on the report card meant until the second six weeks when I didn't do any better I was sitting the backseat of the car when my mom explained it to me. I felt so awful for doing so bad.

One day, my teacher walked up to my desk, put her hand on it and blurted loudly "this child has problems." I felt so embarrassed but extremely confused to why she would do and say that. I worried that she meant me having problems as being a bad girl. Later that day, I went to her desk (something I never did to previous teachers) and asked her why she said I had problems. She told me that I was immature but had a lot of potential. Although I made poor grades, she could see that I could make good grades, all A's and B's in fact. I asked her how do I do that? She then told me how I needed to do focus on my schoolwork, study for my tests and do my absolute best. So, in efforts to erase her perception of me being a problem child, and get rid of my bad feelings about doing poorly, I made more of an effort and gave more attention to my schoolwork for the first time in my life.

Everything finally began to make more sense to me, the whole concept of "school." Unlike other people who have Asperger's such as Liane Holliday Willey as she states in her book *Pretending to Be Normal* "I am fascinated with the opportunities words provide. I love everything about them, especially the power they yield," I did not understand that vocabulary words had meaning. I was able to read but still could not understand the meaning of it so I found a way to read and still be able to make good grades on tests – the art of memorization! For vocabulary tests I learned to memorize the vocabulary word and the order of words that would be the definition. I didn't need to pay attention to what I was reading. I found an easy way to make good grades. My third report card showed that I made mostly A's and a couple B's. I finally understood what the numbers on the report card meant and what I had to do to get those numbers. I remember my parents being so proud of me with that report card, my dad gave me a hundred dollars and said he would continue giving me a hundred dollars each time I made all As and B's. So from then on I only made A's and B's. In fact, I stayed on the "honor roll" my entire school career.

I call it a "school career" because I perceive children to be trained to become professional students and some are good students while others are not so good and then there is all in the between. A child's career is "school. I made up my mind in fourth grade I was going to be a good student and make good grades no matter how hard it was. So I did. But the way I did it, I realized later in life, was not really the right way. Because I struggled with reading comprehension so much, I learned another way to make good grades and that was to memorize everything, all the words and in what order they were to go in. Every school year I scored way below average on the SAT in the reading and analogy section. However, I usually scored in the above average in math and problem solving. I didn't really have an interest in math until seventh grade; up until then I did it because it was part of school.

In our seating arrangement, Kimberly, the girl who tried to be my friend in first grade sat right next to me. We became the best of friends that year. I greatly enjoyed her and her friendship. She liked to be silly like me and laugh a lot. I made sure I didn't talk during times that I would get my name on the board; however, I did get my name on the board five times that year. Each time I got my name on the board I realized, well having my name on the board isn't that bad after all, as long as I don't get a check next to it, and it was worth the fun I had talking with Kimberly. I made one more friend in that class that year too. However, looking back on it, the other friend was always asking me for the answers to Math homework and I gave her my paper to copy. Although she may have been using me for my answers, I still was happy we were friends.

Another thing I did in school was daydream. I remember clearly daydreaming through most of fourth grade and ended up doing so throughout the rest of my school career during the boring times. I found being at school and the teacher talking while sitting in a desk to be on the extreme side of boring. The feeling of being bored was horrible, and I couldn't stand it at all. To compensate for those feelings, I doodled on paper, wrote notes to my friends, took my pens apart and put them back together over and over again and mostly daydreamed. Daydreaming became such a habit that as soon as the teacher began to talk I would immediately begin to daydream. When she stopped talking, and if she didn't write the assignment on the board, I asked my friend Kimberly sitting next to me what we were supposed to be doing and she would tell me the assignment.

I learned that the textbooks gave the lesson before the written assignments so I would read through the lesson in order to learn how to do the assignment – particularly for English and Math. I could not learn by listening to the teacher. I had to read it and see it. I needed to see it as a whole rather than a little at a time. When the teacher wrote things on the board I felt impatient. I daydreamed until she was completely finished, and then I would examine it all at once for better understanding.

During the second half of the school year, the teacher taught us what a spelling bee was and said that we the class was going to having weekly spelling bee's. To my surprise I won many of those class spelling bee's. I remember feeling so surprised that I won. I didn't think I was smart enough to win a spelling bee. The teacher picked me to be in the school spelling bee. I was really scared to be in the school spelling bee. I felt so nervous, and when it was my turn in front of a whole lot of people I didn't know, I became petrified. I was not able to spell correctly; it was like I was in a different body with a mind that didn't work. The method my mind used to spell wasn't available when I was nervous. I felt so awful for letting my teacher down. I continued to strive to make good grades in order to make the teacher and my parents happy. I felt so happy that my parents were happy because of me.

I had gotten sick often as a young child but did not get sick hardly at all during fourth grade. One night, I remember lying in bed missing the special attention I got from my parents when I was sick. I thought I could make myself look sick so they would give me that special attention. I got the thermometer, got back in bed and held it in my mouth a long time thinking if it was in my mouth a long time the temperature might show as a fever. I didn't think it would and I was right when I looked at the thermometer so I put the tip of it to the reading lamp light bulb on my bed. In just a second the thermometer exploded and all these little silver balls went all over my pillow, bed and the floor. I picked up some of the little balls and examined them thinking that is weird that all those little silver balls were in that thermometer. After playing with all the silver balls, I just brushed them off my pillow and threw the broken thermometer away. It wasn't until I began working with children who had autism that I learned thermometers had mercury in them and that mercury vapor was extremely toxic. Who knows how long those mercury balls were in my bedroom while I breathed in the mercury vapor while sleeping.

Fifth grade – a perfect year!

I had a very easygoing fifth grade teacher (I later found out that she was fired from her job the next year). I really liked this teacher because she liked me. I was the only one in her class that made straight A's on the report card. She announced this to the class and therefore gave me special attention that I loved. She called on me to do little errands for her and bragged to the rest of the class what a good student I was. My friend Jenny was in the class, and we were so happy to be together again. She still had a lot of problems with academics, and the teacher frequently asked me to help her, and I was so happy to do so.

There was another girl named Dorothy who sat by me. I noticed that she was very quiet. In fact I began to observe her and she never said a word. She didn't seem to have any friends. I was very curious about her and felt sorry for her that she didn't have any friends. One day I leaned over and asked, "Do you want to be friends?" She nodded, and we got to know each other very well. I was so happy that year. Another girl named Jaime began to talk to me, and I was thrilled at the attention of her. I thought she was so pretty and nice so I decided to let her be my friend also. I had three really good friends! The four of us spent as much time as possible together. We ate lunch together and even spent the night over at each other's houses. Now that I look back, Jenny probably had a learning disability, Dorothy probably had a form of Asperger's and Jaime may have had some of the characteristics of Asperger's but not enough to be considered as having Asperger's syndrome.

There was a boy in the class who frequently got into arguments with the teacher. He frequently corrected her while she was teaching. The teacher would get on to him every time we were to write definitions to our vocabulary words because he refused to look up the definition in the back of the book and write them like it was next to the vocabulary words. He insisted that he already knew what the words meant and that he write his own definitions. This happened every week. He seemed like a very smart kid but didn't make good grades. I noticed that he didn't talk to the other kids and sat alone at lunch. I felt a bad for him that he didn't have any friends but I also thought he was not a good student for giving the teacher a hard time.

When we were in seventh grade I told this boy that I thought he had a very large head (his head was very large compared to other people's heads). I wasn't making fun of him I just thought he had a large head and so I told him one day. I had a tendency to say what I thought without thinking if what I say would hurt someone's feelings. He said, "The larger the head, the bigger the brain, and the bigger then brain – the smarter you are." I thought that was very interesting so I began to add to my bedtime prayers for God to give me a bigger brain so I would be very smart. I remember during the school years that boy would wear star trek uniforms to school and the other kids would make fun of him. He said he liked star trek. I actually became friends with this boy during 12th grade when he sat next to me in chemistry class. I enjoyed talking to him because we liked the same topics, chemistry and math. He was a very nice person when I got to know him. When I first learned of Asperger's syndrome, I immediately remembered this boy. No doubt did he have Asperger's.

Again, in fifth grade I frequently won the class spelling bee's and was sent to the school spelling bee and again I was not able to spell on my first turn. I wondered why I couldn't spell in front of a whole bunch of people but it didn't bother me as much as it did the year before.

Close to the end of the school year, the school made it mandatory that everyone receive a measles vaccine. I received mine just like everyone else. A little later that day Jenny said, "Hey, your arm looks very purple." Yes, it was very purple looking around where I received the shot. It went away by the end of the day and I didn't think much of it. The next day at recess my face broke out in a terrible rash! The teacher sent me to the clinic. My face broke out into rashes frequently after that. This was a huge turning point in my life.

Sixth grade – a horrible year!

This was the first year I had a locker and had to change classes. The schoolwork was much harder than the year before and I had to spend much more time memorizing words and paragraphs to maintain honor roll. I had seven different classes and seven different teachers so it took me six weeks to analyze each of the teacher's expectations and figure out how to meet those expectations. I made mostly B's my first report card but the rest of the year was mostly A's.

Something very bad was going on with my body. I began to experience a lot of pain in my back and felt really uncomfortable sitting at my desk. I remember pressing my forehead on my desk as hard as I could because the pressure helped take away the uncomfortable feeling. I had to sit on my knees almost all the time or I just couldn't stand sitting at all. I felt like I had to be moving or stretching all the time to avoid feeling so painful and uncomfortable. I remember squeezing my arms to relieve pain. I became very clumsy and almost lost my ability to dance that year. I could not stand wearing blue jeans because they hurt. The seams of my socks hurt. I couldn't stand wearing a jacket even on cold days. My eyesight became so bad I had to wear a –7.5 prescription glasses. My eyes changed color from dark brown to hazel green. I could not focus at all at school because of the pain in my body (I later learned to be inflammation). My parents thought all of these issues were pre-puberty.

One night, when my mom was trimming my hair, my attention was brought to the discomfort in my brain at the sound of my mother's breathing. The perception was almost unbearable. I couldn't tell her to stop breathing! I remember asking her to stop breathing so loudly. The sound of people chewing began to bother me and I would tell my mom and dad to stop chewing so loud and they would say that they weren't chewing loudly. Also during this time I was not able to go outside without sunglasses anymore because my eyes hurt so badly from the brightness of the sun. The brightness was like a tornado hitting my eyes and unbearably painful. Another change was my perception of being hugged and touched. I had always been extremely affectionate and love hugs and kisses all the time. Not anymore. I couldn't stand for my mom or dad to suddenly touch or hug me but sometimes I would try to make myself tolerate the discomfort to eradicate the feelings of guilt I had for not hugging my parents back. The kissing sound threw me over the edge. No more kiss noises. AAAAAH!

Another interesting thing that was happening to my body was that I felt incredibly silly and also had a drunken feeling after I ate a meal. I wanted to make animal sounds, pretend to be a sheep or cow, jump up and down making turkey sounds, and laugh hysterically. I thought it was so funny!

The friends I had would laugh at me and sometimes would join in with me making animal sounds. I remember telling my parents I literally felt drunk that I couldn't help but act that way. I remember after lunch at school I would feel so silly and goofy and the other kids in the class would tell me how weird and strange I was. But I didn't care because I felt so goofy and drunk! This continued on until I changed my diet in my early 20s. I didn't know that my body was probably converting gliadin from gluten in wheat into alcohol! I didn't know that yeast build up in the intestines contributed to problems with digesting food and released its waste in the bloodstream. I really was drunk! Ever wonder why a child with autism suddenly begins "stimming" like crazy?

During this year, I remember while at home I would get the family photo albums and go to the bathroom and lock the door. I would sit on the bathroom floor and cry my eyes out while looking at pictures of me with my parents when I was a little kid. I didn't want to grow up. I didn't want to shave my legs, I didn't want to wear a bra, I didn't want to start my period; I wanted to be a little kid again.

I had taken dance lessons since I was three years old and greatly enjoyed dancing. I greatly enjoyed anything physical because it made me feel good. I played softball for nine years of my childhood and practiced to become pitcher because I thought it was the most active and important position. I received a trophy for being the most valuable player on the team the year before. I participated and won dance competitions the years before. This year was different. Very different. My pitching aim became off and it was much more difficult for me to get it right. I became clumsy and lost my rhythm and coordination at dance. The dance teacher took me off the competition team. I was devastated but determined to get my talent back and I did, but it took several years. I also re-gained my pitching ability with a lot of effort over the next couple years but it was never the same as before. I tried out for the school dance team that year but did not make it. When looking at videos of me dancing that year in regular studio dance, I was extremely off beat and looked terrible compared to previous videos. What happened to me that I suddenly began experiencing so much pain and loss of coordination? Nobody had any idea at the time except that I was probably experiencing pre-puberty. After working with children with autism and hearing the same "my child was fine until he received that vaccine" story from almost every family I worked with and after doing thousands of hours of research on the subject of vaccines, mercury and autism I knew without a doubt that measles shot I had just a few months earlier provoked these problems. I suffered with terrible back inflammation and pain until I was in my mid twenties and tried the gluten free diet.

Another baffling thing that happened that year is that I suddenly became able listen to a song and learn how to play it on the piano. I had taken piano lessons for a few years but made really slow progress with reading music and playing the piano without looking at my hands. Then all of a sudden the sounds on the piano made sense to me – I saw an abstract picture of each sound and when I heard the sounds in the songs I could see the abstract pictures. It took me about an hour to be able to learn to play a song from listening to one. I couldn't just listen to it once then play it. I had to listen to it a little at a time while I memorized the sequence. I made it a rule to always play the piano in the mornings that I had a test that day at school.

Sixth grade was a very challenging year. I remember looking at myself in the mirror at home looking at a stranger. Who is that person? That is not who I used to be. I don't know myself. Who am I? The only good thing about sixth grade was that Kimberly was in all of my classes. Dorothy and Jaime were in a few of my classes also so I had a few friends. Kimberly and I really related to each other, we were both goofballs, silly girls who liked to make silly noises, animal sounds and have tickle fights. We both enjoyed playing softball as well. Jaime and Kimberly are still my great friends to this day. Jenny and Dorothy moved away and I missed them dearly. We stayed connected for a while with writing letters to each other and then reconnected again after college though the Internet.

Seventh grade – determined to overcome anything

Seventh grade was a little better than sixth. I enjoyed having Kimberly and Jaime as my best friend as well as Jaime since we were in many of the same classes. I enjoyed seeing them and writing and receiving letters with them throughout the day. Kimberly, Jaime and Casey (remember her from meeting her at dance age three, then becoming best friends in first grade and our parents became best friends) and I spent all weekends together doing things such as roller skating, slumber parties, going to the mall and movies. I had three best friends and they remain my three best friends to this day.

I memorized my way through school not having any idea of what was going on and what I was supposed to learn. I was able to comprehend what I read because I enjoyed reading library books, however, I could not pay attention to things I had to read in school so, therefore, was not able to answer questions unless I spent time memorizing the words and the order they were in. In school, if I wasn't reading or writing a letter to Kimberly, Jaime or Casey (Casey was never in any more of my classes but we saw each other in the hallways between classes to exchange letters) I was day dreaming. I continued to have the back pain and discomfort all over and tried to get used to it. I had to sit on my knees all the time. I guess I looked pretty weird with my legs tucked under me all the time at school. I continued to feel silly and drunk right after I ate a meal. I began to eat and crave sour candy all of the time. I ate at least two packs of skittles or starbursts a day. I had them with me all the time and popped one in my mouth all throughout the day. During my research on autism I found that the stress response uses up sugar and depletes serotonin, the brain chemical aiding in emotions and eating. In order to restore balance, sugar is craved and the more prolonged the stress, the more need to restore serotonin (Diamond, 1979). I also didn't know my body was becoming addicted to the food dye in the candies I ate. The cravings were intense and I felt so good when I ate candy.

One day, the second part of the year my math teacher called me and two other children out to the hallway. I was worried I was in trouble for something but the teacher basically told us that we were really good at math and asked us if we were interested in being in the algebra class. I didn't think much of it but agreed to be in the algebra class.

One day, my history class got a new student. He spoke only Spanish. His seat was next to mine. I carefully observed him and recognized that he was really scared. I remember thinking "He must be really scared." So, before class started I said "Hi." He said "Hola." I held up my pencil and said "pencil." He held up his pencil and said "lapiz." We smiled at each other as the teacher began class and I then slipped into my normal daydream. I remember getting a lot of pleasure at knowing that I made him feel better on his first day at a new school. After experiencing this, I befriending many new students throughout the rest of my school career. I became very attracted to the new kids and to the kids who didn't have any friends because I enjoyed making them feel better.

I tried so hard to dance better and was very determined to get my dance talent back and by the end of the year, I tried out for the school dance team and made it! I was thrilled! But when the list of new dance team members were called out on the speaker at school, all the kids in the class began making statements like "how did Kristi make the dance team?" "Kristi made the dance team, that is a shocker, she is so weird." I knew that they were surprised because I was so different and weird, they knew it and I knew it so I didn't let it bother me because I was so thrilled I MADE the dance team! The dance team consisted of 20 girls. I had no idea what was coming.

Eighth grade – rumors of being gay and introduction to boys

I first began shaving my legs in eighth grade solely because of the dance team. I really didn't want to because I knew once a girl started shaving her legs, then she had to always shave her legs. I tried to pick a girl on the dance team to be friends, but she wanted to be with all the other girls on the team. They all wanted each other as a group and I didn't understand that. So, I went to the practices and didn't talk to any of them because I didn't know what to say. I remained quiet but enjoyed the dancing. I hated the before and after. I made sure I did not arrive early and made sure I left immediately when practice was over. Most of the time I didn't pay any attention to the other girls, however, occasionally with intense desire to be accepted and fit in, I would attempt to speak to them but when I did they all would get silent and look at me with strange looks. So my attempts to fit in usually failed. There were times I would be walking down the hall to practice and hear them talking about me – I tuned it out and pretended I didn't hear.

Then one day after school, one of the girls (the same girl I tried to be friends with originally) stopped me by my locker. She said she had to tell me something but it was hard to tell. I said "it's ok, what is it?" She said she has talked to her mom about it and her mom had advised her to tell me what the other girls on the dance team thought of me. She said that the other girls on the dance team thought I was gay. I was shocked! GAY?! I knew that gay meant that girls had sexual relations with other girls. Why would anyone think I was gay? I was only 13. I told her thank you for telling me and immediately left. I didn't want to talk to or confront the girls so I asked the dance team instructor to tell the other girls I was not gay. This was the first time I actually spoke to the dance team instructor.

Instead of dancing at practice that afternoon, the dance team instructor had us all sit while she talked about puberty and growing up and that it wasn't nice to talk behind people's back and assume things about people and that nobody on the dance team was gay. At the end she asked me if I had anything to say, I didn't want to say anything at all but since everybody in the room was staring at me I said quietly "i'm not gay." That night when I was thinking about it all, I began to worry if I really was gay. This caused a lot of anxiety over the next few years.

My friend Casey was very boy crazy. She always had a boy that she "was going with." She tried to get me interested in boys but I had no interest at all. But when I found out the dance team perceived me to be gay, I said yes when this boy in one of my classes asked me to "go with him." So I had a boyfriend but didn't really want one. I was really happy that I was meeting the social expectations of the other girls and also made Casey happy. I made sure that the girls on the dance team saw me holding hands with the boy after school. This boy was kind of cute but Casey told me he was not "fine" and that she would never go out with a boy that she wouldn't french kiss. Yuck! The thought of french kissing a boy disgusted me. Casey was very popular and had many friends. I felt so privileged that she was my friend. However, I don't think we would have become friends if we had met later in life rather than when we were three years old. When I make a friend, I want to keep a friend and so I made sure that we stayed friends.

One day in one of my classes I had with Kimberly, a really popular boy put a note on my desk that said "will you go with me" and had a box to check yes or no. Kimberly told me that he and the rest of the class were playing a trick on me that it was just a joke. Deep in my mind I knew she was right, but my hopes of being accepted and fitting in provoked me to take the chance so I checked yes and put it on his desk. He turned around with a huge fake booger in his nose and everybody laughed. Well, Kimberly was right – and she was able to interpret social cues.

I began to wonder why I was so weird and different no matter how hard I tried to fit in. After hearing so many people tell me "you are so weird," "you are so strange," and "you are so crazy" over the past few years, it finally occurred to me that something might be wrong with me. Throughout the rest of my life I fluctuated between being ok with my being different and not being ok.

I was also in the school band that year and played the flute. On the night we went to band competition a boy asked me to go with him. So I said yes because I was thrilled that he was interested in me. I made sure to break up with the other boy because I knew that it was only proper to go with one boy at a time. One day in the school hallway the new boy asked if he could kiss me. I thought that everyone was wanting me to kiss a boy and that it would make them happy to see me be like a "normal" girl so I let him kiss me but not stick his tongue in my mouth. If I had it to do all over again I wouldn't have gone out with any boys that year – I wasn't ready for that, but my desire to be accepted socially and eradicate the rumor that I was gay was so strong I was willing to go out of my comfort zone to be accepted.

Regarding school that year, I again memorized and daydreamed my way through. The word "school" brought nothing but tension and anxiety. I loved being at home. My parents never made fun of me. There were no difficult social situations to figure out. I greatly enjoyed my algebra class but paid absolutely no attention to any of my other classes. I just did what I had to do to please the teachers and make good grades to get it over with. Kimberly, Jaime and Casey were my best friends and we spent all our weekends together.

By the end of the year, I clearly recognized that I was not like the other girls, but had the desire to be accepted so instead of ignoring them and tuning them out, I tried to carefully observe them and make myself act like them although I felt so stupid and usually presented myself as idiot. I changed the way I dressed and started wearing blue jeans like everyone else although I hated them so much because they were so uncomfortable. I experienced constant tension being at school and made sure that I was never alone anymore, I had to be with or pretend to be with a friend all the time so everybody else wouldn't think I didn't have any friends.

Ninth grade – trying real hard to fit in

I didn't have any friends at lunchtime. I was so embarrassed. My ability to make new friends had diminished and I knew it. So I went outside during lunchtime to avoid all the other kids judging me for not having any friends. I ate only vending machine food that year. However, I did meet a boy outside who was a senior who didn't talk to anyone. So he and I talked and 'hung out' during lunchtime that year. Looking back on it, although I thought he was real nice, he probably had Asperger's or even autism. Throughout the school year, I met a few more "outsiders" that year. It never crossed my mind while I was in school that typical girls avoided people who are different because they didn't want to be seen with unpopular kids (I learned this just prior to writing this book). I never felt embarrassed or avoided the quiet, new or strange kids; it was the opposite, I enjoyed befriending them. Those kids who seemed very quiet or strange usually were very nice people.

I soon figured out that high school was not at all about "school." It was not about academics or learning how to be real human beings in the world. It was all about social groups and "cliques." There were so many. From what I understood, there were the headbangers, the dorks, the nerds, the devil worshipers, the popular and the goody two shoes. It was all so confusing trying to figure it all out and decide which one I wanted to be in or attempt to be in. I decided I didn't like any of them but would rather just have friends. I had a few friends so that was ok. I didn't know at that time that most of the students already chose a clique and didn't really associate with students outside their clique. It all seemed so ridiculous to me. I had the fear and anxiety of being alone or better worded, perceived to be alone. So if I didn't have a friend during the transition times, I would pretend to be in a group so everyone else would see (although I wasn't actually participating in that group). I tried so hard to blend in and fit in and this became my main preoccupation. I would plan in advance who I would walk next to in the hallway or stand next too while waiting for the bell to ring.

I made the dance team again and Jaime also made the dance team! I had a buddy on the dance team. Now, the other girls couldn't think I was so different because I had a friend too. Jaime and I had a good time together. One day I overheard some other dance team members talking about Jaime that she looked like a beaver. I never thought she looked like a beaver. In fact when I first met her in fifth grade I thought she was one of the prettiest girls I had ever seen. Jaime and I stuck together and supported each other that year. During class time I wrote notes to Jaime and Kimberly or read notes they had written me. We tried to plan a route where we would see each other on the way to our other classes although we had no time to talk. We would then exchange our notes to each other.

I didn't pay attention to school. I rarely talked to my teachers. Well, there was one teacher that I like to aggravate. Her name was Mrs. Tarter and I frequently asked her if she liked tarter sauce. I loved her name and wanted to laugh every time I said or thought about it. I told her that her name was my favorite of all my teachers. She smiled and laughed with me. She was the calculus and the computer-programming teacher for the school. She must of thought I was crazy, but thinking about her makes me wonder if she had Asperger's. She didn't sit with the other teachers at lunch; she ate her lunch in her classroom by herself. She was very sensitive to any noise and she would give the class candy every day as long as we agreed to be quiet. She also had terrible allergies, always having to wipe her noise and rub her eyes. I had her for at least one class every year during high school.

For academics, I just memorized what I had to in order to make A's on tests. The only classes I remember enjoying that year were geometry and computer programming. I continued to have sensory issues, and silliness after eating but I learned to control my behavior better when I felt so silly in knowing that everyone else was watching me and judging me. I saved my silliness for being at home. I loved being at home because I could dress comfortable and act myself.

I had many boyfriends that year. All the boys I went with were either from another school or a different grade. None of the boys from my grade asked me out; guess they knew my social status. I learned that the social thing everybody did was "go with each other" for a period of time until one of the partners grew tired of the relationship, or was asked out by another partner that was more interesting. Lots of girls and boys "going together." When a boy asked me to go with him I usually said yes because I loved to get to know new people. I learned that getting to know a boy was really a lot of fun. When another boy was interested in me I would break up with the previous boy because going with two boys at the same time was breaking a rule. I did have a crush on this one boy but he was going with somebody else. I really had feelings for him. I had feelings for a lot of other boys that would not have anything to do with me. However, my feelings would go away after some time and if my feelings went away for a boy I was going with, I had to break up with him. By the end of tenth grade I had gone with 17 boys. I remember them all. I never had sex with any of them although a few tried. Some would never talk to me again. I already made up my mind that sex was for marriage only. I had a strong conviction for that.

When I think about all this now, the social set up in high school for girls and boys going together is a recipe for divorce. It teaches children to go steady with one boy until you get tired of him then go out with another boy until the break up and so on. Children are practicing divorce! No wonderful the divorce rate is so high!

10th grade – careful observation

I just didn't know how to socially connect with groups, especially girls. It was easy socializing with just one person. I preferred to spend time with each of my three best friends individually. I thought that if I could talk with each of the dance team members alone, then we could connect socially. So I tried that solution and it worked pretty well. I targeted a few of them that I liked best and looked for opportunities to talk with them. I didn't understand "small talk" well and thought it was a complete waste of time talking about things that were not important but I learned how to somewhat do "small talk" by careful observation of other people doing it. So I engaged in small talk with some of the other girls individually. A big plus was that Casey was on dance team this year, although I missed Jaime who didn't want to be on it again. Casey got along very well with the other girls and she was like a catalyst for me to blend in with them. The other girls seemed a little more open to me and few of them even said hi to me in the hallways between classes.

Things were good for a little while. I tried out for soccer team and made it. I loved soccer and running made my body feel so good relieving inflammation and pain. Kimberly, Jaime and Casey all made the soccer team and we had a wonderful time during soccer season. I had played soccer before on AYSO teams but this was my first year being on a school team. It was much more competitive than AYSO but I did it because it was fun. Any physical activity made my body feel so much better and relieved my back pain. When I was in college doing some research on the subject of inflammation, I discovered that exercise reduces inflammation therefore reducing pain. This is why I loved dancing, softball and soccer so much. I also had a big trampoline that I jumped on all the time at my home.

Instead of ignoring and tuning out the girls on the dance team as I had done previously, I began to carefully observe them. I watched how they interacted with each other and listened to what they talked about. I became concerned and stuck with a decision. First, I wondered why I couldn't interact that way in a group. Then I thought things like "how in the world can they think that shoes, lipstick and purses are the most important topics in the world?" That is what they talked about. Clothes, makeup, and those silly quizzes in those teen magazines thrilled them. I hated purses. It was a terrible nuisance to carry around purses. I didn't care about clothes or makeup. Do I really want to be like them? I have to make myself act like them and pretend to be interested in what they like. Why can't they be interested in what I was interested in? I wanted to talk about life and it's purpose and meaning, the universe, the planets, ancient Egypt. Well, I did get to talk about similar things with my best friends although at that point they were becoming interesting in popular music and clothes as well. I was confused to why all of a sudden my best friends were becoming so social with other groups. I thought about this carefully whether or not I should become like all the other girls or remain weird and different.

Regarding school that year, I moved through the motions because it was mandatory. There was one class that I had problems with – CP English.

The only problem I had was the vocabulary tests. It wasn't the typical write the definition to the word test like I was used to. It was fill in the blank! The only way to fill the right word in the right sentence was to know and understand the meaning. Oh this was so hard for me. Since fourth grade I had the habit of just looking at words and memorizing them and in what order they went in. I struggled with this tremendously and even became proud if I made a C on that weekly test. I didn't have much of a relationship with my teachers but I did ask my CP English teacher for help in writing an essay. I knew that I would have a bad grade on my report card if I didn't. She spent two hours after school showing me how to write an essay, which helped me learn to write well in college. I am so thankful to her for her help. I am really glad I asked her for help.

I still danced at a dance studio. One thing I didn't like about dance was the girls would talk badly about other girls they knew. They would make fun of their friends at dance class then go to school acting like their best friends. Why would they do that? One day when they were talking and making fun of another girl by "mimicking" her I blurted out "how would you feel if you knew that everybody in this class talked bad about you when you left the room?" They stared at me. Have they ever even thought that it is possible that other people talked bad behind their backs? I could only imagine the things they said about me when I wasn't there.

I began dating that year. Dating was different than going with boys. When you went with a boy, you wrote special notes to each other or talked on the phone. I began real dating when the boy comes and picks me up and we go out to a movie and dinner. I only dated one boy from my school and he was a senior. We went on three dates then he stopped calling me. After a week I called him and told him it was ok he wanted to break up with me but that it was not ok to fail to clearly communicate it. He told a friend of mine at school that I was too prude, didn't like the way I dressed and didn't like that I didn't carry a purse. My heart was broken. I made a little more effort to dress better but I just couldn't get myself to carry a purse.

I met a boy at a water park that summer and we ended up being together for over two years. He was one year older than me and lived 30 minutes away but we could drive to see each other. We saw each other on weekends and holidays. He respected that I wanted to wait until marriage before having sex. He said that he liked that I didn't carry purses. We had a deep and meaningful relationship and I really loved him. He asked me to marry him shortly before my graduation and I said yes and he gave me an engagement ring. I was already like part of his family and he was part of mine.

The month before college started I decided to break up with him. I think it was one of the hardest things I have ever done. I loved him so much, but he had a temper sometimes and I was really scared he wouldn't be a good father to my children. It was very important to me that my children have a wonderful father because I saw the results from families who had poor fathers. Because we knew each other so well and had developed such a close relationship it was hard to stop seeing him. Although we were technically "broke up" we still spent a lot of time together. He frequently asked me to date him again but I couldn't let myself because my prediction of the future if we stayed together was not the perfect family life I desired. I knew that not everyone was perfect but since I was still young, I believed I would find someone who would be a great father to my kids. We both eventually began dating other people. There came a point and time where I decided that I had to stop talking to him because feelings were still there. It was when I got married to my husband! It wasn't right for me to be talking to any boys at all after being married. I decided not to even look at another man ever again. Choosing to marry someone meant choosing to reject all other males in the world.

I sure do wish somebody had taught me the way dating and getting married was really designed. But nobody knew how it was designed. That generation of parents thought that what their kids did in school was the norm. It may have been the norm, but it wasn't right. I don't blame my parents at all, they didn't know. I have learned that there is only one right way to do things and many wrong ways to do things. I also have learned that most people don't know the right thing because they think that what they are doing is the right way because it is what everyone else in society does. I mean, getting a divorce is considered normal now because so many people do it. But it's not supposed to be that way.

11th grade – pretending to be like them

Ok, I so badly wanted to be accepted and to fit in with the girls on the dance team. I began learning that clothes and shoes had brand names and certain brand names were very important to these girls. I began to wear a little bit of lipstick and eye shadow and began listening to popular music and learning all the different music styles and groups. This was not natural for me and I didn't enjoy it but I did enjoy the knowledge that I was fitting in. I felt like I kind of related to them since I could imitate them although I knew they didn't relate to me at all. I knew I was being somebody different than I really was and constantly felt like I had to put so much effort in order to fit in. Pretending was exhausting but worth the security of knowing that I was fitting in and they accepted me.

I liked school better that year because we got to choose our classes. I loved chemistry and decided to become a chemical engineer. I hated homework and so I figured out how not to have any homework at all. I would do my assigned homework from another class in next class while the teacher was lecturing. I never paid attention to the teacher lecturing so it was good that I could make good use of that time and it was wonderful that I had all my homework completed before school was out. I learned that all problems have a solution if you think hard enough. Homework was a big problem for me because I hated it, so I found an effective solution.

I took art class because I thought it would be less homework for the day. When I was in art class I learned that I was able to draw what I saw. The teacher came to my desk frequently and made nice comments on my artwork. I won the art award for that year. I also won a science award that year. I didn't know I could draw. But when I tried I could and it was fun and easy and made sense. My handwriting had always been very messy, but I never cared that it was. However, I learned in art class that year that if I focus hard enough I could very well control the pencil and draw anything.

I began student teaching at the dance studio. I greatly enjoyed teaching the children how to dance. I developed a love for being with and teaching children. Little children were so sweet and nonjudgmental. I didn't have to work hard to fit in because they all loved me the way I was. They look up to grown ups so much and want to be like them. I wanted to be a good model for them.

12th grade – happier with being myself

I was on dance team again. Just a couple months into the school year I became too exhausted of trying to be like them. I was able to now, but it took so much energy and I was tired of feeling ridiculous making myself pretend to like shoes, clothes, their choice of music, popular movies and everything in those magazines. I quit dance team. I continued to student teach at my dance studio. The next year I became a regular dance teacher and taught for three years before getting married and moving away from the studio.

My best friends Kimberly and Jaime were slipping away from me. They were doing what the other teenagers were doing. They had joined in with their own cliques. I tried to go to one party with Kimberly but it was awful. Too loud, too stinky and teenagers drinking too much. It was a very sad reality for me, my best friends had their own social agendas and I couldn't be a part of it. By the end of the school year, we barely even spoke to each other. They had no idea how much I missed them and when I tried to approach them, they acted like they didn't know me anymore. The next year after graduation, Jaime and I began doing things together again and restored our relationship. Kimberly and I restored our relationship when she moved back to town after going to college. I will always cherish them.

I took Calculus A the first semester and Calculus B the second and easily made A's. I had an overall GPA of 3.8. I greatly anticipated school being over and getting on to college. I remember the school fire alarm going off frequently that year due to some technical problems. The sounds of the alarm hurt my ears so bad it brought tears to my eyes despite holding my ears as hard as I could. None of the other kids were holding their ears. Why wasn't it painful to them? How could they tolerate such pain?

That year was a relief for me knowing that it was almost over. I didn't care anymore about trying to fit in. I couldn't care anymore. I recognized that it wasn't all that important after all. High school was almost over. Most of the girls got into fights arguing about things and they spoke badly about each other behind each other's backs. I didn't want to be like them anymore. My mom once questioned me about not attending teenage events. I told her I didn't like teenage events; they mostly drink alcohol and smoke and act stupid. I had already known that going away to college meant parties and drinking in loud social atmospheres so I decided I would stay at home and go to my local college. Besides, I liked living with my parents; they gave me freedom, didn't make fun of me, accepted me the way I was most of the time and cooked the most awesome meals.

I was still addicted to sour candy and had to get three cavities filled the last month of school. I had no idea that the fillings consisted of at least 50% mercury. I didn't know that mercury was to most toxic metal to the human body. Over the next year I began to develop severe pain in my abdominal area. I didn't go to the doctor for this until I was 20 when I was diagnosed with endometriosis and said it would be difficult for me to get pregnant. The pain was so bad that I had to take hydrocodone sometimes. Even then, the pain was so bad I couldn't do anything but lay in a fetal position. I also began to get really weak, faint and dizzy at times, especially after I ate sugary foods. I didn't go to the doctor for this until I was 21 and it was thought to be hypoglycemia. I had lost weight but I was eating so much, even more than my husband. The doctor mentioned it might be hyperthyroidism and wanted me to go to the hospital for testing. I agreed to the doctor, but I knew that there was no way I was going to the hospital for testing.

Summary of "school"

Sitting here and thinking back to my school career and comparing my life, rate of acquired knowledge and understanding since graduation from high school, school was a total joke. I know that teachers and parents reading this will not like reading it and maybe you can help your children appreciate school and get through all the social difficulties etc. Although I appreciate the learning experience (I like to perceive every experience to be an experience to learn from) I perceive that school was a complete waste of time for me. I didn't pay attention in class so I learned very little. The emotions I experienced with all the social difficulties and trying to fit in with the other girls was traumatizing. High school was a total nightmare.

My experience with high school left me with feelings of being a defective girl, weird, crazy, and strange person. However, I accepted that I was all those things. None of my teachers ever recognized that I didn't pay attention or had social issues. I covered it up. I think if somebody would have helped me and talked to me about all my struggles, it would have been so much easier. I had a constant fear of the friends I did have deciding to not be my friend because of something I did wrong or said wrong. Whenever there was a social gathering or a dinner I analyze everything I said and did in response to the other people trying to make sure I didn't do or say anything that would have offended or cause them to discontinue their friendship with me. This prevented me from sleeping and caused a great deal of tension and anxiety. I was too embarrassed to tell my parents about my social difficulties. I kept it all to myself. I didn't even tell my very best friends because I was so ashamed of myself. I think they knew deep down since we slipped away from each other the last year of high school. Maybe I assumed they wouldn't accept me anymore and shyed away from them. I am not sure how it happened. I believe there are so many girls like me out there who have learned to cover up their struggles due to feelings of shame and embarrassment. Girls can learn how to overcome these struggles, they can learn to understand themselves and appreciate themselves. They can learn to have a happy life once their focus is on obtaining the truth about life and find that truth.

I don't want my experiences in school to define who I am. Although high school was a difficult experience, life outside of high school was good. I loved to mountain bike ride steep slopes and jump off high cliffs into lakes and rivers. I had so much fun hiking for hours in the woods. I greatly enjoyed camping and building campfires. I had a love for adventure and a desire to explore. I wanted to try new things, even if they were considered a bit eccentric.

I asked my mom and best friends to write a letter for this book because I wanted to illustrate how well I covered up my struggles, pain, anxiety and insecurity. They thought I was pretty normal and had no clue to what I really was experiencing. But thinking back, there were characteristics they noticed.

Letter from my Mother

When my daughter first asked me to write a letter about her childhood, I panicked because I felt like a bad mom. I did not think anything was really wrong with my child. None of her teachers, coaches or other parents ever said anything to me about her. She met all her milestones on time. She made wonderful grades. She was a very good daughter.

As a child she was very hyper, a regular wiggle worm and loved to play games, run, swim, ride bikes, jump rope and dance. She was a very silly girl. She would find certain words to be so funny and would laugh for hours. I thought this was cute and thought she was such as happy child.

She had some interesting behaviors that I thought proved that she would one day be a scientist or a surgeon. For example, once after fishing she cut all the eyes out of the fish and put them in ice cube trays, filled them up with water and put them in the freezer. I opened the freezer and one of the trays fell out with ice cubes that had eyeballs scattering all over the floor. It scared me at first, but then I thought it was really funny. One time when our cat killed a snake, she got a knife and dissected it. There was a period of time when she saved the blood from her nosebleeds to feed some plants she was experimenting with.

I knew she struggled in social situations. I tried to help her by encouraging her to invite friends over. She had a few very good friends, which stuck by her and today are still friends. I admire her loyalty to her friends; she demonstrates what true friendship really is. She had problems answering questions in a group of people and wanted me to answer for her. I could tell she was out of her comfort zone. I thought she was just shy and bashful.

I thought she was a super sensitive child. She complained about loud noises and hated sleeping anywhere close to her dad and me because or our snoring. I can remember her holding her ears with her head down. She complained a lot about her joints and her back hurting. I thought her pain was from her dancing and playing sports. She hated to wear socks and tight fitting clothes. She hated the clothes she had to wear for dance but tolerated them.

She hid a lot of her emotions. In high school, she hid her feelings from me, but I could see she had a terrible time trying to fit in but I did not know why. I just thought it was normal for other kids to be unkind. Although some of her classmates in high school were mean, I was very proud of her for being herself and not following the leader. She did not change, they did.

I always thought she was so smart to be able to memorize her schoolwork so quickly. I did not know she didn't comprehend what she was reading and didn't pay attention in school, not after fourth grade anyway. She and her dad could carry on deep conversations about the meaning of life and some of it was really interesting.

She was a loving, sensitive, sweet and smart child as well as an adult. I have a very close relationship with my daughter and I love to spend time with her. She is a very good daughter and very loyal to her family. I am happy that she is secure and happy in her role as a wife and mother and that she wants to help other girls who experience what she did. My advice to other parents would be to be patient, accept their daughter as she is and the great joy that she can bring. Never make fun of her and gently explain things she does not understand such as jokes, puns and kidding around. Be there when she is sad and let her know its ok to be different. Show her and teach her to make friends and how to act in social situations as the need arises.

Letters from my Best Friends

From Kimberly

When I recall my fondest memories, my thoughts always drift to our time together as little girls. I often wonder if there are girls today that have a friendship like ours was as children. I doubt it. Our friendship was special, a kind of relationship that only comes around a few times in a lifetime.

I wasn't a risk-taker as a child. Instead, I was cautious, and I spent too much time worrying about insignificant details in life. Kristi, on the other hand, was a risk taker, and she didn't seem to worry about anything in the world. I remember her telling me long ago to let loose and take chances in life. She said, "Let's do it and not care!" Drinking pickle juice from glasses, spray painting our hair, being buried in a pile of leaves and eating fried pickles until our stomachs hurt are all things that we did that spawned from her spoken words and carefree lifestyle. She loved life as a child, and her upbeat personality told me so everyday. I also loved my life, especially being her best friend.

One thing is for sure. We weren't the most popular girls. I knew that, and she knew that. But we soldiered on like any awkward middle-school girl. Dealing with preteen issues was horrible - but we got through it together. We confided in each other, we supported each other and we stuck up for each other through thick and thin.

Looking back, I had no idea she was dealing with Asperger's. Although she was a quirky child, she was also vivacious and energetic. And while I'm sorry she battled the symptoms of Asperger's alone, I would not have changed anything about her personality. And I certainly would not have changed anything about our friendship.

We've been friends for 23 years. She is my oldest friend, and when I die, she'll still be my oldest and most cherished friend. Twenty-three years ago, I would never have predicted that we'd still be friends to this day. I would have never guessed that she'd be a successful psychologist, wife, daughter, mom and friend. Thank you so much for being my friend.

From Jaime

Growing up together, I found Kristi to be very sweet, thoughtful, caring, and entertaining. During high school I didn't notice her to have difficulty making friends. I now notice her being uncomfortable when I introduce her to someone new. I found her making animal sounds to be hilarious and silly. Sometimes she would do them too much and be annoying, but if it did I would tell her or change the subject and we both would forget about them. When I get silly I get antsy and do silly things like talk a lot and jump around.

Kristi has a way of communicating something bad but in a caring way. She listens to people and is there for them even when they aren't necessarily there for her. She is emotionally strong and resourceful.

Kristi is very analytical and although I appreciate it she can do it too much. I am the same way. Analyzing things too much can cause massive harm to self-esteem and cause.

In high school I had fun with Kristi. I didn't have to worry about her getting me into trouble. I felt that she accepted me for who I was and I did her. I trusted her. Now, Kristi and I have a different kind of friendship. A friendship that deals with adult issues such as kids, health, politics, and finances. We are pretty much on the same page with all the topics. There are times when I may disagree or I may not go as far as her. However, if that is the case I listen to what research she has done on the topic, I do my own and then I come to my own conclusion. I think she respects decisions that I make just as I respect hers. This makes for a good friend that won't get upset if we don't always agree.

From Casey

Kristi and I grew up together. She was like my sister. We first became friends when we were three and all my childhood memories have her in them and they are all amazing and fun. I didn't notice that she struggled in social situations, although now thinking about it she did have weird reactions if pointed out in front of a group of people. I did think she was a shy person around other people, but with me she wasn't shy at all. She also seemed to be gullible at times. I thought she was a very picky person, wanting to wear socks and pants that were way too big for her. She liked soft clothing and blankets. She didn't like makeup and would frequently tell me I wore too much "glop" on my face. I thought it was funny. I thought she was so smart, so good at art and always thought outside the box. She was really good at mimicking animals. I loved it and wished I could have sounded as good as her. She taught me not care about what other people thought about me.

References

Diamond, J. (1979). *Your Body Doesn't Lie.* New York : Warner Books.

Chapter 5

The Real World, College and Autism

In this chapter, I share the "slap-in-the-face" experience I received after high school graduation when introduced to the real world. I also describe a few interesting experiences during college and my amazing experience being initiated with children who have autism. It was my work with children who had autism that lead me to the realization that I had Asperger's. Those children gave me the incredible desire to learn everything I could about autism, what it was, what caused it, how to recover from it and how to prevent it. I would be a different person if it were not for those precious children I helped learn to talk. They gave me a passion for existing. If it were not for my research in autism, my kids, especially my son, would have most likely developed autism.

Another world

I spent most of my life in a classroom. I had been training to be a professional student my entire life. That was all I knew how to do. Sit in a classroom, memorize stuff and make good grades. I didn't know how to live. I was only comfortable sitting in a desk taking a test. I didn't know anything about anything. I didn't know about insurance, taxes or bills. I didn't know how to cook a meal, didn't know the names of trees, flowers or herbs. I didn't know there were natural effective alternatives to health problems. I didn't know which plants were poisonous and which ones were edible. I had no knowledge of being self-sufficient and I didn't know basic survival skills. If by chance I were left alone in the wilderness, I would have died. I didn't know how to exercise self-accountability. Why is everything so complicated all of a sudden? Did they teach all those things in school? Have I daydreamed throughout my life? I was officially a "grown-up" but felt like a little child. Although I hated school, I wanted to go back. I knew how to be successful in school. But what I soon learned and continue to learn is that the real world was, and is, a totally different world than the world of a classroom. It is a better world and a different life. It's a world of real learning, real living and finding truth and knowledge than the fake world within the walls of a school building.

A welcomed wake up call

I attended the closest college to my home. Even though I was aware that going away for college was the "thing to do," I absolutely did not want to go away. I approached my college classes the same way I did my high school classes and I made two C's my first semester. I was absolutely devastated! It was literally the end of the world for me. My methods for making all A's in school did not work in college. This was a huge wake up call. I couldn't just memorize my way through college and expect to maintain a perfect GPA. I had to create a list of different steps to reach my new goal. I was going to have to comprehend what I read and be able to apply and generalize it to other situations. But the problem was I couldn't understand some of the terminology in the journal articles and research studies. I could memorize the words but I didn't know what they all meant. I had a tendency to read while skipping over the hard words but realized I didn't understand the full meaning. I wanted to receive the complete meaning. There was only one thing to do to fix that problem. Get the dictionary. I remember attempting to read AND comprehend every word in an assigned journal article. I perceived the task to be a challenge, and I aimed to accomplish this challenge. As I began reading, I underlined all the words that didn't make sense to me and would stop at the end of each paragraph to look up the words in the dictionary. To my further surprise, I didn't understand some of the words used in the dictionary to describe the words I was looking up. Therefore I had to look up those words as well. It took me about 30 minutes to read just one paragraph. Although I did not like how much time it took to read a journal article, I was delighted in the understanding I was receiving from the hard work.

As time went on, and as I applied my new method of studying, my need for the dictionary decreased and my grades during the second semester and throughout college remained near perfect. I was pleased that real learning was taking place in my life. Now, true meaning was permeating throughout my entire life. I felt like I just began living. I wondered how I went so long getting by in the world and I wondered why my teachers during my school years had never recognized that I wasn't paying attention. I wondered if I didn't find school interesting but I wanted to make good grades so I developed a habit of ignoring the content while memorizing the words. This habit stayed with me throughout my school career, but college was the remedy.

I loved college. There was freedom in college. College was a refreshing restart or new beginning in life. The material I was learning was very interesting. I did have some trouble paying attention in class because I couldn't receive the full lesson by hearing it from the lectures, but I was able to completely absorb the lessons by reading the books and articles for myself.

Just as college was a whole new experience after high school, graduate school was a whole new experience after completing the first four years of college. There was even more freedom to pursue my own interests. In fact, two of the classes were for students to read and research their areas of interest. It was so much easier to pay attention to things that interested me. In fact I would become so absorbed in my readings that I forgot about everything else. This is how I feel when I am doing other things as well like drawing or painting; I have no awareness of anything else going on around me.

Join a sorority?

I was aware that it was most common for girls to join sororities when they began college. A sorority is a girl only group comprised of women who may share common interests. The goal of a sorority is to create a group of women who are bonded by their membership and friendship. When I first began college I knew that joining sororities was the thing that girls did in college. I had read about sororities on the Internet that members were entitled to certain benefits, including residence in a sorority house, access to scholarships, and the ability to network with current sorority members and alumni. So I went to the first meeting and I absolutely hated it. Being there reminded me of the terrible struggles I had always dealt with around groups – especially groups of girls. I learned that it costs a lot of money to be a member of a sorority, $70 dollars a month when I first began college. That would make it $840 a year and $3,360 for the four years of college. That sure was a lot of money to be in a group. At the meeting I observed all the girls just talking away, they did not notice me nor did I attempt to talk to any of them. The room was so loud and everybody was talking at the same time. I felt dizzy and nauseous. As my anxiety increased, my desire to be in a sorority decreased. I left immediately and never regretted not becoming a member. I felt much better when I mentioned to a girl in one of my college classes the next day that I went to the first sorority meeting but decided not to become a member and she said, "Sororities are not for me either. I don't believe in buying my friends."

I didn't make a conscious effort to make friends in college. I perceived my attending was to get educated so I could have a career. However, along the way I made many acquaintances without even trying and even made a few friends with common interests.

One of them?

I had accepted an invitation to join a psychology group Psi Chi. I went to the first meeting mentally preparing myself for the tension and anxiety I experience in groups. To my delight, it was a small group with only nine people. The other students welcomed me with smiles and acceptance. I got to know a few of them one by one. We were all invited by one of our psychology professors to attend a conference and were told that the experience would be very beneficial to our professional development. I decided to go along. When we got there, I found I had to share a hotel room with three other girls, and I had to sleep in the same bed with one of them. I lay as still as possible at the very edge of the bed awake all night long. What a miserable night.

The conference was very interesting and meeting some of the well-known scientific researchers was a wonderful experience. I dreaded the conference to be over because that meant our group would re-unite to go to dinner. We walked to a restaurant and I did my best to follow the conversation and participate. I found this to be very difficult and exhausting while at the same time trying to tune out all the loud sounds typical of restaurants and all the other people talking at the same time. After we ate, we walked back to the hotel. I needed to relax a little so I walked behind everybody else. When we were about halfway there, one of the students looked back and saw me far behind the group and said "come on Kristi, your one of us." Those words made me feel so accepted, and so included. I replayed that phrase over and over in my mind.

That night the group gathered in one hotel room for what I learned a few minutes later to party/hang out. One of the guys brought out some whisky, orange juice, rum and coke. I thought about what one of the others said about me being one of them and I briefly wanted so badly to stay there and be a part of their hang out. The guy fixed me a drink and handed it to me. Everybody else was relaxed and enjoying themselves. I took a little sip of the drink, yuck. When I didn't think anybody was looking, I made my way to the sink, poured out my drink and slipped out the door. I was so disappointed in myself, but I just couldn't stay in that room. I looked down the empty hallway and suddenly felt so embarrassed. I wanted to hide, I wanted to disappear. I got on the elevator and went to another floor. When I got to the floor above, I walked down the hall feeling a little safer thinking that they won't find me up there. To my delight, I walked right past an exercise room. I went in and began to lift weights, which decreased my tension and anxiety. Afterwards, I went back downstairs to the room I was in, took a shower and hid under the covers pretending to be asleep when the other girls came in. I guess I really wasn't "one of them."

Foreword by Liane Holliday Willey

Introduction to the world of Autism

One day I turned on the TV and found the last half of the movie *House of Cards* about a little girl who had regressed into autism after her father died. I had heard of autism and I always had great desire to meet a child with autism. I had missed the first half of the movie so when the movie was over I immediately went to the movie rental store and checked it out. I watched it three times before returning it. The little girl's sudden loss of eye contact, loss of language, necessity for sameness and her sudden ability to do the incredible – build a house made of cards was astonishing. I was fascinated by all the other children in the movie who were at the clinic the little girl was taken to.

I found another movie about a boy with autism, *Mercury Rising*, about a brilliant child with autism who became a target for assassins after he figured out a top government code. I thought the title of the film was weird for the movie and now that I think about it, I wonder if the producers named it *Mercury Rising* as a clue to the rise in mercury and the rise of autism. I developed an incredible desire to meet a child with autism and wanted so badly to play with him, talk to him, interact with him, and help him…

I went to the counselor's office at my university to see how I could get connected to the world of autism. He didn't have anything for me except that he knew of a professor who had a student who worked with children who had autism. And to my delight, it was one of my professors! Before class that day I approached her and asked her if she had a student who worked with children who had autism and she said "yes, as a matter of fact, she is coming to talk to this class today about the possible job opportunity." Wow, God is the master of timing! The girl came to our class and described her experiences with children who had autism and described the type of therapy she used to help them. I absorbed every word she said, and we exchanged contact information. A couple weeks later I received a phone call by a mother who had a three-year-old child with autism. She asked me if I was able to come receive training in applied behavior analysis.

When I saw him, I thought he was the most beautiful child I had have ever seen. Those big blue eyes pierced into my soul, especially when he made eye contact. I sat on the floor and watched the other therapist run a few programs with him. He had been in ABA therapy for six months and knew the structure of coming to the chair and play. The therapist said, "Ok, you can go play." He walked over and sat on my lap. What an awesome feeling. "He is sitting in your lap," the therapist whispered. She went to get his mom. His mom came in and said, "He must really like you" and handed me his favorite book to read to him. My very first child, I will never forget my experiences with him.

Benson was receiving 20 to 30 hours of therapy a week. His compliance was exceptional. He would come sit at the table immediately when asked. He had some language, but didn't use it. Benson would repeat anything if asked. He could label a few things out loud, but had great difficulty focusing. He loved to give and receive backward hugs. His "stimming" behaviors included verbal sounds, tissue rubbing, and twirling things. As Benson grew and continued to receive therapy, his tantrums decreased dramatically, and his attentiveness improved. His family provided an excellent work environment.

Benson appeared to be making good progress over the next six months after I began working with him. He was easy to reinforce because he loved little toys, especially little cars and Slinkies, and he loved little pieces of chips. Then, I noticed a change in his progress; his progress seemed to slow down and even regress. It became more difficult to reinforce him because he showed little interest in toys. Come to find out, tickles and physical play, such as throwing him on the bed a few times helped him become more attentive. I was told that as a child with autism grows, it becomes more evident to what extent of autism the child has. Benson's ABA consultant informed me that he was a child with severe autism. I now believe that his immune system was bombarded and his terrible allergies and frequent infections caused his regression.

Benson appeared to me to be aware of what was going on around him. He was a very friendly little child. I began shadowing him at a local preschool a couple hours of our sessions. He adapted very well to the structure of the class, such as circle time, snack time, gym and outside time. He did not at all freely interact with any of the other children. He was not able to use his words for communication, although he could imitate the words someone else said. He required the most help during free time. If left alone, he would run back and forth, stand by the door, or twirl long objects in his hand. He would play in the areas that there were other children as long as someone engaged him in some type of toy play such as puzzles or Legos. Most of the other children were very nice to Benson, especially the girls, and would try to play with him. Many children asked me many questions and I encouraged them to ask questions and play with Benson. One day his class went on a field trip to a garden palace. Benson required me to hold his hand the entire time because if I let go, he would run straight for the ponds or he would kick gravel. I wondered what attracted him to the water. Benson loved verbal praise, so when I said, "Great job, that's the way we walk!" he would smile.

Benson was not able to attend a typical classroom. ABA therapy gave him excellent behavior and compliance skills; however, his level of cognition was not high enough to do the level of schoolwork in a typical classroom. He could expressively label things when asked and he could identify his numbers and letters, but math, counting and reading were overwhelming for him.

Just a few months after administering therapy with Benson, I began to also work with David and several more children. David was almost three years old when I first began working with him. I was extremely amazed at his rapid progress, especially in spatial skills, imitative actions, object manipulation, and his receptive skills. I thought he was a very gifted and remarkable child. Every now and then during our sessions, I would hear him say certain words under his breath, but I was unable to get him to speak or say any words clearly. Before even introducing his alphabet to him, I noticed that he already new his ABC's! He had this toy that when you pressed the letter, the computer would say the letter out loud. I went through every letter asking him to touch one at a time, and he knew them all. Shortly after, when I read books to him (which he always appeared to pay close attention to) he began pointing to the words and followed the sentences as I read to him. So I asked him to point to certain words, and he could do it! I was deeply intrigued to see a three year old identify words and possibly even read. He learned how to do this on his own. I was very amazed.

Although David appeared to be cognitively gifted receptively, he struggled greatly with speaking. He sometimes would open his mouth but nothing came out. He also was clearly in his own world when not engaged with a therapist. He would jump up and down and flap his arms. He did not make eye contact with anyone for about six months after his ABA program began. Even after that, it was still difficult for him to make eye contact.

I loved working with David because he was easy to reinforce, and easy to gain compliance. At about age four and a half he began to show signs of verbal speech. He would imitate a few sounds. And those sounds eventually turned in to single words and those single words eventually turned in to multiple words. I thought that he was cured from his autism. However, when I took him to church one day and went with him to a Sunday school class with other children his age, he was clearly different than the other children. He would stare at the walls, jump up and down flapping his hands. He would climb on top of chairs and under tables. He didn't even seem to notice the other kids.

His parents didn't take him anywhere because they were embarrassed by his behavior. They told me that when they would go to a restaurant, he would stuff his mouth with food instead of taking little bites at a time. So upon their request I spent time with him trying to teach him to use a fork and to take small bites at a time. He learned how to eat; he just needed some teaching.

After about a year of ABA, David's parents lost interest in his ABA program. One afternoon when I arrived at his home, his mother told me that she didn't think David needed ABA therapy anymore. She told me she already spoke to his ABA consultant and decided to discontinue his program as it was very expensive and he was already way above average intellectually. I later called his ABA consultant, and she said that she felt he still needed ABA because he still had many behaviors that would make it difficult for him in group settings and needed to continue working on his expressive language, but the parents had made their decision.

I really missed working with David and I frequently imagined what behavioral and language progress he would have made if his parents continued ABA therapy. This was my first basic lesson in working with families. I had assumed all families would do whatever it took, no matter how much money or time was needed. After working with many children and getting to know their families, I realized that not all parents have the same perspective; some barely even spoke or interacted with their children while others were involved every minute of the day. Of course, those children with the most involved parents were the ones who made the most progress.

Life has meaning

I could describe every child I have worked with and my experience with each of them and their family members. They each are very unique and different, have their own strengths and weaknesses. They all are very special, precious children. After working as an ABA therapist in the homes of children with autism for several months, I had firmly decided that I wanted to become an ABA consultant and do what was necessary to become a board certified behavior analyst. Most of the parents of the children I saw expressed great happiness with their children's progress. I was happy to see for myself the progress the children could make. I was happy to see many parents and children learning to be with and have fun with each other. Over the years, my responsibilities to the children changed. I began working as an ABA therapist in their homes. I then worked with them at a center-based facility where I learned how to create and develop individualized programs and behavior modification plans. I also trained other people in the principles of behavior analysis to work with the children. This training included teaching the children's parents and other family members the principles of behavior analysis, such as how to teach language and how to generalize and maintain learned skills.

I learned that it wasn't just the number of hours that mattered in a child's life, it was the involvement of the child's parents that made a noticeable difference in the children's rate of progress. I wanted to learn to encourage parents and teach them how to interact and teach their children. Some parents would sit and watch their children's therapy sessions while other parents didn't care to learn.

I noticed a pattern of other factors that contributed to a child's rate of progress such as the relationship between mom and dad, how siblings interacted with them and everyday life structure. I remember one child I worked with was making remarkable progress before his family moved to another house; sadly he regressed to a state that was beyond what he started with after the move. I have worked with children whose parents got divorced and this, no matter how many hours of ABA therapy was involved, contributed to the most rapid rate of regression.

So if parents truly want their child to maximize his or her potential, then they can learn to have a happy marriage, teach siblings good interaction, provide a very structured life, be very involved in their child's life, including playing with them, reading to them and even researching autism and best treatment methods. I also found out about biomedical treatments. One child who was completely non-verbal suddenly began speaking in two word phrases after one month of Nystatin, which is a yeast fighter. The stimming behaviors of one child greatly decreased when beginning vitamin B6 and magnesium supplements. One child stopped stimming when wheat and milk products were taken out his diet. But vitamin B6 didn't work for another child, and there was not observable behavioral change in another child on a wheat/dairy free diet. Why did some biomedical treatments help some children but not others? I greatly enjoyed searching all the research over the years to answer such difficult questions. The answer is in the last chapter.

Every single child I have seen and worked with has truly touched my life and my heart. Seeing the results of the effort I have poured into the lives of children gives great meaning to life. There is nothing on earth more rewarding than to see a child say his first word, his first sentence, write his name for the first time, answer his first question, ask a question, make a friend, look at you in your eyes and say "I love you." I will never forget the time that one of the children walked up to me put his arms around my neck, kissed me on the cheek and said "I love you Miss Kristi." It takes a team of people to help a child with autism. Each member of the team is just as important as the other. Team members collaborate to discuss what are the best methods to help an individual child improve their language and communication skills. I am forever thankful to all those who have touched the life of child with autism.

Chapter 6

Learning How to Effectively Participate in a Family

I always imagined I would get married one day. I don't remember ever considering the option of staying single. I remember frequently praying to God as a little child to give me a good husband – a husband that didn't smoke cigarettes, didn't drink alcohol or do any other drugs. I asked God to give me a husband that wasn't obsessed with football and sports like most men were, a husband who was nice and would be a wonderful father to my children.

I always wanted to have children. I wanted to have four children, specifically four boys. I used to think I could relate to boys better than girls. When I found out my second child was a girl I was a little disappointed. However, after she was born, I so happy to have a baby girl. This chapter describes my experience getting married and learning how to be a wife, having children and learning how to be a mother while keeping the home managed and organized. I hope that my experimenting with and seeking knowledge on how to learn to be a wife and mother will help other girls and women have a wonderful, happy and successful family life. This chapter ends with a word from my husband, what it is like being married to a woman with Asperger's.

Becoming a Wife

I met my husband at a roller skating rink when I was 18. Although roller skating rinks are sensory nightmares to many with Asperger's because of the flashing lights and loud music, I got great enjoyment out of the physical part of roller skating and the way it made my body feel. These feelings helped me tolerate the lights and loud noise, with the use of earplugs of course. I was trying to learn how to skate backwards when a man skated by and said, "Hey, you learn fast." Every time he skated around he would make some comment to me about how I was skating.

We got to know each other better and became great friends. Shane was 15 years older than me but I didn't care. Shane and I became best friends over the next six months, and I found myself wanting to talk with him and be with him more and more. We spent hours every night instant messaging on the Internet, chatting and getting to know each other better. I loved to communicate in words on the Internet. It was so much easier than conversing with people face to face. One day he told me in an email that when he last saw me, he felt like he wanted to kiss me. He had already told me that he hadn't dated in about a decade because he never could find a woman he liked well enough. He asked me out on a "date" and I accepted.

Shane respected my desire to not have sex until married. When I turned 20, he asked me to marry him. I already knew what I would say if he asked me because I had already examined and analyzed whether or not he would be a good Dad, and matched all the other qualities I prayed for in a man. Overall, Shane was a very quiet and calm person. He was very emotionally stable and presented himself in the same mood almost all the time. His presence calmed me. He was not intense about everything as I was which gave me great comfort when I was with him. There have been times when I would get frustrated with him because he did not get so enthusiastic about things as I did. I admired his ability to fix things; he loved tools and knew how to use them to fix almost anything. I am absolutely astounded that he built the fabulous house we live in. We got married when I turned 21.

Shane and I are opposites in personality and temperament. He is stable, whereas I am extremely intense. He is quiet, and I am very talkative. He is highly flexible, and I'm not. He has black and white dreams that he can barely remember, I have very colorful and lucid dreams that I am able to remember every detail. Clutter doesn't bother him at all, and clutter bothers me intensely. He is an auditory learner, and I am a visual learner. Although we are opposites in personality, we share the exact same values when it comes to children, family and God.

Our first year of marriage was a huge struggle and another "slap in the face" in the new real world. Learning how to live with someone is not easy for anyone. My world became out of control that year because his schedule was so unpredictable. I felt like I would flip out when he came home late or left earlier than he said. Many times we had plans to do something and he had to cancel or reschedule because of his work. He had rental property and had to go fix things sometimes unexpectedly. He was used to this, but I wasn't. I thought that if he surely loved me he would make an effort to keep the schedule as planned. So I became emotionally distant thinking he would come get me, but he didn't. Now, I am grateful he didn't reinforce my pitiful efforts to get him to pay attention to me.

After a few years of marriage, I began to get used to married life and somewhat accepted the sudden changes in schedule. I learned how not to show that things bothered me as much. There was no other person on earth I wanted to spend my time with than my husband. I loved being with my husband; quality time was my love language. His quiet and calm presence in the room was comforting. Quality time was not something he could always give me because he was so involved in his work.

There came a point in time that I realized he rarely touched or kissed me and I assumed this was a problem since husbands and wives are supposed to hug and kiss all the time. I asked him why he didn't hug or kiss me anymore and he said because when he did I made a terrible face and flinched so he assumed I wasn't physically attracted to him. He was right that sudden touch bothered me but he was wrong that I wasn't physically attracted to him. I admired his passionate big blue eyes, his dark hair, his strength and his masculine hands. I felt so guilty for not being more "lovey-dovey" but he didn't seem to mind that I wasn't.

Foreword by Liane Holliday Willey

Our communication was difficult sometimes because he would make assumptions about my understanding of what was going on without an explanation. He didn't seem to understand why I needed such specific communication. Shane didn't get upset much but he used to get upset when I didn't understand and laugh when he was joking. He said it hurts a man's ego when his woman doesn't laugh at his jokes. But now we meet in the middle so when he tells a joke or uses sarcasm, he will then tell me it's a joke and so I can pretend to laugh.

I was seeing way too many marriages fail in divorce and way too many unhappy marriages in society. I was afraid that a perfect marriage was not possible. Discovering I had Asperger's during our third year of marriage did not aid in improving our overall marriage. For a while, I used the excuse "I can't help it, it's just the way I am." But my husband would say that it wasn't a good excuse. I desired a perfect marriage and didn't want to settle for less than perfect so I began reading books on improving marriages. And although they were good reads, the advice in them didn't helped our marriage improve. Most of the advice was for both spouses to follow in order for the techniques to work. These books caused me to blame my husband for not "filling my love tank" by speaking my love language as the books said he should. I laugh at that now, how immature I was and the lack of knowledge I had. We took a newly wed class at our church, and although it was worth going and helped us relate to each other better as a couple, it didn't create the perfect marriage I desired.

It wasn't until I discovered my role as a wife that led to a wonderful, happy and joyful marriage. I realized that I just didn't know how to be a wife. I embraced learning how to be a good wife, the best wife possible, as a challenge to accomplish. It wasn't until I read the two books *The Excellent Wife* by Martha Peace and *Created to be His Helpmeet* by Debi Pearl that it finally clicked within me on how to be a good wife – the wife God designed me to be. I didn't care for those liberated perspectives on women. I wanted to be what I was supposed to be. I wasn't offended like some women at the idea of the wife reverencing her husband. Examine the results. Those women who embrace the biblical principles of being a wife are very happy and have the most wonderful, joyful marriages. I learned about the different types of men and learned what type of man mine was, the steady man, and appreciated him for the way he was.

I began to change my own behavior as a wife. I started to see my husband in a different light. I had a whole new perspective, a whole new set of behaviors to follow. I began paying more attention to my husband and his needs and desires. My attitude completely changed. I set out to consistently provide him all natural well-cooked meals. I made sure all his needs were met including his laundry and keeping the house well managed.

Wow, did our marriage turn into a wonderful, heavenly, joyful relationship! In response to my behavior changes, my husband began to become more attentive to me. He wanted to spend more time with me and would even put off his work sometimes to be with me without me asking. I was happy with myself that I was learning to be a good wife, a wife that my husband wanted to be with, and a wife that my husband was proud of. He began bragging to all his friends and family what such a wonderful wife he had. We have been married since 2001 and every year gets better and better with the joy doubling itself each year. I just couldn't settle for anything less than a perfect marriage.

Motherhood

My gynecologist told me that it would be difficult for me to get pregnant because of my endometriosis and recommended me to get a Lupron shot. The minute I was about to leave my college to get my first shot, a classmate was walked by my car and stopped to talk with me. I mentioned to her I was about to get a Lupron shot and she exclaimed "Oh, don't do that, my best friend got a Lupron shot and it was the worst mistake of her life; it caused her to go into terrible rages, have terrible hot flashes, and caused her to have so much pain." So, I decided to call my doctor and tell him I wanted to hold off on the Lupron and see if I could get pregnant first. We prayed and prayed to God to help us get pregnant. Two months later, I was pregnant. Isn't God the master of timing?

I was very sick the first few months of pregnancy. The smell of anything, including soap, made me sick. All the senses were heightened even further. I tried not to care so much, because I was so thrilled that we were going to have a baby. Hearing the first heartbeat and seeing the baby on the ultrasound was absolutely amazing. I was thrilled to hear that our first baby was a boy! I chose to feed my babies with breast milk because a great deal of scientific research showed that children who were breastfed had higher IQ's and a healthier immune system than children who were formula fed.

I wanted all my children to be exactly two years apart in age. I prayed to God to help me meet this goal. I researched methods on increasing our chances of conceiving. We immediately got pregnant with our second child. Her due date was just two weeks before my son's second birthday. Being pregnant with my second child was just as exciting as the first, but I was still very sick the first few months. My third child, a girl, was born just two weeks before my second child's birthday.

At first, I thought I was going to be a good mother and have very well-behaved children since I was a behavior analyst. It wasn't until my son was 18 months old when I realized that behavior analysis was not the best method for parenting. My son was such an intense toddler, very self-willed and what most people would call a "spirited child." Behavior analytic principles did help a great deal with teaching my kids certain behaviors, like good table manners and eating habits, and routine behaviors such as getting dressed, potty training, taking baths and going to bed. However, parenting includes teaching moral and ethical behavior, choosing right from wrong, obedience and integrity and being a good behavioral model.

I wanted so badly to become a good mother so I searched for parenting books. Wow, there were so many books on parenting. Doing a search on Amazon with the words "child raising" over 63,000 books came up. I read as many books on parenting as I could. I checked them out from the library and ordered them off the Internet. While some of the books were terribly written and had very poor advice, many of the books provided excellent advice. I learned a lot of information while searching and reading about how to teach moral intelligence in children, emotional stability, obedience and a list of other character traits such as integrity, attentiveness, authenticity, love, compassion, hardworking and developing good habits.

It wasn't until I read the books *Where's Mom? The High Calling of Wives & Mothers* by Dorothy Kelly Patterson and *Passionate Housewives Desperate for God* by Jenni Chancey and Stacy McDonald that my role as a mother clicked within me. Again, I had a whole new set of behaviors and rules to follow, and I was very happy to have discovered what a good mom is supposed to do.

One day, my husband mentioned that we might want to consider home schooling our children. "Absolutely not!" I exclaimed. I wanted my children to go to school, have the best education possible, go to college and go as far as possible when it came to education. My husband tried to reason with me and asked me to just consider it. So I considered it. I checked out books on home schooling at the library and purchased some from the bookstore. I was absolutely astounded at what I found and read!

The main concern people have with home schooling is that children will not make friends or learn social skills if they don't go to a school. Research shows that testing of home-schooled children suggests above average social and psychological development. And anyone who has observed home schoolers will notice a high level of sharing, networking, collaboration and cooperative learning (Lines, 2002). There have been research studies done in which home schooled children score high in self-concept, leadership skills, and community involvement which are reflectors of positive socialization (Houk, 2002). Many studies have established the academic excellence in home-schooled students. Statistics show that home schoolers tend to score above the national average on SAT and ACT tests. Numerous studies consistently show that home-schooled children score between the 60 to 90th percentiles on academic subjects, with the more years of home schooling the higher the percentile (Smith & Farris, 2004).

As part of my job as a behavior analyst, I frequently shadowed children in typical classrooms. I was becoming increasingly bothered at the structure of the classroom, at how so many children were being ignored during the day because of the student-to-teacher ratio and I was even more disturbed by the lack of teaching on moral and ethical behavior. I began to feel irritated when parents would pressure their children on the autism spectrum, "Do what the other kids are doing," "Watch the other kids and do what they do" or "JUST BE LIKE THE OTHER KIDS!"

I understand parents who have children with autism do not like the fact their children are different and they want their children to be "normal" like the other children. But what I saw is that these children were presented with almost constant stress, confusion and disappointment in themselves at failure to meeting the grown-ups' expectations. One would argue they are doing these children a good service by teaching them to be like everyone else so they can participate in the world. While I believe they can learn social skills, I also believe that the world needs to be more accepting of people who appear different.

What I also observed in the classroom was that children get into trouble and are sent to time out when they speak to each other at inappropriate times. There was one particular child I was teaching social skills to, including how to begin and continue conversations with his peers. One day during circle time, he suddenly looked at the child next to him and asked him a question. This was a HUGE breakthrough for him! I was so happy! But his teacher sent him to time out for talking. I later talked with the teacher about what happened, and she said that although it was a breakthrough for him, he had to follow the rules just like the other kids. I was so disappointed in this situation.

I learned that school was NOT the best place to teach conversation and social skills. Could there possibly be another way to teach them social skills without causing them such stress and frustration? Play dates are a great way to teach social skills, where the child has friends come to the home engaging in play activities led by a parent or therapist. What about home schooling? There had been several families who opted for home schooling I had worked with, and were very happy with the results in their children. Not only were their children learning more, but they also were making close friends rather than just having a few acquaintances. Being presented with all types of people of all different ages, rather than the people of the exact same age all the time is a great method for teaching good social skills. I would have to write another book on this subject. Home schooling is not for every family, but most families don't even know it is an option.

After praying to God for guidance, reading many books on home schooling, looking a great deal of research that has been done on home schooling, talking with adults who were home schooled as children, analyzing my own experience with school, my husband and I decided that home schooling was the best option for our children. I looked back to all my time at school, daydreaming and doodling my time away until the bell rang, how much I began learning when I went to college, and how much I have learned since graduation from high school and figure that home schooling is best for our family. So many people have questioned me as to why I have decided to home school because they feel the same way I used to feel about it. But I smile and kindly reply to them that, "I believe it is best for my children." If they continue to question me then I go into more detail about my reasons for home schooling including: teaching at my children's level on each subject, being able to provide for their physical needs, their socialization needs, their academic needs, their creative needs, their intellectual needs, and a primary focus on moral intelligence, emotional stability and biblical principles.

Home schooling my kids means that I won't have time during the day like most moms have while their kids are at school. My time is spent teaching them. I try to see every situation as a teaching opportunity. I want to teach my children how to help children who have autism. My goals in life have changed to raising my children to the very best I possibly can. It is the truth that *I have no greater joy than to hear that my children walk in the truth* (3 John 1:4).

I think my biggest challenge as being a mother is the sudden sensory stabs I receive throughout the day. I have to put a blanket on my ear when I read to my son because he is such a loud person in general making noises, such as making little smack noises with his mouth. When he brings me a book to read to him, he also brings a blanket for my ear. I would use earplugs but since we have had a baby in the family I don't want to accidentally lose one and the baby find it and choke on it. Sometimes I wear earmuffs. I try so very hard not to let the sudden loud noises disturb me. Most of the time I can shake it off after a minute when reminding myself how much I love my kids. Another challenge, that I have been improving on according to my husband, is sometimes I am so tuned into my thoughts that I forget what I am doing, where I am and who I am with for a few moments. When someone in my family is trying to get my attention they end up having to raise their voice because I didn't hear them the first few times.

I absolutely delight in my children. They are a true blessing from God. They love me no matter how I dress, how I wear my hair or if I am silly sometimes. I am determined to be the best mom possible teaching my children everything I know and how to learn anything they want. My prediction that my husband would be a good father was correct. He is an amazing father. He gave up TV to spend time with his kids. He took the TV out of our house and our family has been growing closer and closer everyday. My husband and I have been learning how to be good parents together.

I have a record of every single time my kids have gotten sick, the symptoms listed, where they probably got it from, treatment (which is usually extra vitamin C and D and specific herbs), length of illness, and date and age. When my kids get married, they are going to know exactly how many times they got sick in their lives, when they got sick and how they recovered. I talk about my children's behavioral and medical clues and how my husband and I think we prevented them from developing autism in the last chapter of this book.

Organizing and managing the house

Learning how to organize and manage our home was not easy. It was a challenge that took several years to come close to mastering. I grew up as an only child and my only responsibility in life was to make good grades. When I got married, I didn't know how to cook, didn't know anything about taxes or any type of insurance, and didn't know much about money management or record keeping. Record keeping and bill paying is so hard for me, so frustrating and so stressful. I am very fortunate that my husband does the record keeping. But I am able to successfully manage our home.

Keeping the housework managed used to be a challenge, and I hated the problem of having to do the same things over and over to find that they needed to be done again. I needed a change in perspective and solution to this problem. A schedule, yes, that's it! I made a list of all the things that had to be done such as each person's laundry, cleaning the bathrooms, the kitchen, vacuuming and dusting. Then I assigned a chore to each day of the week. Mondays are for cleaning the bathroom and doing the kids laundry. Tuesdays are dusting and cleaning up the clutter days. Wednesdays are my husband's laundry and vacuuming days. Thursdays are my laundry, mopping and kitchen cleaning days. Fridays are washing the towels and bedclothes days. My kids all participate in these chores and we get them done in a very short time. They are much more fun doing them together! Of course I had to spend a lot of time teaching them what to do and how to do it when they were first learning. Even my one-year-old helps clean up clutter and puts laundry in the washing machine. I had taught my other children to fold washcloths when they were two. Now, they know how to fold their own clothes. I would not have ever known to teach them to help with the chores if it weren't for a ministry called No Greater Joy Ministries that gave me a new perspective on teaching responsibility. "Train up a child in the way he should go: and when he is old, he will not depart from it" (Proverbs 22:6).

I used much of the advice that Liane Holliday Willey offers in her *Pretending to be Normal* book in the *Organizing Your Home Life* section. Making my way through the day without stressing myself out by making lists of assignments and using visual reminders. I shop online as much as I can in order to avoid going to the store. I always hated shopping. When I was a kid I used to get bad headaches and get dizzy and nauseated in stores. I wanted to get out as soon as possible and I remember getting so impatient with my mom for taking so long. When I was a teenager I became aware that "shopping" was a favorite activity for most girls and women. I agreed to tag along a few times with invitations from friends, having to make myself bring a purse because the rest of the group did. Once we were there, the girls would pick up shirts, hold them out and say "awww, this is so cute don't you think?" I tried so hard not to roll my eyes and scream "YOU HAVE GOT TO BE KIDDING!?" Somehow I managed to get a little "yeah, it's cute" out because I knew they wanted a response similar to that. I am so grateful for online stores and yard sales.

Because I home school, I work outside the home much less than I used to. So I have had to learn to be more frugal with money. Learning to be more frugal has been a lot of fun! I learned how to budget the grocery list, how to look for sales and clearances, shop at yard sales, buy in bulk, and I've even learned what the prices are on various items at different stores. I found books that helped with money management and wise spending such as the *Miserly Moms* books by Joni McCoy. My husband became very interested in Dave Ramsey's *Financial Peace*.

I look forward to what the future holds for my family and me as we continue on this journey of life. I look forward to teaching my children everything possible, look forward to seeing them continue and grow their relationship with each other as siblings, look forward to raising my kids with my husband teaching them moral intelligence and emotional stability, look forward to improving my ability to be a better mom and wife, look forward to all the future Thanksgivings, Birthdays and Christmas's with my family, look forward to improving my relationship with God and teaching my children how to have a relationship with God.

A Word from My Husband
What it is Like Being married to a Woman with Asperger's

Shane Hubbard

What first attracted me to my wife was that she was very pretty and nice. She wasn't conceited over her looks, nor did she obsess with putting on too much makeup or wearing designer clothes. She seemed like a down to earth girl. She liked to learn and have fun by being silly. She was really fun to be around. I really liked how outgoing she was and how nice she was to me. We seemed to click right off from the start. I liked her interest in God. We would have conversations for hours each night on the Internet. I first began to fall in love with her personality on the Internet.

I asked her to marry me because I thought she would make a great wife and mother. She seemed and acted very caring and had a quest for knowledge and truth. Her closeness to God really attracted me to her. I had been asking God for years to bring someone like her into my life. My prayers were answered and I continually thank God for bringing her into my life. She is only the best mother I have ever seen. Now that I have seen what a good mother is, I couldn't imagine having anyone else raise my children. Marriage was hard at first, but since she has read those books about being a wife, she has become a wonderful wife and gets better every year. I am very happy in my marriage. I believe the closer to God we become, the better our relationship develops.

I did notice some unusual behavior in her early on in our relationship. She would avoid small talk. Many times she would just walk off when the conversation in a group became meaningless and uninteresting, "chitter chatter." I would sometimes avoid gatherings of my friends because I knew my wife wouldn't fit in well with all the small talk and candid jokes being said. I would rather spend time around her friends because they were already used to her behavior. Some people thought she was being rude when she would seem uninterested in their small talk. Some would ask her a question or say something sort of funny and she would just give a blank look, not answering or responding. She does not understand sarcasm hardly at all and is not able to tell when I am joking. That was very difficult for me to understand. I didn't know whether to stop them myself or help her understand when something was a joke, so she could laugh anyway to make others and myself feel good. She sometimes would also just stare into space, inattentive to what's going on around her. She would drift into her own world even during one-on-one conversations, if the topic didn't interest her much. Her attentiveness has greatly improved since I first met her.

She complained about lights being too bright, noises too loud or certain noises irritating to her. She would not tolerate certain lights being on in the house and could not stand the volume I liked for music. She would squirm away if I touched her neck or made smacking sounds to close to her ears. She would also complain about certain smells that to me seem very mild. She complained about the smell of the shampoo I used. I didn't understand any of these things. Her sensory issues were difficult to accept at first, I sort of thought she was just being a little over dramatic, but after learning about many others with the same issues, I began to understand and accept her sensitivity.

My wife is very well organized and researches everything to keep our family healthy. I don't think Asperger's is a bad thing. Now that I understand it better, it can be good sometimes. The advantages outweigh the disadvantages.

Suggested Readings

- *Asperger Syndrome in the Family: Redefining Normal* by Liane Holliday Willey (2000)
- *The Excellent Wife: A Biblical Perspective* by Martha Peace (2001)
- *Created to Be His Help Meet: Discover How God Can Make Your Marriage Glorious* by Debi Pearl (2004)
- *Where's Mom? The High Calling of Wives & Mothers* by Dorothy Kelly Patterson (2003)
- *Passionate Housewives Desperate for God* by Jenni Chancey and Stacy McDonald (2007)
- *Revolutionary Parenting: What the Research Shows Really Works* by George Barna (2007)
- *Shepherding a Child's Heart* by Tedd Trip (1995)
- *To Train up a Child* by Michael and Debi Pearl (1994)
- *Raising Your Spirited Child Rev Ed: A Guide for Parents Whose Child Is More Intense, Sensitive, Perceptive, Persistent, and Energetic* by Mary Sheedy Kurcinka (2006)
- *The Little Book of Big Reasons to Homeschool* by David & Kim d'Escoto (2007)
- *The Homeschooling Book of Answers* by Linda Dobson (2002)
- *Miserly Moms: Living on One Income in a Two-Income Economy* by Joni McCoy (2001)
- *Miserly Moms: Living Well on Less in a Tough Economy* by Joni McCoy (2009)
- *You Can Afford to Stay Home With Your Kids: A Step-By-Step Guide for Converting Your Family from Two Incomes to One* by Malia Ccawley Wyckoff and Mary Snyder (1999)
- *Financial Peace Revisited* by Dave Ramsey (2003)

References

Houk, K. (2002). Have there been any studies about how homeschooling affects a child's ability to get along with others and make the transition into the real world? The Homeschooling Book of Answers. Revised. The 101 Most important questions answered by homeschooling's most respected voices. By Linda Dobson. Prima Publishing.

Lines, P. (2002). Have there been any studies about how homeschooling affects a child's ability to get along with others and make the transition into the real world? The Homeschooling Book of Answers. Revised. The 101 Most important questions answered by homeschooling's most respected voices. By Linda Dobson. Prima Publishing.

Smith, J.M. & Farris, M.P. (2004). Academic Statistics on Homeschooling. HSLDA Legal Research Supplement. Retrieved on November 14th, 2009. http://www.hslda.org/docs/nche/000010/200410250.asp#xviii

CHAPTER 7

Perception, Thinking, Recognizing Patterns and More

Other people with Asperger's may or may not be able to relate to the characteristics described in this chapter. I am certain that each individual will at least be able to relate to some of these. For many of these situations, I have been able to effectively apply solutions. I hope this chapter provides understanding, relation and tips to others with similar issues. Characteristics discussed in this chapter: solving problems verses showing empathy, difficulty converting meaning into expressive language, repetitive thinking, auditory processing verses visual processing, bluntness verses authenticity, intense interests and focus, literal perception, way of thinking and memory, being resourceful, trying to understand typical behavior, keeping friendships and loyalty, recognizing friendships and acquaintances, small talk, anxiety, obsession with knowledge and facts, sudden changes in schedule, asking repetitive questions, difficulty following movies, the necessity of figuring out a cause from an effect, recognizing patterns that can be seen and unseen and whether or not to join the mainstream.

Solving peoples problems vs. showing empathy

Many people have accused me of not being "compassionate," "sympathetic" or "empathetic." I admit that I may have trouble showing these things in the way that people would expect. Showing empathy in a way others expect is very difficult. It is not that I don't feel compassionate, sympathetic or empathetic; I do feel these emotions to a tremendous degree. However, I feel the incredible urge to offer advice or provide a solution to the problem the other person is experiencing in efforts to eliminate their struggle, sadness or unhappiness.

For example, when a friend calls and tells me that her young child is coughing uncontrollably and has a high fever, her husband does nothing but lay on the couch, she is struggling financially, her mother in law is always telling her what to do etc. I want to provide my friend with possible solutions to all those problems so that they can be solved. Therefore, she would be happier and less stressed. Instead, I have learned the hard way with hearing people say "just listen" so much, I recognize that my friend is more likely needing someone who will listen to her while she relieves stress and frustration by expressing her problems. I so badly want to tell her what herbs and methods to use to help her child with coughing, how to be a good example for her husband and how him love instead of nagging him, and give her the names of the books that have been published on managing finances. But she doesn't want advice; she wants a friend to listen to her.

Now that I know this and can apply it, I sometimes have trouble distinguishing whether or not to just listen, offer advice or a little of both. Something that helps me distinguish what I should do is to only give advice when asked. If advice is not requested, I try to just listen and ignore the impulse to offer suggestions. For some reason that I don't understand, some people do not want solutions. Maybe because what they really want is for their emotions to return to normal. One way to do that is to vent (talk about what is causing those emotions).

On the news, in the newspaper and on the radio, tragic things are frequently reported such as girls being raped, children being kidnapped, people dying in tornados and hurricanes etc. Emotions generated from hearing those things are so overwhelming; I have to shut out those things from my mind in order to protect myself from overload. I choose not to watch the news or read the newspaper because of all the tragic things being reported. I have certain people tell me, or I look on the Internet for recent political or other current events in order to avoid hearing the tragedies. Because I don't talk much about these tragedies or make comments, some people have assumed I am not compassionate.

Difficulty converting meaning into expressive language

I remember as a child, having great difficulty finding words to use that described what I was trying to say. The meaning was there in my mind, but I could not effectively communicate that meaning. As my vocabulary increased, I was better able to express meaning.

Another issue that interferes with expressive communication, is that the process of "thinking" is much more rapid than the process of "speaking." Therefore, having to pick and choose what parts of thoughts to say expressively in order to get the communication across while at the same time speaking, can slow down the speaking and limit full expression. I didn't realize until I was 24, that sometimes what people intend to communicate and express, other people may not perceive or receive exactly as intended. This happens to everybody at times and that is how misunderstandings take place. Many of the problems that occur in relationships are a result from misunderstandings. Sometimes, people assume others are receiving and interpreting exactly what they are trying to say. And sometimes others assume that what they perceive is exactly what was intended. Don't assume people fully understand what you are intending and that you understand exactly what they are intending. When an argument develops as a result from a misunderstanding, give the other person the benefit of the doubt because you know how easy misunderstandings can happen.

Repetitive thinking

During my preteen years, my thinking began to change. When I experienced a heightened emotion, whether it be angry, surprised, embarrassed, excited or happy, I had a tendency to replay the event that caused the emotion over and over in my head. For example, if my mom said, "Tomorrow, we are going to the Smokey Mountains for a week," I would feel excited about it and replay her saying it over and over and replay our last trip to the Smokey Mountains over and over. Or if someone told me that I was good at something such as, "You're good at pitching during the softball games," I would replay the person saying this over and over, while experiencing the emotion over and over. This repetitive thinking would cause me to not be able to sleep at night. Also, people have often told me I appear spaced out at times. I perceived this to be a problem and gave effort to not repeat the events in my head. However, it seemed the more I tried to stop it, the more difficulty I had to control it. As an adult, I sometimes have this problem. However, I have learned that if I can't sleep because my mind won't stop thinking and replaying events, I will type it out. This relaxes me, and I typically fall asleep with no obsession. This helps during the day as well, but I have learned that changing the subject or focusing on something else such cooking a meal for my family, or doing a physical activity such as taking a walk helps my mind refocus.

Visual processing vs. auditory processing

When I first began working with other professionals in the field of autism, one of them mentioned to me that I might have an auditory processing disorder. So, I researched what and auditory processing disorder was and realized that I was not able to process everything I heard into meaning. Auditory processing disorder (APD) is not being able to process information from hearing in the same way others do it. It is not a hearing impairment. There may be a problem with the ears taking in the sounds and the brain interpreting them and converting them to meaning. Although I have had sensitivity to sounds and can hear people talking, sometimes I don't understanding exactly what they are saying. My mom used to frequently tell me that, "You don't listen to the whole conversation."

What causes auditory processing problems? There is not a specific cause that has been identified, however, possible causes include: frequent middle ear infections, lack of oxygen at birth, damage to the brain, and it is specifically linked to the autism spectrum.

It is important to note that sometimes a child may not receive what is being told to them because they are not paying attention. This should not be confused with not being able to make out exactly what people are saying. I know that many times in my life, I was not paying attention. Therefore, I did not receive the whole conversation. However, there were times I would give a great deal of effort to paying attention, but could not fully comprehend what was being said. I wonder if I did not pay attention because I knew I couldn't receive or learn from what was being verbally taught, or because I was not interested. I admit I had trouble paying attention to things I wasn't interested in but my desire to make good grades led me to compensate for not paying attention. I could learn the lesson by seeing it in the textbook. This led to the discovery of different learning styles and that individual children have easier ways of learning. I have found that children with autism learn much preferred by having a visual aid paired with the verbal teachings. Having a visual schedule can make transitions much more tolerable. Learning by doing, kinesthetic learning is also a learning style that most all children greatly benefit from. It is possible to strengthen a weaker learning style by consistently pairing it with a strong learning style.

I am aware of not being able to perfectly process everything by hearing, so I give effort to closely attend when people are speaking to me. But if people speak very rapidly I have trouble segmenting the words and only receive some of what they are saying. I have great difficulty following conversations in groups. Having conversations with just one person at a time is what I prefer because I can follow and participate in the conversation better. I think this is one of the many reasons why people with Asperger's generate so much anxiety in groups.

Bluntness vs. authenticity

Many people have told me that I am "too blunt" and that I can easily hurt people's feelings. For example, if I perceived somebody to be bossy I said, "You are bossy." I remember saying to my cousin one time "that boy can't walk" looking at a boy in a wheel chair. I remember telling a friend that her mom was crazy. There are many times where I just said what I saw or thought without any intention or realization of hurting anyone's feelings.

My mom was good at helping me learn that saying what you see or think can hurt people's feelings so it is important to think before speaking. I try to think about how a person would feel before saying anything. I have absolutely no intentions on hurting anybody's feelings.

It can be hard to not always speak directly when I am trying to communicate certain things. I feel silly saying things that are not the truth, like telling someone their haircut looks great, when I am thinking that it doesn't. I do believe that it is important not to hurt people's feelings, however, I think people just get their feelings hurt too easily. Personally, I would much rather people tell me exactly what they were thinking and get my feelings hurt than for them to tell me they liked the haircut but thought that it was bad. I would much rather know the truth and deal with the hurt feelings. In fact, I have learned that feelings can be a choice. I can choose to let my feelings hurt or I can choose to appreciate the other person's honesty. I would rather have the truth than a false compliment. The saying goes, "treat other people the same way you want to be treated." Well, for me the saying goes more like this, "treat other people in the way *they* want to be treated."

The word "authentic" means to be real, true, genuine and trustworthy. It does not mean to be false. I perceive "authenticity" to be a character trait that is important for people to have. I try to be authentic with people, however, if I am too authentic this can cause them not to want to be my friend or socialize with me. This can cause other people to dislike being around me. I have found a solution to this problem. Since I don't want to hurt anybody's feelings and I want to keep my friends, I try not to say anything that would hurt a person's feelings. But I do find something to say that would make them feel good. For example, if my friend just got her hair cut and fixed and asks me how I like it, I mention something that I like about it and make a comment on that such as "the color looks great on you" or "I like the length." If another friend asks me how I like her new outfit that I truly dislike, I find something I do like about it such as "I love the designs" or "the fabric looks pleasant."

There is a way to be true and genuine without hurting other people's feelings. Focus on what you do like and give them the compliment. And if you truly want others to be completely honest with you, tell them that you appreciate their complete honesty and assure them that it would not hurt your feelings if they told you the exact truth.

Intense interests and focus

Throughout my life I have had very specific interests that would sometimes cause me to not pay much attention to other things. When I was smaller I had an incredible interest in cats. My bedroom walls were covered in posters of cats. I had many picture books of cats I frequently examined and a ceramic cat collection. I have never been without a pet cat. I thought cats were the cutest, intriguing, most precious creatures on earth. I had many shirts with cats on them and wore them until some girls from high school told me that my cat shirts made me look like a child. I think sometimes my cat focus prevented me from attending to other things or ideas. I remember going to a bookstore, rapidly scanning the bookshelves to spot a cat book to look at rather than look at what other books there were.

When I was in middle school I had an intense interest in farm animals. I did not look at pictures of them or collect them, but I pretended to be them. I thought it was the most hilarious and fun thing to do, pretending to be a cow, sheep, goat and turkey. My best friends would tell me I was crazy and goofy but sometimes they would join in with me making animal sounds. I remember wondering why all the other children didn't enjoy making animal noises. Even to this day I find making animal sounds amusing, although I am able to completely control any impulse to do so. I like working with little children because it is socially appropriate to sing songs like *Oh McDonald had a Farm*.

Sometimes having intense focus in something can be a good thing. For example, when I sketched something, I am able to focus so intensely to get the lines just like I see them and when I painted something I can precisely mix the colors to match what color I am trying to make. When I first began playing songs on the piano by listening to them, I was able to attend to the song and isolate the different sounds and match them to the piano.

As an adult, I have an intense interest in searching for the truth and gaining knowledge. I greatly enjoy reading research articles, self-help books and non-fiction books. I have an incredible interest in learning to be a good wife and a good mother. There are things in life that are truly important and many things that don't really matter. It is good to be able to distinguish between what's important and what is not. Having a happy marriage and having emotionally and morally intelligent children are extremely important. I have learned that people are very sensitive to the methods their parents use to raise them. A child's character begins to develop as a baby and parents have the most influence over how a child will be when they grow up.

If you have an intense interest in something, I think it is great to attend to and enjoy what you're interested in. However, make sure it doesn't distract you from other important things such as family and friends. Use your interests to build on your strengths and discover your talents. People will appreciate your determination and talents. Just make sure you don't forget what is truly important in life. Although things can sometimes seem more interesting than people, people are more important than things.

Literal perception

Since I can remember my mom made comments to me how I took everything so seriously and literally. I didn't even know what the word literal meant until high school. It means understanding things exactly as they are said. People with literal perception have difficulty understanding figures of speech, inside jokes and use of idioms.

"It's raining cats and dogs!" my Mother hollered one day while I was playing Nintendo. I immediately got very excited at the thought of cats and dogs being all over the yard, especially cats. I got up and looked out the window expecting to see cats and dogs everywhere but only saw rain. How disappointed I felt. "Mom, there are no cats and dogs, why would you say that?" "It is a figure of speech, honey," she would reply. When I became aware that I had trouble understanding sarcasm or figurative speech I got a book of idioms to help me interpret many of those sayings.

Now that I have studied many of the idioms and their intended meanings, I can convert the picture I have in my mind to the actual meaning. For example, when I hear the phrase "I'm all ears," my mind pictures a person with ears all over them, but I convert that picture to the meaning "that person is really listening." I was 24 when I first learned what the phrase "two faced" meant when one of my co-workers told me that many girls are two faced because they will say something about somebody to another person but then say something totally different to that person's face. I never cease to be amazed at how there are so many sayings with specific wording and how people so greatly enjoy using figurative speech.

Even though I am now very aware of myself perceiving things literally and not understanding subtle jokes or sarcasm, I still have moments where I believe exactly what is said or don't recognize when a joke is being told. Sometimes, if I give myself a moment to think about something that doesn't make sense, I can figure the intended meaning. For example, my husband recently told me "don't let the kids eat on the new carpet." I immediately thought "why in the world would the kids eat the carpet, they have outgrown wanting to put non-edible items in their mouths?" After thinking about it a few moments, his intended meaning came to me "oh, he must mean not to let them eat food while they are standing on the carpet." There are still many times when my husband would say something that I don't really get or understand why he would say that and he will see by the blank look on my face that I don't get his joke or even recognize that he was joking and he will tell me "it was a joke. This kind of joking is not the same as telling a joke. It is not saying, "Why did the chicken cross the road?" kind of joke. It is something funny that is tied into a conversation. When we are with groups of people, many people enjoy joking and using figures of speech, so I just pretend to laugh when everybody else does.

Way of thinking and memory

I clearly remember lying in bed one night with a high fever at age 11 (the year after receiving that measles vaccine). My thoughts were clear and began taking on a different pattern. I remember thinking "this is strange, I have never thought like this before." I lay there thinking about life, people, the universe, God and was very clearly seeing my thoughts. They were not clear pictures as you would see with your eyes or on photographs, but they had a sight of their own. Each concept I thought about had it's own picture with multi-dimensional attributes with color, shades, tints, tones and shapes. There are no specific words that can describe them perfectly except that was I was seeing in my mind with my thoughts were like abstract works of art. This became my way of thinking for the rest of my life.

For a simple example, when I think of the days of the week, I see a long parallelogram with fuzzy edges and inside are different blocks, some stand out more than the others and they all have different colors and shades. The beginning of the parallelogram is a block that starts with white at the top and gradually turns to a bright tint of yellow at the bottom. The block is raised forward slightly. This block represents the word "Sunday." Each of the blocks represents a day of the week and has a different color and dimension. The colors and dimensions represent my perception of the day. I like Mondays the least so "Monday" filled with tints of gray and is flat. "Friday" is a tone of red close to maroon and turns black at the bottom of the block. I love Saturdays so "Saturday" has the largest dimension of all and is a pleasant mixture of green blue tints since turquoise is my favorite color. For every thought, there is an abstract picture. Most of them have patterns leading into deeper thought. Sometimes I have trouble converting those abstract pictures into language.

Do you have a good long-term memory? Although I do not have a photographic memory, many people have told me that I have a good memory. My mom told me that when I was three years old she would tell me her phone numbers because I could remember them all. I remember being able to hear a phone number and pair it in my memory with a name. When I later began using the phone to call people, I memorized the pattern of the number on the phone. After seeing the pattern, there was no reason to give effort to remember the numbers. Sometimes I couldn't say out loud a phone number but I was able to dial the number from knowing the pattern on the nine buttons on the phone. I now know that when I was in school I was good at memorizing things using rote memory. Teachers and parents wanted kids to make high grades; they didn't care how they did it.

Resourcefulness

I enjoy making the most out of what I have. I don't like spending money on things I know I can get somewhere else for a lower price. I enjoy buying needs such as clothes at yard sales or on the clearance rack. I don't feel the need for name brand expensive furniture, to drive a brand new car, or to have a huge house. I am happy driving a used car.

I used to have such a problem with throwing things away. I felt like I was wasting something if I threw it away. I also thought there would come a time when I could use it. For example I didn't throw away shoeboxes thinking I could use it to store something in. I didn't throw away the cardboard tubes inside the paper towels and toilet paper thinking I could make something with them. I didn't throw away any scrap paper, plastic bottles or containers. I later realized that having the clutter and trying to keep everything organized was not worth keeping every single little thing. I also realized that years would go by and I wouldn't use most of the things. Recycling or donating to places who do art such as schools are options. Now that I have children, many things get put to temporary use. I let them practice their scissor skills and give them opportunities to create artwork.

I don't like throwing away banana peels, apple cores or any other food scrap item. I throw them all outside into compost for the earth to recycle them. I later use the mesh as topsoil for my garden. I don't like throwing food away. When there are leftovers that aren't enough for a meal, I put them all together to make a soup.

Understanding typical behavior

My intention in this section is not to nit pick at people. I am truly trying to understand typical behavior. When I was in high school many of the other girls thought that having name brand jeans were extremely important. I couldn't understand why girls would pay so much money for one pair of jeans when they could use the same amount of money to buy several pairs of jeans with several shirts at another place. I was probably 18 when I made the connection that girls do this to impress each other.

Girls like to impress each other and buying expensive jeans and wearing them makes them feel important. But this is a puzzle because I have heard many girls say things like, "Look at her brand new jacket, I hate her" and "I can't stand how that girl always has perfect hair, perfect nails and perfect clothes." So, does wearing name brand clothes really impress the other girls or does it make those girls feel jealous, therefore, they have the need to buy their own expensive name brand clothes in order to feel better about themselves? Well, I know that it greatly bothers other girls if other people don't dress well, like not having matching clothes or wearing "old-ladies" clothes. After college I learned in a self-help book that girls don't want to be seen by other people who dress poorly because they feel it would hurt their reputation and reputation is extremely important for girls. I like being able to find name brand items at yard sales.

I notice many people, especially girls, verbally express unhappiness about their vehicles, their homes being too small, needing new furniture and new clothes. Do they want these things to make themselves happier, to impress other people or to meet the expectations of other people? Are we as a nation training our young to feel like the only way to feel important is to impress other people?

I have observed women dressing very pretty with nice matching shoes and expensive looking necklaces come in to a social scene such as church. Other women would come up to them and say things like, "Wow, you look wonderful" and then the reply would be something like, "Oh, I just got out of bed, quickly got dressed and left the home with barely brushing my hair." I have observed women making a nice comment about another woman's dress such as, "That dress looks real nice on you," and the woman with dress would reply something like, "Oh, this old thing?! I've had this dress for ten years." I wonder why women would say things like that when it is very clear that she spent a great amount of time decorating herself to look good? Why can't she just say, "Thank you?" Maybe those are the socially acceptable responses? Do the other women say what they say because they feel that is the expected response? Is it that they are trying to make themselves look humble? I think the easiest thing to do is to simply say "thank you" when somebody gives a compliment.

Keeping friendships and loyalty

When I make a friend, I expect to keep that person as a friend. My best friends today are the ones I made a very young age. When I was able to make new friends, I didn't understand how some of them could just suddenly end a friendship. People make new friends all the time and I have learned that people usually make friends with people with similar interests and similar lifestyles. My best friends and I used to be so much alike as kids. But when we became older teenagers, our interests changed and we didn't spend as much time together. As adults, we respect each other's interests and choice of lifestyles. However, I have seen many people stop being friends with their good friends because their friends would make them mad or because they disagreed with choices they made. This is hard for me to accept, making a friend and getting to know them well and later not be friends any longer.

I do not think that people should act in inappropriate ways just to maintain friendships though. For example, when I was 13, I tried to smoke with one of my friends because I thought she would like me better as a friend. I hated it. I told her I just couldn't do it anymore but we could continue doing the other things we liked together like roller skating and swimming. It is best to be honest with your friends and don't make yourself do things you think are wrong or not good for you just to maintain a friendship. If you lose a friend because you stand for what is right, that friend really wasn't a real friend after all. Focus on the people who do love you, even family members.

Recognizing friendships and acquaintances

An "acquaintance" is a person in your life that you know who would be on a lesser level than a friend. When I was younger I thought that people were either friends or not friends and nothing in between. Later I learned that there are different levels of friendships. There are best friends, friends and acquaintances. Best friends are people who you share you secrets with and spend time with outside of school, church and other activities. You talk on the phone with your best friends and write letters to each other. Friends are those people who you say hi to when you see them and you may engage in "small talk" occasionally. You would invite your best friends and some of your friends to your birthday party. Acquaintances are people you know and they know you, but you don't talk to them on a regular basis. You have a little bit of a relationship with an acquaintance but it is on a much smaller level than a friend or best friend. It is important for you to choose your friends carefully and be able to discern if a person is pretending to be your friend in order to get you into trouble or to use you for your talents.

Small talk

Small talk or "chitchat" is a socially important way of talking with people in a non-personal, non-controversial, non-deep way. Many people with Asperger's have trouble using small talk with people and may even perceive it to be meaningless and a waste of time. Examples of small talk include talking about the weather or asking someone how they are doing. I have always had trouble with the question, "Hi, how are you?" because saying "fine" or "good" is what is expected regardless of how a person is really doing. Some people will ask the question and then continue talking before the person has time to answer.

Do you understand that conversations are structured to have a beginning, middle and ending? Small talk is a tool to begin or end a conversation. I feel the same way Liane Holliday Willey (2001) as she says, "I am never quite sure how to start or leave a conversation. I seem to be more inclined to forget introductions. I have to remind myself that there are certain rules society lays down regarding how we approach and leave a conversation." Liane also says "When I talk to others, I consistently picture a diagram of a conversation that is built around beginnings and endings I have memorized."

Small talk is a comfortable method people use to ease themselves into a good conversation. Small talk is good for those socially awkward moments with people you feel uneasy with. Small talk is the beginning to making a friend. Learning to engage in small talk with people may not come natural but it is the beginning to making friends. If you approach a stranger at a park and ask, "What do you think the purpose of life is?" they would think you were weird and probably avoid you. If you go up and say "Hi, are you from around here, I live three blocks away" they would be more willing to begin a conversation.

Small talk is a method to get to know a person. You don't want to go around blurting out your opinions to just anyone. People don't like that. It is best to get to know a person before sharing your opinion. If you knew a few things about a person, you would be able to better predict how they would respond to your opinions. Small talk is a non-personal way of communicating with people. With better understanding, it can be a very useful tool.

Anxiety

Intense anxiety is associated with Asperger's syndrome. Nick Dublin (2009) says in his book *Asperger's syndrome and Anxiety* "For people with Asperger's, anxiety is often symptomatic of and aggravated by the neurological difference. I have yet to meet a person with Asperger's who does not experience a high degree of anxiety in his or her life. This fact is supported by the research…" Anxiety is feeling uneasy, nervous and worried. Anxiety has been one of my biggest struggles in life. When I was a kid I worried about making good grades, worried I would get in trouble, worried that my parents would die if I were bad, worried that other people would see that I didn't have many friends, worried that aliens were going to kidnap me, felt uneasy and nervous in all social situations and generated anxiety in crowded and loud places. I still feel a great deal of anxiety during social events and if I have something on my mind that I need or want to do, like draw a picture or clean the kitchen, I feel so anxious until I do it. Therefore, I hate to procrastinate.

I generate anxiety by trying to stop my repetitive thinking and have learned to stop that anxiety by stopping the repetitive thinking. Sometimes my anxiety causes me to feel faint, have difficulty breathing, tremble, shake and even generate a fever. Sometimes I feel I am panicking on the inside, that my heart is having an attack and that I am in the process of dying. I later get so mad at myself for becoming that way and wonder why I have such little mental control over it. Crowded places and groups of people cause a lot of anxiety. When I go somewhere and find a group of women together I suddenly feel very nervous. Upon entering restaurants, I always seek the table in the corner.

Nick Dublin (2009) mentions "Perhaps becoming aware your anxiety is a neurological issue verses a psychological one can relieve a burden you've been carrying around for a long time." Shifting my focus to something relaxing can be helpful. If I am at a crowded social area and become anxious, I think about when it is time to leave and what I will do afterwards. When I am thinking about an upcoming undesirable event, such as having to go to the doctor, I try not to think about it by reading or doing an activity that would get my mind off it. Dublin says that people with Asperger's "have to work much harder at managing stress than most neurotypicals." Then he says you may "see yourself in a new light – a warrior, someone with a level of bravery that rivals a soldier heading into battle."

I generate anxiety by fearing things. I fear I will say the wrong thing and will lose a friend. I fear I can't make friends. I fear I will hurt somebody's feelings. I fear getting sick. I fear anyone else in my family getting sick. I fear my mom or another loved one will die one day. I fear fire, spiders, ticks and poisonous snakes. I fear loud noises and strong smells. I fear misunderstandings. I fear scary things such as demons. I fear unpredictability. I fear deception. I fear being alone when I become an old lady. I fear Satan. I fear feeling fearful. STOP IT! "There is no fear in love; but perfect love casteth out fear: because fear hath torment. He that feareth is not made perfect in love" (1 John 4:18). I consistently pray to God to make me perfect in love. "For God hath not given us the spirit of fear; but of power, and of love, and of a sound mind" (2 Timothy 1:7). Ah, finally, relief from anxiety.

Obsession with knowledge and facts

Shortly after graduating high school I began going to the library and became very interested in non-fiction books. My whole life I had to read (memorize) all kinds of fiction for school that I found uninteresting. When I finally had the freedom to choose what I learned, I took advantage of it. I checked out books on astronomy, the planets, the galaxies, the human body, weather, animals etc. Over the next few years I began to become obsessed with learning facts and gaining knowledge. I prayed to God everyday to give me knowledge and truth.

Through learning facts and gaining knowledge, I have learned that all problems have solutions. There are many solutions to a problem, but there are better ones than others. For example, when a child has a respiratory infection, the thing to do is give her antibiotics to kill all the bacteria to heal the infection. This method works, however, it has consequences or side effects. Antibiotics cause upset stomach, fatigue, yeast infections, headaches and a list of other things. What is another solution to treating a respiratory infection? I believe a combination of boosting the immune system and using natural anti-bacterials. There are hundreds of herbs and some of them kill bacteria, relieve congestion and build up the immune system. There are certain foods with certain vitamins and minerals the immune system needs to be able to heal the body. Then there are certain foods with colors and additives that damage the immune system and make it hard for the body to repair itself. Respiratory infections can be prevented in many cases. What causes respiratory infections? They usually follow a typical cold. A cold comes from a virus. When the body is healing itself from a cold, it produces extra mucus to excrete the waste. However, if the immune system has been damaged, it can't do what it needs to do in the amount of time it can do it so a bacterial infection can take place where the mucus is such as the lungs, ears and sinuses. This book is not about giving medical advice, I am just mentioning this in order to express that there are better solutions to problems.

Sudden changes in schedule

Knowing what the schedule is really helps me stay focused and enjoy life. I write monthly schedules and if a day comes that doesn't have a schedule of events, whether it be going somewhere or just doing housework, I plan the whole day in my head before even getting out of bed that morning.

When I was a kid, and there was a sudden change of schedule from a fun event to a not so fun event I had difficulty accepting the change. However, with my dad having Asperger's, being very schedule and time oriented, interrupted schedules usually got compensated for. For example, one time when we took the camper to the beach, it broke down on the way. It took hours for my dad to repair it well enough to get us back home. But instead of canceling the trip, my dad said we would take the car and rent a hotel. When we had other plans, like going out to eat, we always left at a specified time.

When I began work, it baffled me how people could be late to work or not even show up for their interviews. I hated it when I scheduled a gathering at my home and people didn't arrive on time. I also hated it when we were invited to parties and got there on time and the party didn't start until much later. There is the term "fashionably late" that I learned that people feel the need to arrive a little later than scheduled because it is the popular thing to do. People tend to behave in ways that they think is popular and the most socially accepted way. I have learned to be much more tolerant of people being late and also allow myself to not stress out so much if I am running a few minutes behind.

Life is full of changes in schedules from having to go to the emergency room for a broken arm to deciding to go out to eat instead of cooking. Some sudden changes are very inconvenient while others can be nice. That is life. We have to learn to tolerate times of disappointment and focus on the next good thing. I believe that learning to effectively cope and deal with sudden changes of schedule builds a person's character. Although we may feel like we are going to explode, we can control how we behave on the outside and even learn how to change our own feelings. I may suddenly feel like I am going to explode on the inside when the car won't start, but I don't have to have a fit and yell and scream about it. I can choose to say, "Oh well, the car won't start this morning, lets see if I can find out what why?" and then imagine the car starting again after I find out what is wrong with it and fix it.

Asking repetitive questions

I remember asking my mom the same questions over and over even if I knew the answer because I greatly enjoyed her answering exactly the way I imagined. "Are you my mommy?" "Am I your daughter?" "Do you love me?" "Are we going to the park today?" "Are we still going to the park today?" I remember asking these types of questions over and over and laughing when she answered because I loved hearing the expected response.

Many of the children I have worked with, especially the higher functioning ones, would ask me repetitive questions during therapy and laugh when I answered. I knew that they received pleasure out of the response. One little girl I worked with would ask me over and over "Is your name Miss Kristi?" and "Are those your toys in that bag?" I did teach the children the right context to ask questions and to wait until after a program was over then I provided the reinforcement. Working with those children was so much fun.

Difficulty following movies

I remember watching movies when I was an older child and paying close attention to the pictures and graphics. When I became a young teenager I made the realization that I had previously not paid attention to the plot, or the story when I was a younger age. My best friends and I would go to the movie theater often. It was difficult for me to pay attention to the beginnings and sometimes I had to ask one of my friends what was happening. Then I would know enough to have enough interest to pay attention to the rest of the movie. Even after I got married, I would have to pause the movie about fifteen minutes through so my husband could explain to me what was happening. My problem was mainly that I couldn't make myself pay attention to the movie when it first began. But after I learned the beginning and what was taking place, then I could more easily pay attention to the rest of the movie.

At home, I enjoyed watching cartoons like "Rugrats" on Nickelodeon when I was a teenager. I sometimes watched the popular teenage TV shows and I found them to be interesting, but I was disappointed in the immorality. I wonder how many teenage girls get pregnant because of the influence of the media. Why does the world want to teach young teenagers to have sex before they get married? My mother said because "sex sells." TV producers add in sex because more people would be interested. With more people becoming hooked on TV shows, producers get more money from commercial advertisement.

Sometimes the loud music and sounds would distract my mind from paying attention to the story plot. Shows that come on TV have so much loud laughing that it would distract my attention and I would feel irritated. For shows that I became very interested in such as ER, my interest in the plot overruled the loud sounds. As an adult, I no longer watch TV; we don't even have one in our home because it was becoming an unhealthy addiction for one of our children. We do have movie night once a week where we watch a children's movie on the computer screen as a family.

When I used to do home therapy for children with autism, a couple of families wanted me to teach their children to watch a movie at the movie theater. Well, these children would not sit in the movie theater chair very long and would not watch the movie. They were too interested in discovering what was underneath the chairs and what was at the top and bottom of the theater. I tried using edible reinforcement for sitting in the chair but even the edible reinforcement wasn't strong enough to last even through half a movie. Although their parents wanted their children to learn to watch a movie, I didn't feel it an important thing to teach, especially since they were not interested. Working on language expansion, going to the library, the bookstore, improving compliance behavior and social skills were much more important.

A person watches an average of 142 hours of TV a month (Semuels, 2008). That is 1,704 hours a year!!! Just think of all the things you can learn and do in 1,704 hours? Although TV is entertaining, fun and relaxing to many people, what about learning skill and having things to show for like writing books, painting, learning musical instruments, reading and learning, making things, studying the Bible, exercising, exploring the outdoors, developing relationships or investing in the lives of children. I don't think TV watching is a bad thing, especially when someone needs to relax a bit. But I think it can be overused. Watching TV and the number of hours of TV is a choice.

The necessity of figuring out a cause from an effect

I am unable to accept effects as they occur. I have to know what is the cause. What caused the computer to crash? What caused the catfood to spill? What caused her to throw toys? What caused him to bring me flowers? What caused this big rash on my face? What caused her cancer? What caused his autism?

A fever as a symptom (effect) is conventionally treated with Tylenol. Cough is treated with cough medicine. Inflammation is treated with anti-inflammatory medication. However, that fever, cough and the inflammation have causes. Symptoms are clear observable effects that are warning signs that something is wrong. Instead of strictly focusing on the symptom, I like to focus on what is causing that symptom. A virus or bacteria caused the fever, and that virus or bacteria came from somewhere, something is causing the pain and a possible food or environmental allergy can cause inflammation. Something causes that allergy, and it may be a genetic predisposition to not be able to excrete certain toxins with disruption of the methelation process (method body uses to carry out toxins) and toxins are left to do damage to the immune system, circulatory system and neurological system.

Everything has a cause I have always been determined to analyze every possible available detail to figure out that cause. However, if I can't find out for certain what causes something, I will accept a theory. Only the best theory available. I know without a doubt, with all the research I have done on cancer, that cancer can be prevented. Instead of just treating the cancer symptoms the conventional way with radiation and chemotherapy, targeting the causes will increase the chances of overcoming cancer. What can causes cancer? There are a list of things shown to be carcinogens such as cigarette smoke, burnt food, chemicals in spray paint, chemicals in plastics, improper diet, highly stressful lifestyle etc. Treat the causes by cleaning a sick colon, flushing the toxins out an overworked liver and gall bladder, cleaning the blood, eliminating preservatives and artificial ingredients in food, eating raw organic foods etc. These examples give a person a greater chance of overcoming cancer. I believe there is currently enough research on autism that to provide sufficient knowledge that autism can be prevented. Autism can also treated, not only by addressing the symptoms, but targeting the causes in each individual as well.

We as a worldwide nation have been coming together to treat autism as a group of symptoms and behaviors. I believe it is wonderful that so many people want to help all these precious children learn to behave in more socially appropriate ways, improve their language and communication skills and help them catch up on the developmental milestones. Another group of people have been doing extensive research to find out what causes autism. Examples are genetic research, brain research and medical research.

I don't like using the term "autistic children," I prefer to use the terms "children with autism" or "children who have autism." I don't think children are autistic, I think they are typical children who are learning how to operate a body that has been damaged. Therefore, they are children who have autism.

With the children I have worked with, I have enjoyed analyzing their behavior to determine what caused it. The most common behaviors that need replaced are tantruming, throwing things, non-compliance, self-injurious behavior, and disruption. The most common causes are feeling frustrated, feeling tired, not interested in the teaching subject, escaping or avoiding something asked of them, feelings of pain and inflammation, feelings of silliness, experiencing intense emotions such as anger, embarrassment or disappointment, experiencing allergic reactions to the environment or food, an excess or deficit of certain neuro-hormones or vitamin and mineral deficiency. Behavior analysts are supposed to focus on behaviors that are clear, observable and can be easily defined. However, most of those easy to observe behaviors have causes as well. Should we punish a child for throwing puzzle pieces across the room by having him sit in time out for 10 minutes? Throwing puzzle pieces may not be appropriate but why did the child throw to begin with? Was he not able to put the puzzle together and generated feelings of frustration? Has he had a bad experience with puzzles in the past and developed a dislike for puzzles? Did he get enough sleep the night before? Is he getting sick? Is it too hot in the room? Are there too many people in the room? Was there an interruption in schedule prior to being presented with the puzzle? Determining the cause of a behavior will better help anyone determine how to respond to the behavior in order to either prevent the behavior from occurring again or teach the child a more acceptable behavior. The same approach can be applied to problems in the body, problems in relationship, problems in families, problems in the economy, problems in the world. Problems have solutions! But is treating the problem or treating the causes of the problem the best choice at solving the problem? Maybe a lot of both. Preventing the problem would be even better.

Recognizing patterns

Do you see patterns that are unseen? I get distracted by looking at wallpaper and carpet. My eyes continuously and repeatedly go over the lines, colors and shapes recognizing the multiply overlapping patterns. These patterns jump out at me and look three-dimensional. When I attend conferences and workshops I tend to want to stare at the walls, carpets and the light fixtures. The lines and shapes jump out and my eyes want to follow them over and over. I greatly enjoy looking at chandeliers as they have limitless patterns.

There are time patterns. When I began to drive, I recognized the patterns in the stoplights at the intersections I frequently drove through. I learned to be able to predict exactly when the light would turn green and when the turning arrow would show up for each of the directions. I learned that there were different patterns according to what intersection it was and what time of day it was.

Many of the children I have worked with seem to recognize patterns to a greater degree. For example several children who have visited me would become so fixated on the gravel in my driveway that they could not focus on anything else. One of them began to cry when his mother forced him away from it. He wanted to examine the patterns he saw in the gravel. I have noticed many children staring at trees and watching the leaves blow in the wind.

Not only are there physical and time patterns, there are unseen patterns such as behavioral patterns, societal patterns, work patterns, health patterns, business patterns, family patterns, and patterns in the Bible. If you can examine the patterns in a person's behavior, you can learn to predict that person's behavior. This is much easier to do in children than adults. Adult behavior is a little more tricky to figure out especially the reasons why they do things they do. There are methods to use to learning to predict behavior. First, figure out why the behavior is occurring. Consider the person's motivation; analyze events that come before the behavior and events that come after, look for patterns in time (time, day, week or month) and in the environment (people, temperature, place, any visual or auditory distractions etc…) and pay careful attention to the frequency of the behavior. There are common reasons for behavior such as getting attention, getting one's own way, feelings of frustration or other intense emotions, to avoid or get away from an unpleasant activity and self-pleasure. I have heard from many parents that their children have difficult days when there is a full moon at night. Why is that? Is it because when the moonlight shines through the window, decreasing the body's ability to make melatonin (sleep hormone)? Therefore, the child doesn't get enough sleep that night? I know I have a very difficult time sleeping with any light or sound so I either cover my eyes with a blanket or I cover the window with a thick blanket during nights of full moon.

There is a pattern in society that is leading many people in a difficult direction. If this pattern is not stopped or interrupted then disaster might take place. Popular TV shows are full of teenage sex and drug use. Teenagers think it is "cool" to have parties drinking and smoking. Teenage magazines advertise to young girls that being skinny and looking beautiful is the best. Emphasis is being placed on what materialistic things a person has so people are struggling to make lots of money so they can afford expensive TVs, brand new cars, name brand clothes and furniture etc.

Many people have told me they can't afford to have more children; yet, they drive brand new cars and go out to eat several times a week. Many women feel they have to work, that they have no choice because they have to make money. Many have to maintain a sense of self-esteem by having a career. I have noticed many men slacking in their desire to work and provide for the family. Divorce rate is higher than ever, it is becoming the normal thing to do rather than the exception as it used to be. Teenage TV shows have an enormous amount of influence over teenage behavior. Teachers and parents teach their kids to say no to drugs, yet, they continue to give their kids drugs for being too hyper, depressed, anxious etc. Adults too are increasingly relying on drugs to balance out the havoc created in the body created by increasing problems that they can't deal with because they don't know how. These generations of parents are losing, or have lost, their ability to parent. There are thousands of books on parenting and many parents are consuming them like crazy trying to figure out how to be with their own kids. Many people have mentioned to me that their children are a burden to them, rather than a blessing as intended to be.

People trust everyone in their own professions because they lack the common knowledge in these specific areas. Look at the results. The rate of autism has greatly increased; the rate of ADHD, OCD, ODD, asthma, diabetes, allergies, autoimmune conditions and cancer are on the rapid rise. All these patterns are leading to the destruction of the family and to increased governmental control. Do you really want to join in this pattern? Lets take a look at two different kinds of lives; the typical life society is trying to train you to live or a life where you are happy, joyful and productive with the ability to apply solutions to any problem.

The standard modern mainstream

Are you happy with the way the standardized lifestyle that is taught to people? I like to pay attention to the results of applications applied. When I see the long-term results of the lifetime pattern of modern day society, I feel unhappy. It is the standard developing pattern I see that may possibly lead to unhappiness. This kind of lifestyle is what most people perceive to be the "normal" sequence of living. Most people don't seem to realize there are other lifestyle options. The descriptions below do not apply to everyone. If people are sincerely happy living the modern mainstream life, then I am happy for them. I just want others to know that if they are unhappy, they have different options. The first description is the common taught lifestyle that many people are living because it is the standard. The second description is just one example of another kind of life. I had spent most of my life following the standard lifestyle until I realized there were other options. Once I found another way, I began to gradually jump out of the standard pattern of living to another kind of lifestyle. I am much happier with the results in people who have found another kind of life.

Foreword by Liane Holliday Willey

Standard modern day living pattern – a general description

Children begin life going to daycare, preschool or mother's morning out programs while both parents work or do other things. Doctors are trained to tell parents that vaccines are good for their children. Parents fully trust what their doctors tell them. Children suffer side effects and frequent infections. Parents are not aware that infections can be prevented and there are natural alternatives to healing. Children go to elementary school coming home with hours of homework each night. They spend the rest of their time participating in extracurricular activities (sports, music classes, dance, etc.). There is little or no time for play and establishing real relationships. Children spend little time with their parents. Parents work most of the time. Children and parents spend most of their time feeling stressed out. Children learn to hate learning because school is perceived to be work. Then there is high school, pressured to make the honor roll and to participate in after school activities. Children are constantly exposed to premarital sex and bad language. Children will experience peer pressure to attend parties, smoke drugs, drink alcohol, participate in sexual activities, date whomever and whenever, and will likely do so to maintain feelings of importance and self esteem to fit in.

Then it is time for college. Some continue with the high school party life while others learn to get serious about making good grades. Most people can't find a job in what they majored in college. Many have to go to grad school because society now perceives bachelors degrees to be almost worthless and because a good paying job will require at least a Masters. (However, we are very thankful for those led by God to learn to save human lives that have had to go to college for 15 years). Then find a job working for someone else that makes nice money so you can pay off those college loans, get a new car and new house with new name brand furniture. You are constantly aiming for pay raises and promotions so more stuff can be bought. You tell your kids who are constantly begging for your attention and time, that you are working to make money for them; that you are providing them plenty of food, a nice home to live in and more toys to play with. I have heard people who live in $500,000 houses say they can't have kids because they can't afford them.

Get married to someone who you feel you are "in love" with regardless of character even though you have already had sex with many other people because society thinks it is normal to have sex with everybody you come into contact with. Run up credit cards and have lots of bills to pay. Feel obligated to buy all family members and friends name brand stuff for birthdays and Christmas. Money will always be difficult to manage regardless of how much you make.

Most people will have 1-2 children and get on the waiting list for a daycare to pay someone else to care for your children or hire a nanny. Having more than two kids in this life pattern is greatly challenging. Look for a church that will minister to your needs. Go to church on Sundays and argue in the car in the way there and on the way back. Stress out over what to wear and what clothes to put your children in. Husband and wife constantly battle for control. If the marriage is unhappy, the typical thing to do is get a divorce. Then go to the divorce care the churches offer nowadays. Children greatly suffer emotional trauma with the instability of divorced parents. You may try seeing a counselor if you have marriage troubles attempting to find the love feelings again. Then there are problems like unhappy marriage, unruly children, or other mental and behavioral problems and physical problems – pay someone else to fix the problem because you don't know how. Get on anti-anxiety and anti-depressant medication (drugs) for a quick problem fix and put kids on Ritalin so they will behave better in school. Learn how to pretend that everything is just fine in your life for the public eye.

Eat out most of the time because there is no time to cook healthy meals. The body becomes unhealthy and feels fatigued. Then have to see a medical doctor to get medicine to lower cholesterol and blood pressure. Spending so much time in the car, taking kids to school, go to work, run errands, pick up kids and take them to their extracurricular activities. Stop by fast food on the way home, and make children do their homework. Kids have difficulty concentrating because of all the preservatives and added colors in food. Kids lack essential vitamins and minerals. Then plop on the couch to watch TV until time to go to sleep. What a stressful day, what a rushed life.

Stress will further damage your body and you will contract a health problem such as diabetes, pancreatitis, and arthritis or suffer low immunity. Your kids are likely to have bad attitudes as teenagers because society thinks it is normal for teens to be smart alecks. You feel like you always have to buy the new release movies and all the new technological advanced gadgets thinking it will make life more happy and satisfying. You buy your ungrateful children all these things too thinking that they will like you more if you buy them more stuff. Kids move out, you continue with work and plan to take an early as possible retirement. When you do retire, you become very depressed because you have nothing to do. You wonder why you spent your whole life rushing and stressing out. You wish you spent more time with your family. Ask any elderly person. They will tell you that their main regret in life was not spending enough time with the people they love. What was the point of trying so hard to accumulate expensive materialistic items when we all end up in old bodies? Do you like the result of this standard mainstream lifestyle? Do you really want this life? Is there any other life than this one? Most people don't know there are alternatives.

Another life

Young children stay by their parents learning everything their parents do, learning responsibility and real life skills. There is plenty of time to play. Children learn to love learning because it is full of excitement and true discovery and spending time with parents and siblings. They have a chance to learn anything they want to rather than what they are forced to. There is time to focus on personal talents.

There is time to go on frequent field trips, visit the library often, visit nursing homes to deliver homemade cards or volunteer in homeless shelters. There are no worries about acquiring new and name brand materials for oneself for a false sense of security, self-esteem issues and to impress others. There is time for learning, developing relationships and finding ways to minister to other people while developing character. One's mind is not constantly on oneself but rather on others. Children can be giving opportunities to make money and develop their talents beginning at young ages. The family finds a church that they can minister in (play musical instrument, sing in choir, teach Sunday school, volunteer to greet people at the door, etc.). There is time to learn real skills and opportunities to learn because children are learning with their parents how to fix anything, how to be a good spouse and a good parent, how to manage money and self accountability.

Be creative when making money. Become your own boss, invest in land, write books, design interiors, make things, create, invent something, and determine what other people need. Make it and sell it to them at a reasonable price. Do what others need but what makes you happy at the same time. Determine your gifts and talents and use them to help others at the same time fulfilling your purpose and meaning. If you desire a profession that requires a college education, then go to college by all means but try to go to the closest to home college as possible to save money and avoid peer pressure. Beware, there will be lots of young adults who are not mature and think that partying is the thing to do. Minister to them by being a good example for them to follow. Help them make wise decisions and get on the right track in life. Teach them about money management, how to study appropriately, how to behave in a mature human manner. Do not attempt to become one of them in order to feel good about yourself by fitting in. Stick to what is true and important no matter what temptation and influences come your way. Instead of following them, get them to follow you.

Try to surround yourself with godly, wise people living in truth who will accept you as you are. Saving sex for the first night of marriage will be so worth it. Get married to someone with good character and who will be a good parent and easily solves problems. Have all the children you want and keep them with you, training them up as they should go. Life is so joyful, spending time with family, developing close relationships, doing chores together, and eating nice meals together as a family at the table. Grow your own garden and see how refreshing it is to watch vegetables grow and how good you feel when you eat healthy. No stress. No rush.

There is plenty of time for communicating and fellowship. Joy is filled in every heart of the home. Time will be managed, happy marriage, well trained children; gratefulness to the blessings God has given you. No worry about what other people think of you if you drive a used car or wear clothes that are not name brand. Growing gardens and using natural herbs is a pleasure because you do it with the ones you love most. Play games, bike ride, go hiking, go camping, fishing, read books to young children, have family cookouts and invite friends to come visit. Life is not wasted watching seven hours of TV each day. Learn to be frugal and don't waste money. Be happy with less material stuff. Make time for your children. Your time with them is the best investment you will ever make. It is very possible to have a joyful life and to also prepare for eternity at the same time. It is a win/win situation. The life society teachers you to live might be a lose/lose situation (you lose your joy and eternal rewards). Remain focused on what is truly important, God's eternal program.

Children are more important than what society perceives them to be. What they do, who they are with, how they are trained and the model behavior they witness will have an incredible impact on what kind of human beings they turn out to be (their character, emotional stability, moral intelligence, choice of spouse, ability to be a good parent, how they solve problems, how they treat others, their relationship toward God etc.). Wisdom, moral intelligence and emotional stability are more important than modern day "intelligence." "Listen to advice and accept instruction and in the end you will be wise" (Proverbs 19:20).

Suggested readings

- *The North Star* by Peter H. Reynolds (2009)
- *All Cats Have Asperger Syndrome* by Kathy Hoopmann (2006)
- *Asperger Syndrome and Anxiety: A Guide to Successful Stress Management* by Nick Dubin and Valerie Gaus (2009)
- *Your Life is Not a Label: A Guide to Living Fully with Autism and Asperger's Syndrome* by Jerry Newport and Ron Bass (2001)
- *Scholastic Dictionary Of Idioms* by Marvin Terban (1998)
- *How to Win Friends and Influence People* by Dale Carnegie (1998)
- *How to talk to Anyone: 92 Little tricks for Big Success in Relationships* by Leil Lowndes (2003)
- *Don't Sweat the Small Stuff with your Family: Simple Ways to Keep Daily Responsibilities and Household Chaos from Taking Over Your Life* by Richard Carlson (1998)

References

Dublin, N. (2009). *Asperger Sundrome and Anxiety: A Guide to Successful Stress Management.* Jessica Kingsley Publishers.

Semuels, A. (2008). *Americans Now Watch more TV than Ever.* Los Angeles Times. Retrieved October 24th, 2009. http://latimesblogs.latimes.com/technology/2008/11/americans-now-w.html

Willey, L.H. (2001). Asperger Syndrome in the Family. Redefining Normal. Jessica Kingsley Publishers, London.

CHAPTER 8

Overcoming Sensory Issues and Social Difficulties

Many people with Asperger's have sensory issues with noises, lights, touches and smells. In my experience with providing therapy for children with autism, I have noticed that almost all of my clients have had specific sensory issues. My personal sensory issues interfere with my ability to participate in social events, especially those that are loud and crowded. Throughout my life I have developed effective methods to tolerate, deal and cope with sensory sensitivities. I am going to describe sensitivities in hearing, seeing, smelling and touch. I am also going to explain the methods that can be applied to overcome and even prevent these sensitivities. I will then discuss what sensory integration is and reasons why many people with Asperger's have sensory sensitivities. Lastly, I will discuss overcoming social difficulties, making and keeping friends, taking advantage of one-on-one interactions, goal setting and improving relationships. Tips for conversation will be included.

Are you sensory sensitive?

- Do certain noises bother you that don't seem to bother other people?

- Do certain lights bother you that don't seem to be a problem for others?
- Are you bothered by certain textures?
- Is it difficult to make eye contact while having conversations?
- Do you easily get car sick or motion sickness?
- Do you dislike crowded areas?
- Do clothes bother you, such as tags, seams, turtlenecks, tight or rough?
- Do you easily get dizzy?
- Do you feel discomfort with light hugging?
- Do you have any problems with balance?
- Are you extremely active?
- Do you tend to avoid social situations?
- Do you frequently feel panicky?
- Do you feel anxious often?
- Do you experience insomnia?
- Is it difficult to calm down after a stressful event?
- Do you easily get irritated?
- Do you easily get frustrated?

If you have answered yes to many of these questions, you may be sensory sensitive.

Noise

The neighbor is mowing his lawn on Sunday afternoon, oh PLEASE not Sunday afternoons! The chewing sounds of people chewing gum feels like the un-insulated wires in my brain are being electrocuted. The sounds from the dishwasher, washing machine, and even running water distract my attention from what I am doing. Crickets make it impossible to sleep, the sounds rotate and segment throughout the brain, become four dimensional, vibrating every single nerve. The sounds of everybody talking at once during parties distract me from having a conversation with one person. People are laughing, talking and having fun, and I can't make out precisely what anyone is saying. The treble is turned up too high, and it feels like the sounds are clawing at my brain. A sudden loud noise of something falling, like a book falling from a shelf, causes a ripple throughout my body and eardrums. I can't get too close to fireworks. The loud sudden bang noises prevent my enjoyment of watching the beautiful colorful lights.

Sounds are so loud, sharp, pointy and distracting. Not all sounds. Bass is nice sounding. Waterfalls are refreshing. Soft sweet piano music is pleasane. The sounds of walking on dried leaves in the fall are exciting. Praise and worship music is uplifting.

What does a person do when they are typically inflicted with pain? They get away from it or at least take measures to reduce it. Moving away from every sensory disturbance is not possible. Tolerance. I have learned, and am still learning, the best ways to handle painful and sudden sounds is to simply tolerate the issue. Many methods of tolerance come from traits such as love, mercy, understanding, gratitude and optimism. Peeking into the future and anticipating the time the sound will stop helps. I remind myself that the sensory disturbance is only temporary and a quiet time will soon come. It usually takes about an hour for my neighbor to mow his lawn – so I can endure it that long. I can tolerate the sounds of chewing from my kids and my family because I truly love them. I can tolerate the sounds of the washing machine and dishwasher because I am gracious that I have those machines to lighten the work load. I can tolerate the sounds of everyone talking at once because I understand that they greatly enjoy parties and crowds. They are having fun. I want them to have fun. I can learn to participate in social events because I can learn to tolerate and control sensory disturbances. Tolerating and controlling sensory disturbances takes a great deal of effort and energy. I try to enjoy as much as possible while at the same time anticipating when it will be over so I can go home.

Sometimes, the perception of noises being loud and painful can cause a lot of anxiety and stress. So when the noise or event is over, my body remains stressed. There are many things I can do to alleviate this problem including running and doing other sensory activities. Every problem has a solution. And every solution may not work for every person's problem. But people with the same problems can use similar methods to find solutions that work for them. Being able to focus on what is truly important helps to decrease the pain.

Earplugs are a wonderful for cutting the sharp edge off loud noises. I don't care that earplugs may look funny. Since I love to roller skate, I have to wear earplugs when I go to the skating rink or I just can't tolerate being there. I have never attended concerts. When I was a teenager, I was invited to a couple of concerts but I didn't go. I wondered why so many people loved them so much with such loud music. Earplugs are great to help tolerate snoring sounds, lawn mowers, washing machines, hair dryers, and other machines.

The intensity of most noises does not cause me to have to hold my ears. Fire alarms, police car sirens and fire truck sirens, I do have to hold my ears. I have seen almost all the children I have worked with hold their ears at some time. Some children cover their hears at the sound of other people clapping. Some hold their ears at the sound of a toilet flushing. I have seen children in school settings sit there and hold their ears during free play. Very small children I have worked with would scream and cry when their mom would turn on the vacuum, blender or hair dryer. Different children on different levels of the spectrum have various perceptions of pain intensities regarding sensory sensitivities. Many of the children with high-functioning autism do not display the same observable intense stress response than the children with more severe autism do. This makes me wonder if the intensity of sensory sensitivity is related to the severity of the autism. In addition, while many children are sensitive to almost all sensory stimuli, I have noticed that different children have particular sensory sensitivities. For example, one child appears to be auditory sensitive but not light sensitive or touch sensitive; another child appears to be touch and smell sensitive but not auditory or sight. People can't assume exactly how another person perceives something and to what extent.

Another interesting thing I have observed in children with autism is that although they seem very sensitive to certain noises and some types of high volume sounds, they seem to like specific high levels of sounds. For example, I have observed children hold a musical toy to their ear and laugh. They would hold it to their ear for a long time laughing and sometimes jumping up and down. I wanted to see what was so funny about it so I would put my ear up to the toy to find an unbearable noise level. So, a particular child may hold his ears at the sound of a toilet flushing but he loves the sound of a loud toy? That is interesting. There have been times when I would turn my bass up and the volume of music when driving and it was very pleasing. I wondered why I like it so much considering most of the time I am so sensitive to certain noises and volumes.

Although most sounds seem too loud, I have trouble making out what people say sometimes. I hear them clearly and asking them to speak louder will not help me better understand what they are saying. Speaking slower and more articulate will help me better understand. Many times when I miss something in a conversation I try to piece in that gap by what I understand of the conversation as a whole. And using this method, many times I misunderstand some of the conversation. Sometimes I just ask people to repeat their comment.

Summary of methods for overcoming sound sensitivities:

- Tolerance
- Love for friends and family
- Mercy for people
- Understanding others
- Gratitude for having modern technology to help lighten the work load
- Optimism for the future
- EARPLUGS!
- Remembering the sensitivity is only temporary and quiet time will come soon
- When the sensory experience causes anxiety and stress, do other sensory activities such as running, walking or exercising

Bright

There are powerful streams of white glowing sharp light rays bouncing all over the place when the sun is out. Even sunglasses don't take away all the pain. Adding a hat with sunglasses makes it more tolerable. Even on cloudy days, I can't go outside without sunglasses. Certain lights blind my eyes from seeing anything else in a room. There are certain lights in my home that I can't turn on. I learned that the ones that bother my eyes so much are incandescent lights. They not only bother my eyes, but they also bother my brain. It feels like sharp metal fuzzes are permeating into my eyes and throughout my brain.

What does a person do when lights are painful? Cope. I cope with the sun by wearing sunglasses and hats. I cope with the incandescent and even fluorescent lights by, well, leaving them turned off most of the time. I use lamps in the corners of my house. This gives the atmosphere a very pleasant lighting. Not too bright but not too dark. But if I go to someone else's house with painful lights, I try not to focus on the discomfort from the light, but on the people there instead with the knowledge that I will be there just a little while. I remind myself that people are much more important than that silly light. If I focus my attention to the light, then it seems to get brighter and more bothersome, but if I am able to focus my attention on other things, the light becomes more tolerable. There have been times I would have to put on my sunglasses while being inside.

When I began driving, I had a lot of trouble driving at night because of the oncoming lights from the other side of traffic. The lights were so bright I wanted to close my eyes and I did at times when people had on their bright lights. I knew that closing my eyes while driving was not a good solution, putting others and myself at risk for wrecking. So I wore sunglasses while I drove at night, and this helped a great deal but it also made it more difficult to see in general. I figured wearing sunglasses at night while driving was a bad idea. The best solution I came up with was to look at the right side of the road to avoid directly looking at oncoming traffic lights. When an oncoming car has their bright lights on, I look at the line on the right side of the road.

I can detect when a fluorescent light or a computer screen is blinking. My husband used to have a computer monitor that I couldn't look at for more than a minute without getting a headache, feeling dizzy, or nauseated. I insisted to him that his computer screen was blinking on and off really fast, but he wasn't able to see it. I remember when I was at school sometimes a fluorescent light would be blinking on and off rapidly. This was very distracting and uncomfortable and when I mentioned it to the teacher or to some of the other kids, they didn't see it.

Years later, in my professional life as a consultant, I was called in one day from the center I contracted with because a child was having disruptive behavior during a therapy session. The child was knocking over his therapy materials, he wouldn't sit in his chair appropriately, and he wouldn't comply. I came to the center, and when I entered the room, I immediately saw the overhead fluorescent light blinking. I told the staff members that his disruptive behavior was likely due to the blinking light, and moving him to another room may solve the issue. The child's difficult behaviors diminished quickly in the other room, and he was able to better focus. He didn't have the verbal skills to tell anyone that the light was bothering him. This incident makes me wonder just how much children with autism are misunderstood.

I have noticed many of the children I have worked with squinting their eyes inside of buildings. Many people assumed that this was a stimming behavior that needed to be redirected. I said it was a sensitivity to light that he needed to learn to tolerate. I have learned to help young children with very severe sensory sensitivities learn to cope with and tolerate some of the pain they perceive by pairing highly reinforcing toys, activities, edibles with those sensory experiences. I find it also interesting that some children enjoy the colored lights in their toys. They will keep pushing the same buttons over and over while staring at the flashing lights while laughing and jumping. Two extremes; hating certain light and loving certain light.

Not all light is painful. Glow in the dark things are pleasant, especially the blue night sticks. Although light is direct and obvious to me, my vision is terrible. I am very nearsighted with a prescription of –7.5. I can't see anything without wearing corrective lenses.

Summary of methods for overcoming light sensitivities:

- Use lamps in the corners of your room or home
- Wear sunglasses and hats when going outside
- Remember the sensory sensitivity is only temporary
- Remember people are important
- Don't focus on the light; focus on anything else; this takes practice

- When driving at night look at the right side of the road and the line if necessary on the road to avoid directly looking at the oncoming car light (NEVER close your eyes)

Smell

I can't walk down the cleaning supplies aisle at the store without getting dizzy and feeling faint. A workable solution to this problem is that I make sure I know exactly what I am getting in that aisle, hold my breath before darting down the aisle, grab the soap or laundry detergent I need and dart back to my buggy for breath. I can't use many cleaners when I clean in my home because the smell is just too strong. I have to use a scent free laundry detergent. The smell of certain soaps, shampoos, deodorants and perfumes are very overwhelming. Sometimes I feel very dizzy and sometimes I get nauseated. I try to use all natural and scent free items.

Cigarette smoke. There are no words to describe just how painful, unpleasant and agonizing cigarette smoke is. On a scale from one to 10, my sensitivity to cigarette smoke is a 105. My parents used to smoke and I used to cry and scream at them for smoking. They tried not to smoke around me but the smell would linger on them and get on my clothes. I don't blame them. From what I have observed, most typical kids don't pay any attention to cigarette smoke. When I researched addictions, I learned what was going on inside of my parent's bodies when they were being depleted of nicotine and what they felt like before and after a cigarette. So I understood why they smoked. My understanding and love for them helped me tolerate it somewhat. But it is the most difficult smell to tolerate and I try to avoid it as much as possible. My mom quit smoking and she has no idea how incredibly proud I am of her. It must have been so hard for her, but she did it. She and I have a much closer relationship now that we can spend more time together. And she has a much more closer relationship with her grandchildren than she would if she continued to smoke.

Many young children with autism do not have the expressive verbal skills to say when smells are bothering them, and they may engage in puzzling behavior. I wonder just how much of this behavior is from uncomfortable sensory experiences. It bothers me when some professionals and parents see these behaviors and perceive them to be some kind of bad symptom, a bad behavior that needs to be extinguished. I do understand that parents and professionals have the best intentions and they only want to help children in the best way they know how. I want people to know that those behaviors have causes. I understand behaviors that come from not getting their own way and tantruming because they don't get the candy they wanted. But what about crying because a certain smell hurts or flapping their hands because the light is too bright? I have met some professionals who are very good at doing pattern analysis, functional analysis and descriptive assessments, determining why behavior is occurring and then write a behavior modification plan to replace it or extinguish it. But very rarely do any of them conclude a behavior is a result from a sensory sensitivity. I think it important to consider this possible cause because I think it is important that children learn coping strategies, toleration and what to do or say when they are overwhelmed.

There was one child I worked with who was diagnosed with high functioning autism that did something I rarely saw the other children do. He smelled everything. I mean he would smell the walls, the blocks, the markers, the crayons, his clothes, people, paper etc. His mother said his constant smelling things were his stimming behavior. During therapy we immediately redirected him, kept him engaged in activity and gradually increased the amount of time that passed before he smelled things. I also think his smelling was a habit and habits are hard to break. Going longer and longer amounts of times without smelling helped him break the habit of constantly doing it. I included this story because I found it extremely interesting that a child would get so much pleasure out of constantly smelling things. Autism is full of deficits and excesses.

Summary of methods for overcoming smell sensitivities:

- When needing to buy detergents or soaps, look down the aisle to find what brand you want, rapidly obtain your item and quickly return to your cart at the end of the aisle.
- Don't use soaps, cleaners, toothpastes, deodorants, or perfumes that make you feel dizzy, lightheaded or nauseated. Use all natural, and scent free items.
- If you don't like smoke, then get away from it. If you are in a situation where you can't get away, like being in a car with

someone smoking, kindly tell the person that you are very sensitive to cigarette smoke. They will likely put it away for later. Be sure to say "Thank you."

Touch

Sudden touch almost always startles and distracts me. Nick Dublin (2009) says "many people with Asperger's startle easily…the fight-or-flight response begins pumping all kinds of chemicals, such as cortisol, into our nervous systems to get us ready for battle. But sometimes there is no battle."

I get very distracted when someone suddenly hugs me without me knowing first. I greatly enjoy hugs from people I love such as my husband and my children. I prefer hard over soft hugs. I love to wrestle, tickle, give high fives, give and get back massages. When I am bothered when people suddenly and lightly hug me, I remind myself that they are expressing their love for me.

Growing up, I had big problems with wearing certain types of clothing, including shoes and socks. I hated blue jeans, and anything that came close to my neck. I remember my mom trying to get me to wear jeans and turtlenecks; "it would look so cute on you," she would say. I couldn't stand them at all. I liked to wear sweat pants and flip-flops. When I became a teenager, I made myself wear jeans because all the other teenagers were. But I immediately took them off when I got home. I also hated to wear make-up. Rubbing all that liquid foundation on my face made my face feel like it had a thick layer of plastic on it. I had acne and very oily skin and wanted to hide it somewhat so I found that powder was a good alternative.

I have noticed a wide range of responses from children who have autism in regards to tactile experiences. Some of them seem to absolutely love to be hugged and tickled while others absolutely can't stand it. Whenever I do an initial reinforcer assessment I like to find out if the child likes hugs or tickles or not because I don't want to hug them as reinforcement when they hate being hugged. I have also noticed that little children who liked to be hugged and tickled most of the time do not like it all the time. They have days they don't want to be touched. I think we all humans have days we don't want to be touched. Another interesting thing I have observed is that many children like to hug backwards. I like hugging backwards because I like the pressure on my back.

Many times my body feels a need for something very sensory, and anxiety and stress will suddenly increase. Deep pressure, pulling, pushing or lifting weights is what I crave. Sometimes I put an ice pack on my back or walk outside in freezing weather for a few minutes wearing just a t-shirt. The temporary intense cold makes me feel better afterwards. Using a handheld massage tool on my back helps as well as running and exercising. I like to be squeezed; bear hugs much better than soft light hugs. One thing that many occupational therapists do is use a special brush and brush the arms, legs and backs of the children. I found that doing this to myself with a hairbrush helps me go to sleep on nights I just can't sleep. And there have been many times I felt anxious and stressed and I would get a hairbrush and brush my skin. Afterwards I would feel much more calm. There are other tactile issues other than touch, such as the textures of food.

I have never had any food sensitivities that I can remember. When I was a little kid I loved to eat raw oysters. I didn't know that this was a weird behavior for little kids until I got older because most all kids I have known don't like raw oysters and they would call me weird and strange for liking them. I loved raw oysters and I loved the squishy slimy feel in my mouth. Except for being pregnant, I have never had any food aversions. I always ate my fruits and vegetables. But I do have big problems with using silverware. I hate using silverware, and much rather eat with my hands. I have tried to learn to like eating with silverware since it is the polite way to eat but when nobody is looking I use my fingers.

Now, my experiences with many of the children on the spectrum are a different story. Some of them will not touch anything soft like mashed potatoes, pudding, or Jello and only eat hard crunchy things such as chips and crackers. Some of them will not touch anything hard or crunchy and will only touch and eat soft foods like baby food. I have seen several children shiver and shake when they touch a soft food. One little boy I was shadowing at school one day touched the icing on his cupcake and he shivered, screamed and immediately wiped the icing on his clothes. Many children who have food texture sensitivities benefit from sensory integration therapy and feeding therapy. I have learned to teach a child to tolerate and even like certain foods utilizing the principles of shaping, prompting and reinforcement. Ok, so a child can't stand soft foods and only tolerates hard crunchy things. I get a bag of Doritos, the child's favorite food, and a bowl of mashed potatoes. The child touches a small spoonful of mashed potatoes with his finger – he gets a Dorito. Then in order to get another Dorito, he has to tolerate me putting a very tiny amount of mashed potatoes on the very tip of the Dorito and eat the Dorito. After that, I gradually increase the amount of mashed potatoes on the Dorito until the child can eat the Dorito with a spoonful of mashed potatoes on it. The Dorito is gradually faded out. Mashed potatoes aren't so bad after all. There are other methods too. One time a parent requested me to teach her child to eat an oatmeal cookie. I broke the cookie into small pieces, put them on a plate on the table. I got the child engaged in imitative actions and then I said, "do this" and put one of the pieces of cookie in my mouth. Without thinking, the child did exactly as I did. Then she realized there was something in her mouth, made a yucky face followed by a pleasant face, then chewed and swallowed the cookie. Then she ate the remaining pieces of oatmeal cookie on the plate with a big happy smile.

Summary of methods for overcoming tactile sensitivities:

- Remember that when people hug you, they are expressing their love.
- If your body feels in need of sensory input, try a temperature extreme such as ice on your skin for a few minutes or hair dryer for a few minutes. Try massaging tools and brushing. Also try activities from the list of sensory activities listed in the prevention section below.
- If you have trouble sleeping, try brushing your arms, hands, legs, feet and back with a bristle hairbrush.
- If you have food sensitivities and would like to be able to eat more foods, pair sensory sensitive food with your favorite foods while gradually increasing the amount of the sensory sensitive food.
- Applying a thin layer of powder make up is an alternative to wearing liquid foundation.

Prevention

I have learned by experimentation that doing certain sensory activities before sensory sensitive events can help prevent sensory overload during those events. You can take note of when you feel the most sensory sensitive in your normal daily routines. I feel the most sensitive in the afternoons between 2:00 p.m. and 4:00 p.m. Not only do I feel very irritated at every little sound, noise or smell, my body hurts badly all over. So and hour before I try to do activities that will decrease the sensitivity I would usually feel. Depending on the weather I do a variety of things, but my favorite things are exercising such as bike riding, jumping jacks, push-ups and lifting weights. I involve my children in the activities or I join in their activity. They love for me to jump on the trampoline with them and they love to go bike riding. I always set my bike to the hardest speed for a deeper pressure as I pedal. On days I am not home, I will run up and down stairs, or find somewhere I can stretch my muscles where nobody will see.

I have also learned to be able to predict when children with autism would become the most sensory sensitive. Just before that time I would have them walk around the building with me, pull ropes, play with Playdoh, silly putty, and shaving cream or let them do a puzzle. For some children, doing a puzzle can be very calming. Sensory activities are selected on a very individual basis.

Something else that helps with the intensity of sensory defensiveness is diet. By eliminating foods with preservatives, artificial ingredients and high sugary foods the body naturally feels better. I try to shop the parameters of the grocery store and buy fresh. I avoid eating from cans and drinking sodas. I also try to avoid consuming anything that is not natural, even artificial sweeteners such as aspartame.

Many people with Asperger's have food allergies and/or environmental allergies. The relationship between allergies and sensory defensiveness is well established. If you are sensory sensitive, then you likely have food sensitivities you may not even be aware of. Food sensitivities can cause confusion, dizziness, fatigue, anger, irritability, anxiety, mood swings and headaches (Hellar, 2002). You can have your blood drawn and sent to a laboratory such Great Plains Laboratory, Alletess Medical Laboratories

Foreword by Liane Holliday Willey

or Immuno Labs to see what foods you are sensitive and allergic to. The results to my blood tests show that I am allergic to wheat, eggs, cow milk, soybeans and peanuts. The results also show that I am sensitive to baker's yeast, brewer's yeast, gluten and 10 other foods. When I eliminated my allergic foods for several days, my sensory sensitivities were reduced by about 50%.

Sensory activities

- Swinging on a swing
- Jumping on trampoline
- Jumping rope
- Skipping and galloping
- Spinning in spin chairs
- Running
- Walking
- Riding bikes
- Rocking chair
- Going up and down stairs
- Doing sit-ups
- Jumping jacks
- Lifting weights
- Massage/vibrating tools
- Playing with silly putty
- Walking in the grass on sand barefooted
- Walking in mud
- Pet animals

- Chewing gum

- Arm wrestling

- Bear hugs

- Hug a big pillow

- Pull a tied rope

- Pushing or pulling heavy loads

- Do a puzzle

- Gardening

- Squishy balls

Why the sensory sensitivities?

I wanted to know why I was sensory sensitive. The number of sensitivities and the levels of intensity vary within individuals. One mother of a child I worked with told me that she thought that autism was a "disorder of the senses." I wondered if children would be able to communicate, socialize, and learn in typical environments if they didn't have such sensory problems. I believe that the sensory issues are a large part of what autism is, and contributes to "autistic behavior." But something has to cause those sensory problems. I am going to discuss sensory integration and sensory integration disorder and then explore reasons why people on the autism spectrum may have sensory disturbances.

Our brains constantly receive sensory information, then process the information and tell us what is going on. Movement, touch, sight, hearing, taste and smell are the main senses. Our brain interprets the sensory information and tells us what it sounds like and how loud it is, what it feels like, what something looks like and how bright, what it tastes like and smells like and to what intensity. Touch the surface of an iron and the nerves sends the signal to the brain; the brain processes it, and tells you it is hot and painful. Eat a potato chip; it is crunchy and salty. Listen to a clock ticking, a car starting, the air conditioner or heater turning on, no big deal. Go to a party or to a restaurant and talk with friends and family paying no attention to the other people talking and the sounds of the silverware hitting the plates. Watch fireworks, the lights are so beautiful, paying no attention to the bang noises they make. The smell of perfume is very sweet and pleasant. This is "normal" sensory integration.

What is happening when the brain processes information and the response is not "normal?" The iron may not feel hot and you will get burned. The potato chip tastes sweet. Can't talk to friends and family at parties because attention is on how loud everyone else is talking and those high pitched clanging noises. Can't enjoy fireworks because the noise blasts your eardrums. The smell of perfume makes you dizzy and nauseous. This is called a sensory integration dysfunction. This condition affects people in different ways and to various degrees (Morris, 2003).

Why does the sensory dysfunction occur? It is a neurological disorganization that can occur in three different ways: the brain doesn't receive information due to a disconnection in the neuron cells, sensory information is received inconsistently or sensory information may be received consistently but doesn't connect properly with the other sensory information. What happens as a result of the neurological disorganization is inefficient behavior, motor, language, or emotional output (Bright tots, 2003).

But what causes the neurological disorganization? Mercury poisoning is thought to be one of the major biomedical contributors of autism, ADD, ADHD, Asperger's, pervasive developmental disorder and sensory integration dysfunction. I did not say that mercury is the "cause," I said "contributor." Exposure to mercury can cause immune, sensory, neurological, motor, and behavioral dysfunctions (Bernard, et. al, 2001). The type and degree of symptoms depends on the dose, the method and duration of exposure. From doing multiple searches on different search engines on the Internet, there are many numerous conditions that are associated with mercury toxicity involving psychological disturbances, oral disorders, gastrointestinal effects, systemic effects, neurologic effects, respiratory effects, immunological effects and endocrine problems that would take a whole book to write on, which there already are.

A great deal of children I have worked with had their blood tested for heavy metals. Their parents shared with me what the results were and I have never had a parent report that their child did not have high or toxic levels of mercury in their blood. Some children had other toxic metals in their blood such as aluminum, lead, aresenic and cadmium. The children with additional heavy metals seemed to have a more severe expression of autism than the children with just high levels of mercury.

I don't remember having any sensory issues to light, noises or smells when I was a small child. I just a sensitivity to sudden touch. I began having terrible sensitivites to everything when I turned eleven, just a few months after receiving that mandatory measles vaccine at my school. I had already been exposed to the mercury in a thermometer I broke when I was nine that spilled all over my pillow. When I had more dental amalgams put in my mouth, the sensitivities got even worse. When one of my amalgams broke from biting on a cherry seed, I began having an awful metal taste in my mouth followed by hand tremors and increase in back inflammation pain, and even more increase in noise sensitivity.

Allergies

Why are food allergies associated with sensory defensiveness? The most common cause of allergies is leaky gut sundrome, which means there is excessive permeability of the digestive tract allowing undigested food particles into the bloodstream. When this happens, the body perceives itself to be sick and will experience an array of symptoms (Heller, 2002).

What causes leaky gut syndrome? Yeast overgrowth or candida overgrowth. What causes yeast overgrowth? A poor immune system. When there is a poor immune system, infection is more likely, and when infection is present, doctors will prescribe antiobiotics. Antiobiotics kill the good bacteria in the intestines making the environment perfect for yeast overgrowth. Yeast and the imbalance of bacteria results in food cravings for sugar and breads which further contributes to constipation, diahrea, muscle aches, ear or upper-respiratory infections, irritability, mood swings, rashes, etc. These sympoms may contribute to the degree of sensory sensitivity. See the pattern?

Can this cycle be broken? Can this problem be fixed? Yes, but it is hard. Eliminating specific foods such as yeast, sugar, wheat, oats, barley, rye, and dairy products as well as all the foods that a blood test reveal allergy or sensitivity; use natural remedies to kill the yeast such as grapefruit seed extract, caprillic acid, cranverry extract, take probiotics which is beneficial bacteria. I think it best that you research this for yourself and find a qualified health care professional. Not all doctors are familiar with yeast overgrowth so you have to find just the right doctor. I prefer seeing a DAN (Defeat Autism Now) doctor.

I think it helps people on the spectrum to know what causes their struggles. Although it is more difficult for them to learn social and communication skills than typical people, they can still learn to the best of their potential. They may need a more logical way of learning communication and socializing than typical people, but learning to overcome social difficulties and developing better relationships is possible.

Overcoming Social Difficulties
Making and keeping friends

Making friends may not always be easy. There are books about making friends, maintaining conversations and influencing people that have greatly helped me. The two most important things you should know about people is that they like to feel important and they like to be appreciated (Carnegie, 1936). If you can make a person feel important and appreciated then you likely have a friend. People like to talk about themselves. I have learned to always remember something that a person talks about during our conversation in order to bring it up again in the next conversation. For example, if a person mentions that their dog had broken his leg, the next time I see that person I ask them how their dog is doing. People love it when you remember their concerns. People will much more likely talk to you again and more and more when you show an interest in their life. You make people feel important when you remember what is going on in their life. I try not to talk about myself too much. I ask people questions, make comments on their answers and answer their questions.

It is good to give effort to remember the name of a new person you just meet. Next time you see them, greet them by name. People like hearing their names. Although there are tremendous tips and strategies organized in many books that you can read, my top three simple methods of making and keeping friends are: 1) Remember their name and greet them by their name. 2) Smile. 3) Remember what is going on in their life and ask them about it next time you see them. The more you talk to someone, the more you will get to know him or her and they get to know you. The more you get to know each other, the closer the friendship.

Many people make friends through shared interests. If you are interested in dancing or playing a sport you will be around other people interested in the same thing. The opportunity to make friends is greater because you have something in common. People like to talk with other people they have things in common with. As you live life and reach new stages you will make new friends depending on what stage you are in. If you are a mother with young children, you are likely to make friends with other mother's with young children at places like the library or the park. Meeting new people in those situations will create opportunities to find out more about them. If you are a college student majoring in biology, you will likely meet other college students with similar interests. If you like to play golf, you will meet other people who like golf on the golf course. It is good to plan activities around mutual interests.

After making friends, sometimes it may difficult to keep friends for the long run. This is because there are different phases in life and people's interests change. If you want to remain friends with someone, you have to stay in contact. My best friends and I went through this stage where we had become such different people since childhood, that we didn't have much to talk about anymore. As children we did more things together such as swimming, dancing, riding bikes and playing softball, but as adults we don't do those things any more. I wanted to keep our friendship and they did also so we decided to meet for dinner once a month. We know each other more than anybody and would support each other in anything. As adults, we have developed different and new interests, but we still remain friends because of our strong foundation. Other friends will come and go through the life stages. It is important to know that family members can be good friends as well. My husband is my very best friend.

If you desire to have a lot of friends, you want to make sure that you are not making yourself appear as someone you really are not. You will have to continually work so hard to make and keep friends. I don't think that it is the number of friend that you have that is so important but the quality of the relationships you have with the people you are friends with, even if there are just a few friends.

One-on-One

I have always had a much easier time having conversations with and developing relationships with one person at a time. Making friends in groups has always been difficult for me. I can pay attention to just one person at a time much easier than two or more. There is too much information to process at once with groups of people. There have been times in my life where I would pick out a certain person from a group such as in college and church. I would invite her over, call her on the phone or try to find a way to speak with her one-on-one without the others. Many times after doing this, she will say things like "it has been nice getting to know you better, I used to think your were extremely shy" or "wow, you are much different than what I first thought of you." Girls will form their perceptions of other girls, but getting to know someone first hand without any interruptions or competitors will give a much better idea of whom someone really is.

If you are struggling in group social situations and don't have any "friends" in the group, consider choosing a girl you think would be most likely to accept your invitation. Make sure this is a girl you would like to be friends with, possibly have similar interests as you. Many times when you can connect socially with one person in a group, that person will likely bridge the gap between you and rest of the group.

Goal setting

Many people I have known with Asperger's are happy with their lives and with themselves. They don't seem to care much about what others think of them and appear much less anxious in social situations. However, some people with Asperger's have a great desire to participate in social events and have many friends. But the understanding of social situations and social behavior of people can be confusing. I like to see it as something to decode, separate single pieces of information to understand each piece by itself then put the pieces together like a puzzle. I decide what goals I want to meet in the social world, list all the steps it takes to reach those goals, remind myself not to get discouraged if I mess up, and put myself in situations that would lead me to meet my goals focusing on one step at a time.

For example, my husband really wanted to join a Sunday school group at our church. At first, I didn't want to. I didn't want Sundays to be days of anxiety with having to try to participate in a social setting. Going to church was great, but the thought of having to go to a Sunday school class afterwards was very overwhelming. My husband really wanted to go so I went with him. It was just like any social situation, many people talking to each other in small groups all at the same time. There was one woman in the class who was very friendly, someone I would consider very socially gifted. To my surprise, she was very nice to me and often talked to me. Because of her incredible acts of friendliness, I decided to try to be a part of the class after all. I made it a goal to be "one of them." I wanted to participate in the after church and weekend activities with the group. My husband was already making friends some of the other men and I wanted to make friends with each woman in the class. Reaching this goal was going to take many steps so I made a list of steps to follow:

1. Get some books to help me with conversation skills and making friends.
2. Invite the really nice woman to dinner with me one evening in order to get to know each other a little better one-on-one.
3. Get to know each of the other ladies one at a time starting with the ones who seem to be really good friends with the really nice woman.
4. Remember conversations I had with each of them so the next time I saw them I could ask them a question about what we last talked about. For example if one of them mentioned that they were going to the lake with their family, the next week at church I would be sure to ask them, "how was your visit to the lake?"

5. Determine which women would be easiest to be friends with and invite her and her husband over for dinner. Invite one family at a time.
6. Care about the others in the class. When they got sick or needed help, bring them dinner and offer assistance.
7. Participate in the group as a group member.

For most typical people, participating the group would have been easy to begin with. I was able to meet each of these steps one at a time until I reached my goal; participate in the group as a member. This was a rather lengthy process – it took a couple of years, but I was really happy to have met my goal and to be able to, without intense anxiety, participate in the group. In the process, things would happen like I wouldn't be able to completely follow a conversation when several were talking. I would feel guilty and discouraged but I tried not to let myself stay discouraged. I would sometimes feel discouraged when I observed how easily they conversed with each other and how happy they appeared to be. I wanted it to be that easy for me and I wanted to be that happy. The group had monthly social events where each family in the group would take turns hosting a social. Sometimes the socials were hard for me because they were often crowded and loud, but I didn't give up. My desire to be a part of the group was much stronger than letting the sensory sensitivities prevent me from doing so. There were times where I would have to go outside or go to the bathroom for a few minutes. But after all of that, I became "one of them."

- Set your goals
- Decide the steps to reach the goals
- Don't get discouraged
- Put yourself in social situations so you can focus on your goals and reach them.

Improving relationships

Are there specific people in your life that you would like to have a closer or a more meaningful relationship with? People such as your parents, spouse, children, coworkers, individual friends, classmates, cousins, aunts, uncles, neighbors, etc. I have learned that most people are usually afraid of people they don't understand. Everybody has people in their lives they really like, people they somewhat like, people they don't like and people they really don't like. Why is that? I believe the people on their dislike list are people they don't understand. When they get the opportunity to get to know that person better and develop a better understanding, a better relationship develops.

I have seen many parents and teens dislike each other. They lack understanding. Their relationship would be better if they each, or at least one of them tried to better understand the other's point of view. If there are people in your life you would like a better relationship with, then the first move is yours. You don't have to let your social difficulties prevent you from having happy relationships. Use one-on-one, sensory tolerance, and goal setting. Invite the person to do something with you, just the two of you. Get to know what the other person likes. Plan something you both are interested in. If you can't think of anything, then go out to eat. Everybody likes to eat. Just spending time with someone helps to get to know each other better. Focus on what you like about the person and make positive comments, but don't overdo.

There are probably just a few people you would like to improve your relationship with. Don't rush into it. Focus on one person at a time. If the other person is just too busy, then focus on another person.

After your relationship improves a little bit, you can inform the person of your sensory issues. You can tell them that high pitch sounds like shouting hurts your ears. You can mention that you wear sunglasses because they sun is too bright for you. If the person wants to hug you all the time, kindly inform that although you appreciate their affection, sudden touch bothers you. Or, you can tolerate the hugs knowing that the person has good intentions. Typical people may not be able to relate to your sensory sensitivities. You can help them relate by giving them scenarios such as "imagine washing the dishes wearing a thick wool sweater in the middle of summer with the sun shining in your face through the window, with the radio turned up all the way, the water is as hot as it will go, the soap smells like pure bleach, the kitchen is crowded with people all talking at the same time and they keep bumping into you." People may be able to relate better with scenarios.

Tips for conversation

- Don't be afraid to introduce yourself.
- Remember the person's name.
- Show interest in the other person.
- Offer honest compliments.
- Make comments and ask questions.
- Remember people like to talk about their work, their goals, their hobbies, or vacations.
- Find out about the person to see what you have in common by asking a question such as "what do you like to do during your free time?"
- Don't think while the other person is talking. Listen.
- Listen to keywords such as people and places. You can bring these up in the next conversation.
- Remember details and facts about the other person.
- Be aware of your body language. Research shows that over half of face-to-face conversation comes from nonverbal body language (Gabor, 2001). Smile don't cross your arms, lean forward, make eye contact and nod your head.
- Pay attention to others body language. Are they interested in what you are talking about?
- Don't complain too much or only talk about your troubles.
- Don't be too aggressive, pushy, critical or blunt.
- Don't interrupt the person while they are in mid sentence.
- Don't be fearful about saying the wrong thing and become anxious.
- Be careful not to over exaggerate your good qualities while hiding all your faults.
- Make sure the conversation is well balanced. Don't talk the entire time and don't allow the other person to talk the whole time.
- Don't always assume you are right while the other person is wrong.
- Remember that making friends is not always easy for anyone.
- Don't allow yourself to get too upset if you are rejected. There are others.

- When the conversation is ending, make a positive statement before closing such as "it was nice talking with you, the persons name" or "let's talk again soon, name."

People tips

- People want to feel important
- People like to be appreciated
- People like to be understood
- People like attention for their interests
- People like to see other's smile
- People do not like to be told they are wrong
- People like respect
- People like sympathy

Suggested readings

- *Too Loud, Too Bright, Too Fast, Too Tight: What to Do If You Are Sensory Defensive in an Overstimulating World* by Sharon Heller (2003)
- *The Sensory Team Handbook: A hands-on tool to help young people make sense of their senses and take charge of their sensory processing* by Nancy Mucklow (2009)
- *How to Start a conversation and Make Friends* by Don Gabor (2001)
- *How to talk to Anyone: 92 Little tricks for Big Success in Relationships* by Leil Lowndes (2003)
- *How to Instantly Connect with Anyone 96 All-New Little Tricks for Big Success in Relationships* by Leil Lowndes (2009)
- *How to Win Friends and Influence People by* Dale Carnegie (1998)
- *Getting Along with Almost Anybody: The Complete Personality Book* by Florence & Marita Littauer (2000)
- *The Unwritten Rules of Social Relationships: Decoding Social Mysteries Through the Unique Perspectives of Autism* by Temple Grandin and Sean Barron (2005)
- *The Hidden Curriculum: Practical Solutions for Understanding Unstated Rules in Social Situations* by Brenda Smith Myles, Melissa L. Trautman, and Ronda L. Schelvan (2004)

- *Social Skills for Teenagers and Adults with Asperger Syndrome: A Practical Guide to Day-to-day Life* by Nancy J. and Ph.D. Patrick (2008)
- *Solutions for Adults with Asperger's Syndrome: Maximizing the Benefits, Minimizing the Drawbacks to Achieve Success* by Juanita Lovett (2005)
- *Amalgam Illness, Diagnosis and Treatment: What You Can Do to Get Better, How Your Doctor Can Help* by Andrew Cutler
- *Diagnosis: Mercury: Money, Politics, and Poison* by Jane M. Hightower M.D. (2008)
- *Nurturing your Child with Music* by John Ortiz (1999)

References

Bernard, S., Enayati, A., Redwood, L., Roger, H. & Binstock, T. (2001). Autism: A Novel Form of Mercury Poisoning. Medical Hypotheses, 2001 Apr.56(4):462-71.

Bright Tots. (2004). *Sensory Integration/Occupational Therapy.* Educational Toys & Resource Guide to Child Development. Retrieved November 5th, 2009. http://www.brighttots.com/sensory_integration.html

Carnegie, .D (1936). How to Win Friends and Influence People. SIMON & SCHUSTER @ TRADE

Dublin, N. (2009). *Asperger Sundrome and Anxiety: A Guide to Successful Stress Management.* Jessica Kingsley Publishers.

Gabor, D. (2001). How to Start a Conversation and Make Friends. Simon & Schuster, New York.

Heller, S. (2002). Too Loud, Too Bright, Too Fast, Too Tight. What to do if you are sensory defensive in an overstimulation world. Harper.

Morris, M. (2003). *Just What Is Sensory Integration?* Sensory Processing Disorder. Retrieved November 5th, 2009. http://www.sensory-processing-disorder.com/what-is-sensory-integration.html

Wikipedia (last updated November 1st, 2009). Mercury Poisoning. Wikipedia, the Free Encyclopedia. Retrieved November 5th, 2009. http://en.wikipedia.org/wiki/Mercury_poisoning

CHAPTER 9

The Search for Purpose and Absolute Truth

I hesitated to include this chapter in this book because of all the controversy in the world. With much thought, I decided to incorporate this chapter because I would know nothing without my search for and discovery for life's purpose and the absolute truth. There are so many people who do not know what the purpose of life is. Everyone has their own theory but I am not happy with just theories if there is a real answer. Knowing life's purpose, will give anyone a complete change in perspective. My intention for this chapter is not to preach. I do not intend this chapter to be a Bible study. My intention is for the information presented to help others see that although life may sometimes seem meaningless, life does indeed have a purpose. My intention is to show that I used to be a very confused girl, not knowing who I was or why I didn't fit in and that after seeking truth I now understand life's meaning. This chapter may not be meaningful to some people, but I think some of the content may help some of those who are lost and want to find answers. We all live in bodies that are constantly aging. We will all one day live in old wrinkled weak bodies. Studying history makes me realize just how quickly time passes; generation after generation and so on.

I struggled, was anxious and tense in so many situations throughout life with little understanding. We all have struggles. But what caused life to make sense was when my relationship with God began to grow.

I discovered who God is. I asked God and He answered. I remember as a teen spending a lot of time crying in my bedroom with the door shut and locked. I had feelings that the world was ending. I didn't understand what was happening, why it was so hard for me to peacefully and easily understand how to fit in. Why is life such a struggle? What is the purpose of anything? What is meaningful? What's it worth? God, do you have a will for me, and if so what is it? I would sometimes make my way to the mirror with tears in my eyes looking at the stranger I saw and asked God, "Who is this God? Who am I?" Nobody ever knew what I was feeling or experiencing. I didn't know how to talk about it. I was embarrassed for being the black sheep. My only hope at those times was God. I never felt alone behind shut doors. God was there. I prayed to Him. I talked to Him. I asked Him to please answer my questions. I wanted answers. I wanted understanding. I wanted wisdom and knowledge. I wanted to know if life was meaningful and had a purpose. I wanted to know if I could fix the problems I had. God was there. But he didn't answer me all at once. He answered me by giving me the experience I needed to find the answers. He led me to the answers. He is still leading me to the answers.

There is a pattern in the Bible. There is one big pattern, very bold, concrete, geometrical, symmetrical and definite. There are lots of other patterns, some of which I have been able to follow and some I have yet to follow all the way through. Throughout most of my life, I have been trying to figure out how to behave. Should I behave according to how I think other people want me to act, according to how I want to act, or according to how God wants me to act. How does God want me to be? What if I can't behave in the way God wants me to? How do I know for sure if I am going to Heaven or not? Why do You allow so much tragedy God? Why are there so many different religions, so many different interpretations, and so many different perspectives? Why did You create us if you knew we were going to sin God? Why do You let people suffer in pain and confusion God? What is truly meaningful God?? What is the purpose of life??? Why did You create me???? God, will you please answer my questions? I never cease to be amazed by how God works. God has never failed to answer any of my questions. Although I would like for Him to blurt out the answers, He usually has a master method for answering.

I remember when I was 13 years old praying to God one night. I asked God if he really loved me. I wanted God to tell me that he loved me. Before I fell asleep I asked, "God I really need to know that you love me, will you please tell me that you love me?" The very next day I went to the grocery store with my mom. We were checking out and she said, "we forgot the eggs, can you run and get the eggs?" I darted off for the eggs and on my way back up the aisle there was a book facing me on eye level with the big words that read "GOD LOVES YOU." I stopped, stood there and stared. I stopped breathing for a moment. I silently asked God, "God is this you answering my prayer from last night?" Suddenly, a penetrating, piercing warm feeling filled up my heart, a feeling impossible to describe with words. It was almost as if my spirit was being hugged. "Wow, thanks God. You really do love me."

When I was 17, I had made the assumption that 333 was God's number. Somehow I was led to the verse Jeremiah 33:3 which says, "Call unto me, and I will answer thee, and tell thee great and mighty things, which thou knowest not." I thought maybe God was wanting me to call unto him with this verse so I did and somehow got led to the verse Matthew 6:33 "But seek ye first the kingdom of God, and his righteousness; and all these things shall be added unto you." Seek the kingdom of God? Is there a kingdom to be sought? What things shall be added? I repeated this verse over and over and over as well as the Jeremiah 33:3 verse all the time, every day all throughout the day. Everyday and before any event I would repeat these verses.

It wasn't until I was 18 that I learned that the Bible was a book of multiple books and had perfect structure to it, with chapters and verses all labeled and numbered. I had always prayed to God growing up and spent a good deal of time talking to God, asking him for help and thanking God for answering my prayers. But I didn't read the Bible at that time. Sometimes I would hear people say the word "Jesus" but I didn't really know what it meant. One night I asked God, "God, who is Jesus and why do some people say he is so important?" The very next morning, happened to be Saturday morning, I woke up and flipped on the TV to watch cartoons as usual and when I sat back down, I noticed a Bible sitting on the bookshelf. It looked so bold, so vivid, so inviting almost like it was glowing. I turned off the TV and grabbed that Bible and began reading the first book in the New Testament, Matthew. Wow, I thought, I understand what I am reading. I read the entire chapter of Matthew as Jesus walked out of that Bible and straight into my heart. I sat there in silence, in amazement and in shock. "God, thank you for telling me who Jesus is," I whispered as tears filled my eyes and love penetrated my heart.

I am not a Bible scholar or anything like that. I am not a religious person. I am a person who just wants the truth and will do whatever it takes to find it. I hate deception. "But from there you will seek the Lord your God, and you will find Him if you seek Him with all your heart and with all your soul" (Deuteronomy 4:29). Although I have found the answers to many of my questions, I still have much seeking to do while discovering answers leads to the development of more questions. I look forward to continuing my seeking as I am greatly becoming satisfied with what I am finding. I am going to share some of the things with you what I will share with my own kids. I am going to discuss patterns in the Bible, learning who God really is, developing a relationship with God, God's eternal purpose, the purpose of life and scientific evidence.

Patterns in the Bible
Obedience vs. disobedience: blessing vs. punishment

No matter what people say, the Old Testament is still important. Very important in learning who God is and how God speaks and deals with humans. It appears from stories in the Old Testament that God desires a relationship with people, but people become disobedient and God has to consequent them, which causes some people to turn back to God. A fluctuation of generations living in harmony with God, God blessing them abundantly, after some time people take advantage of their blessings and become less obedient and less faithful to God. People turn away from God thinking they don't need Him and God provides a punishment, a consequence, for their lack of faith, their lack of trust and their lack of thankfulness and obedience. There are behavioral patterns in the Bible of people and of God. I have to sum up this in one chapter so I will have to be as brief as possible to communicate what I am trying to communicate.

Adam and Eve lived in the Garden of Eden, had everything they needed and did not experience discomfort. They disobeyed God. God sent them out of the garden so they had to work very hard to prevent their bodies from discomfort. Soon the earth became more populated, and sin increased with violence, sexual sins, and disobedience. God did not like it. God wanted a family to love him, trust him and obey him. After nine generations, God found only one person, Noah, who was faithful to Him. Noah obeyed God when God told him to build a big ark. No matter how much Noah pleaded with all the people to turn to God, that God was going to flood the earth, the people would not believe. All the people were drowned. God flooded the earth as a result of disobedience and unfaithfulness. God killed everybody on earth except the eight people on the ark, Noah and his family.

Noah's children went their own ways and the earth was repopulated. After a few generations, people who lived in Babylon did not want to scatter as God told them to. They were not worshiping God. They worshiped false gods made up of wood and metal. God was angry at their disobedience and caused them to speak different languages so they had to scatter about. But as the earth became more populated, people chose to worship false idols and forgot about God. There was one man, Abraham, who believed in God and not the false statues. God told him to leave his home. Abraham obeyed God and God took him to a special land, Canaan, called Palestine today. God told Abraham he was going to give him and all his children that land and that he will have so many children that they couldn't be counted. Abraham believed God, trusted God and obeyed God. God counted Abraham's faith as righteousness. God told Abraham he would have a son, and Abraham believed him. After 10 years and no child, Sarah his wife convinced Abraham that God meant he would have a child through their servant Hagar. Ishmael was born and later became the father of all Arabic nations. But God spoke to Abraham telling him that He and his wife would have a son. Abraham believed God, although he was already in his upper 80s.

God also told Abraham he was going to destroy a city because all the people were faithless, sinful and disobedient. Abraham tried to reason with God asking to spare the city and God agreed that if there were just 10 righteous people God would not destroy the city. When Abraham went to the city to warn the people, none of them would believe God. Lot, Abraham's nephew and his family were in the city so they left with Abraham as God rained fire on the city killing everybody in it. God told them not to look back at the city, but Lot's wife disobeyed so God turned her into salt. It is becoming apparent that God does not like sin and disobedience. Look at what happened to the people who did not believe and obey God. Fourteen years after Ishmael was born, Sarah had a baby as God promised, Isaac. God wanted to test Abraham's faith so when Isaac was older, God told him to offer his son as a burnt offering. Although Abraham did not understand, he trusted God and obeyed. When Abraham was about kill Isaac, God stopped him and told Abraham that now he new how much Abraham trusted Him. God said that he would bless him and multiply his children as the stars in heaven. It has become apparent that when people obeyed God, God blessed them.

The Bible is filled with stories with God blessing those who obey and punishing those who don't. "The fear of the LORD is the beginning of wisdom: a good understanding have all they that do his commandments: his praise endureth forever" (Psalms 111:10). If you do have faith in God, believe in him, trust and obey, then something good will happen. This reminds me of parenting. If the kids obey me, I want to bless them with rewards, but if they disobey I take away things. If people would just obey God, what blessings God would give them. Doesn't it appear that God is teaching people to have faith in him? Moses obeyed God. Pharaoh did not and looked at what happened to Pharaoh and his city —plaques swept the land and they eventually the death to Pharaoh's son. God answered the prayers of the Hebrews and set them free. God told them that if they obeyed his commandments, then he would bless them. Even with that, many of them began to worship false idols and they got killed. God provided the ones who were obedient with food to eat and water to drink. When the Hebrews finally made it to the Promised Land, everyone but Joshua and Caleb did not trust God enough to enter it. So God punished their lack of faith by making them wander the desert for 40 years. Everyone one of them over the age of 19 died, except Joshua and Caleb, before God allowed them to enter to the Promised Land. Joshua led them in and obeyed God's directions. The land was wonderful and had plenty of food and water. The point of all this is that good things happen when you obey, and bad things happen if you don't.

If you want to learn more, but you are not used to reading the Bible and perceive the Bible to be a bit confusing, the start with the book *Good and Evil* by Michael Pearl. This is a comic/picture book of the Bible that took the author seven years to complete.

The Blood pattern

God told Adam that the result from sin would be death. That is the rule. You sin, you die. After Adam and Eve disobeyed God, God did not immediately kill them. He killed animals in their place. Adam and Eve lived a long life before they actually died. They made animal sacrifices to pay for their sins. The death of the animals and spill of the animals' blood covered their sins. God did not like it when Cain offered a vegetable sacrifice. It had to be a blood sacrifice. Death of the first-born son in each family was the last of the plaques in Egypt. God told Moses to tell the Egyptians to paint the door frames the blood of a lamb and the angel of death will pass over their home. For all those who did not paint their door frames with lamb's blood, their first born son died that night.

There are verses all throughout the Old Testament promising Jesus. The prophets of God wrote them. There were over 350 prophecies to be filled. Here are some of them. Genesis 22:18 says, "And in thy seed shall all the nations of the earth be blessed; because thou hast obeyed my voice." Abraham obeyed God and Jesus is a descendent of Abraham. Jeremiah 23:5 says "Behold, the days come, saith the LORD, that I will raise unto David a righteous Branch, and a King shall reign and prosper, and shall execute judgment and justice in the earth." Jesus was a descendant of David. Isaiah 9:6 says "For unto us a child is born, unto us a son is given: and the government shall be upon his shoulder: and his name shall be called Wonderful, Counseller, The mighty God, The everlasting Father, The Prince of Peace." This verse speaks for itself. Isaiah 7:14 says, "Therefore the Lord himself shall give you a sign; Behold, a virgin shall conceive, and bear a son, and shall call his name Immanuel." Jesus was born of a virgin. Micah 5:2 says, "But thou, Bethlehem Ephratah, though thou be little among the thousands of Judah, yet out of thee shall he come forth unto me that is to be ruler in Israel; whose goings forth have been from of old, from everlasting." Jesus was born in Bethlehem. Isaiah 9:6 says "For unto us a child is born, unto us a son is given: and the government shall be upon his shoulder: and his name shall be called Wonderful, Counseller, The mighty God, The everlasting Father, The Prince of Peace." Jesus is the Son of God. Psalms 22:1 says "My God, my God, why hast thou forsaken me? Why art thou so far from helping me, and from the words of my roaring? This is what Jesus said on the cross. Psalms 22:16 says "For dogs have compassed me: the assembly of the wicked have inclosed me: they pierced my hands and my feet." Jesus was nailed to the cross. Psalms 22:18 says, "They part my garments among them, and cast lots upon my vesture." Lots were casted for Jesus' garments. Very importantly, Isaiah 53:5 says, "But he was wounded for our transgressions, he was bruised for our iniquities: the chastisement of our peace was upon him; and with his stripes we are healed." Jesus took the punishment for our sins.

The beautiful symmetry, perfection in all its pattern and smooth transition with even flow. The sacrifice and blood of the animals covered sins before Jesus. Jesus was promised by prophecy. His *blood* was spilled for our sins. We don't have to sacrifice animals. All we have to do is believe in Jesus.

- But now in Christ Jesus ye who sometimes were far off are made nigh by the *blood* of Christ (Ephesians 2:13).
- Having therefore, brethren, boldness to enter into the holiest by the *blood* of Jesus (Hebrews 10:19).
- Wherefore Jesus also, that he might sanctify the people with his own *blood*, suffered without the gate (Hebrews 13:12).
- Now the God of peace, that brought again from the dead our Lord Jesus, that great shepherd of the sheep, through the *blood* of the everlasting covenant (Hebrews 13:20)
- But if we walk in the light, as he is in the light, we have fellowship one with another, and the *blood* of Jesus Christ his Son cleanseth us from all sin (1 John 1:7).
- This is he that came by water and *blood*, even Jesus Christ; not by water only, but by water and *blood*. And it is the Spirit that beareth witness, because the Spirit is truth (1 John 5:6).
- God "made him to be sin for us, who knew no sin, that we might be made the righteousness of God in him" (2 Cor. 5:21).

God was willing to see Jesus as a sinner in order for Him to see us as righteous. Jesus became what we are so we could become what He is. It was a trade. He traded His righteousness for our sin. He suffered the consequences of our sin so that we can bear the consequences of His righteousness before God (Pearl, 1998). What does one have to do to have this righteousness imputed into his account? "Sirs, what must I do to be saved? Believe on the Lord Jesus Christ, and thou shalt be saved" (Acts 16:30-31). "For God so loved the world, that he gave his only begotten Son, that whosoever believeth in him should not perish, but have everlasting life" (John 3:16).

The Faith Pattern

It is clear that what God wants from us people is our faith, our trust, and our belief in Him. What is faith? Hebrews 11:1 says, "Now faith is the substance of things hoped for, the evidence of things not seen." Wow, faith is a substance, and evidence. God told Abraham that his faith served as his righteousness. In doing a search on Swordsearcher, the word Faith occurs 247 times in 231 verses. Here are some selected verses, which helps us understand faith and how important it is. Follow the pattern beginning with faith healing people, peace by faith in God, definition of faith, and faith examples by those in the Old Testament, with the pattern stopping but beginning again with true faith and actions.

- When Jesus heard it, he marvelled, and said to them that followed, Verily I say unto you, I have not found so great *faith*, no, not in Israel (Matthew 8:10).
- And, behold, they brought to him a man sick of the palsy, lying on a bed: and Jesus seeing their *faith* said unto the sick of the palsy; Son, be of good cheer; thy sins be forgiven thee (Matthew 9:2).
- But Jesus turned him about, and when he saw her, he said, Daughter, be of good comfort; thy *faith* hath made thee whole. And the woman was made whole from that hour (Matthew 9:22).
- When Jesus saw their *faith*, he said unto the sick of the palsy, Son, thy sins be forgiven thee (Mark 2:5).

- And he said unto her, Daughter, thy *faith* hath made thee whole; go in peace, and be whole of thy plague (Mark 5:34).
- And Jesus said unto him, Go thy way; thy *faith* hath made thee whole. And immediately he received his sight, and followed Jesus in the way (Mark 10:52).
- And when he saw their *faith*, he said unto him, Man, thy sins are forgiven thee (Luke 5:20).
- And his name through *faith* in his name hath made this man strong, whom ye see and know: yea, the *faith* which is by him hath given him this perfect soundness in the presence of you all (Acts 3:16).
- To open their eyes, and to turn them from darkness to light, and from the power of Satan unto God, that they may receive forgiveness of sins, and inheritance among them which are sanctified by *faith* that is in me (Acts 26:18).
- That your *faith* should not stand in the wisdom of men, but in the power of God (1 Corinthians 2:5).
- And Jesus answering saith unto them, Have *faith* in God (Mark 11:22).
- Therefore being justified by *faith*, we have peace with God through our Lord Jesus Christ (Romans 5:1).

Hebrews is an excellent chapter for understanding faith. It ties in the pattern from the Old Testament regarding the people who had faith in God. Here are some selected verses.

- Through *faith* we understand that the worlds were framed by the word of God, so that things which are seen were not made of things which do appear (Hebrews 11:3).
- By *faith* Abel offered unto God a more excellent sacrifice than Cain, by which he obtained witness that he was righteous, God testifying of his gifts: and by it he being dead yet speaketh (Hebrews 11:4).
- By *faith* Enoch was translated that he should not see death; and was not found, because God had translated him: for before his translation he had this testimony, that he pleased God (Hebrews 11:5).
- By *faith* Noah, being warned of God of things not seen as yet, moved with fear, prepared an ark to the saving of his

- house; by which he condemned the world, and became heir of the righteousness, which is by faith (Hebrews 11:7).
- By *faith* Abraham, when he was called to go out into a place, which he should after receive for an inheritance, obeyed; and he went out, not knowing whither he went (Hebrews 11:8).
- By *faith* Abraham, when he was tried, offered up Isaac: and he that had received the promises offered up his only begotten son, (Hebrews 11:17).
- By *faith* Moses, when he was come to years, refused to be called the son of Pharaoh's daughter, (Hebrews 11:24).
- By *faith* they passed through the Red sea as by dry land: which the Egyptians assaying to do were drowned (Hebrews 11:29).
- But without *faith* it is impossible to please him: for he that cometh to God must believe that he is, and that he is a rewarder of them that diligently seek him (Hebrews 11:6).

From what I understand in the book of James, a person truly doesn't have faith unless there is some action that follows. In the Old Testament, people believed God by showing that they believed God. Therefore, faith alone, belief alone, without doing anything, without obeying God is not it. Here are a few examples.

- What doth it profit, my brethren, though a man say he hath faith, and have not works? Can faith save him? (James 2:14).
- Even so faith, if it hath not works, is dead, being alone (James 2:17).
- For as the body without the spirit is dead, so faith without works is dead also (James 2:26).

So if a person decides to have faith in Jesus Christ but continues to disobey God, then the faith is not real. Once a person believes and has faith, they trust God enough to do what He says. What does he say to do? He has directions for people to follow. Directions for husbands to follow, for wives to follow, for children to follow, for parents to follow and for people to follow. Examples. For husband and wife "Nevertheless let every one of you in particular so love his wife even as himself; and the wife see that she reverence her husband" (Ephesians 5:33). For children, "Children, obey your parents in all things: for this is well pleasing unto the Lord"

(Colossians 3:20). For parents "Train up a child in the way he should go: and when he is old, he will not depart from it" (Proverbs 22:6). For everyone, "Afterward Jesus findeth him in the temple, and said unto him, Behold, thou art made whole: sin no more, lest a worse thing come unto thee" (John 5:14); "And he said unto them, Go ye into all the world, and preach the gospel to every creature" (Mark 16:15). If a person really wants the truth, will she accept it when she finds it? Many truths presented may be difficult to accept. But I want to have enough faith in God to believe and do what He says despite my own understanding.

The "3" pattern

I have to include this section in this book because it fascinates me so much and I think it will be intriguing to you as well. Below is quoted from Michael Pearl in his book *By Divine Design*.

"All creation bears the stamp of its Creator. Both the physical and the metaphysical world demonstrate an inherent design and therefore reveal a common designer. The similarity of design suggests a purpose and confirms that nothing came about arbitrarily.

The nature of God is the pattern of all that is created, material and non-material alike. The Bible represents the one God as a triune-being. This is a strange concept that one is three and three are one until we see this very enigma represented in the creation, which creation, as we have said, reflects the nature of the Creator. Creation is so thoroughly stamped with God's triune likeness that the apostle Paul was able to tell us that the Godhead is clearly visible through natural creation.

The atom, once thought to be the smallest part of any substance, is three parts: protons, neutrons, and electrons. But now it is known that the protons and neutrons at the center of the atom are composed of three quarks each. Time is threefold: past, present, and future. Our world has three kingdoms: animal, vegetable and mineral. Life on planet earth is divided into three main branches: bacteria, archaea, and eukaryotes. The sun, a symbol of God, emits alpha, beta, and gamma rays. There are three basic elements in soil, causing a plant to grow: nitrogen, phosphorous, and potash. There are three primary colors from which all other colors are derived: red, yellow, and blue.

Like our triune Creator, we are a triune being: body, soul, and spirit. The body consists of flesh, bone, and blood. The flesh has three layers of skin: the Epidermis, the Dermis and the Subcutaneous tissue. Our blood solids consist of three main cells: platelets, red cells, and white cells. Our nonmaterial self (the soul) is mind, will, and emotions. In the emotions, we can love, hate or be indifferent. Human capability is thought, word, and deed. Logical thought, the activity of the mind, demands a major premise, a minor premise, and a conclusion.

All this reflects the image of God who is revealed to us as a triune, singular being: Father, Son and Holy Spirit. Within the Godhead are the Lover, the Loved, and the Spirit of Love. God is a personal soul manifesting mind, will, and emotions-the same "yesterday, today, and forever."

As God's persons are three, His attributes are three: omniscience, omnipresence, and omnipotence. Based on God's nature, space is three-dimensional: height, width, and depth…. God is one essence, composed of three interdependent persons, each essential to the whole and each containing and expressing the whole of the Godhead.

The likeness of God's omnipresence is reflected in our own soul, as seen in our ability to move about within three-dimensional space. The likeness of God's omniscience (knows everything) is reflected in our gift of knowing and our ability to increase in knowledge. The likeness of God's omnipotence (all powerful) is reflected in our inherent ability to exercise creative power within our own environment…the history of man is a chronicle of his struggle to know, to go and to do. Unquestionably, God's triune attributes continue to be reflected in all of creation."

Wow, thought-provoking, amazing, incredible, fascinating, captivating!!!

Plan, purpose and eternity

I am going to share a basic and brief summary of my understanding although I acknowledge that I only have a very small piece of understanding at this point in life. My understanding will grow as I continue to pray for it and study it and as my life continues.

God has a plan and this part of life is a part of his overall plan. God is creating a kingdom. God wants a family. He wants to love and wants to be loved. He wants those who love him to choose to love him, therefore giving them free will. People can choose not to love God or they can choose to love God. We were created in God's image. Most people want to express themselves and expand themselves. Most people expand by having children and some people express and expand through career, adding to the world and/or helping others. God wants children, a family, and He wants to expand his kingdom.

God has been creating long before we existed. There are the angels, cherubim, seraphim and orphanim from what I understand. All of these beings are a part of God's eternal plan.

God cannot create character. Everything that is happening now has to happen in order to fulfill God's plan, God's purpose. People are developing character as they live their lives. God mixed flesh with spirit and soul – an eternal spirit to make man. The soul is the mind, will and emotions. There is a constant conflict between flesh and spirit because the flesh does not know any moral rules; it just wants to be pleased by sleeping, surviving, eating and drinking being entertained. Although the flesh will die because of sin, the spirit was created to be eternal. People allow their flesh to act without regard to values. This is sin. Everybody sins. "For all have sinned, and come short of the glory of God" (Romans 3:23). There are character opposites, good and evil. There is a constant struggle between spirit and flesh. For example, the spirit wants to be hardworking, but the flesh wants to be lazy. The spirit is willing but the flesh is weak. "Watch and pray, that ye enter not into temptation: the spirit indeed is willing, but the flesh is weak" (Matthew 26:41).

God knew that Jesus would be the only perfect man before he even created Adam. God allows Satan to tempt us so that we can choose. We struggle and overcome as we build character. God is a loving, a forgiving and a merciful God. He wants your love and your faith. God hates sin. Sin separates us from God. "But your iniquities have separated between you and your God, and your sins have hid his face from you, that he will not hear" (Isaiah 59:2). The penalty for sin is death, but God gives us a way to live forever. "For the wages of sin is death; but the gift of God is eternal life through Jesus Christ our Lord" (Romans 6:23). Everybody is in need of salvation. Jesus says, "I am the way, the truth and the life. No one comes to the Father except through me" (John 14:6). "And this is the testimony God has given us eternal life, and this life is in His Son. He who has the Son has life; he who does not have the Son of God does not have life" (1 John 5:11-12). "That is you confess with you mouth "Jesus is Lord" and believe in your heart that God raised him from the dead, you will be saved, for it is with your heart that you believe and are justified. And it is with your mouth that you confess and are saved" (Romans 10:9-10). Jesus is the bridge to God.

Imagine, eternal life, existing forever and forever with all of Gods creation in his Kingdom. God gives us a way to eternal life in Heaven by having simple faith. Faith in Jesus Christ. We do things we shouldn't. Jesus took the punishment for those things. We believe Jesus died for us and was raised from the dead three days later. We are going to die, death is the remedy and penalty for sin, but we are going to be raised to eternal life in new bodies because of our faith in Jesus Christ. Once we have faith in Jesus, we have the desire to obey God.

God is pleased when people trust him and have faith in him. He blesses those who trust him. The Bible shows how God is pleased with faith. It seems that faith can be measured since Jesus said in Matthew 17:20, "And Jesus said unto them, Because of your unbelief: for verily I say unto you, If ye have faith as a grain of mustard seed, ye shall say unto this mountain, Remove hence to yonder place; and it shall remove; and nothing shall be impossible unto you."

God has an eternal program. All his creation is for His goals for His kingdom. God wants your faith. God has a purpose for you. Your life is more meaningful than you know.

Life's purpose

You were created by God for a purpose. You will experience and witness good and bad and will constantly have to choose between the good and the bad. There is Satan who tempts you and wants you to do bad things and doesn't want you to have eternal life in Heaven with God. Good always wins over evil. God had created a magnificent being named Lucifer long before people were created. There came a time when Lucifer thought he could be better than God and he became evil and became Satan. God allows Satan to tempt people so people can make a choice. God wants you to choose Him and offers blessings to those who have faith. God gives us a way to heaven through the blood of Jesus Christ as he forgives our sins, as we believe in Jesus. God created all this, everything you know of and much much more. God created everything, including your body, spirit and soul. "For everything comes from God alone. Everything lives by His power and everything is for His glory" (Romans. 11:36).

"You will seek me and find Me when you seek Me with all your heart" (Jerem. 29:13). God created us humans in these bodies for a purpose, for His purpose. He wants you in his family. You need to know your existence is for God's purpose. Read *By Divine Design* by Michael Pearl. Then read *The Purpose Driven Life* by Rick Warren. God loves you. God provides truth in the Bible. "All scripture is God-breathed and it is useful for teaching, rebuking, correcting and training in righteousness, so that the man of God may be thoroughly equipped for every good work" (2 Tim. 3:16-17).

If you choose the bad opposite of the character traits (ex. laziness instead of hardworking, disobedience instead of obedience, lying instead of telling the truth), you are giving Satan some control. Satan will tempt you to follow a modern day flesh pleasing seeking life. "Resist the devil and he will flee from you, draw near to God and He will draw near to you" (Heb. 4:6). Pray to God for the truth. Spend your time drawing toward God.

Be joyful. Enjoy all the things God gives you – pretty grass, flowers, trees, rivers and ponds, a home, food your family members and your friends etc… "In addition to all this, take up the shield of Faith with which you can extinguish all the flaming arrows of the evil one" (Ephesians 6:16).

Remember that God is more concerned in your character development than He is in your comfort in these bodies whenever you ask why bad things happen to good people. "God can use sorrow in our lives to help us turn away from sin and seek salvation" (2 Cor. 7:10). Some people only draw near to God when tragic things happen, otherwise they wouldn't pay much attention to God. So, be thankful in everything you have and praise God for all your blessings. "I look to the Lord for help at all times, and he rescues me from danger. Turn to me, oh Lord and be merciful to me, because I am lonely and weak, relieve me of my worries" (Psalm 25:15-17). You have to trust God when things happen that you don't understand. "Trust in the Lord with all your heart and lean not upon your own understanding" (Proverbs 3:5). God wants your faith. "And we know that God causes everything to work together for the good of those who love God and are called according to his purpose for them" (Romans 8:28).

When you pray, be specific. "Ask and it will be given to you, seek and you will find, knock and the door will be opened to you" (Matt. 7:7). Pray for wisdom, knowledge, understanding, truth, good friends, solutions to problems etc… Prepare for eternity with God. "So we should fix our eyes not on what is seen, but what is unseen. For what is seen is temporary, but what is unseen is eternal" (2 Cor. 4:18). "What good is it to gain the whole world, yet forfeit your soul" (Matt. 16:26). "Whatever you do, do it as if you were for working for the Lord, not for man, since you know that you will receive an inheritance from the Lord as a reward. It is the Lord Christ you are serving" (Col. 3:23-24). Remember, "For nothing is impossible with God" (Luke 1:37). When you feel you can't go on any longer, remember, "I can do all things through Christ who strengthens me" (Php 4:13). Think about God all day, every day in everything that you do. Talk with God all throughout the day. Share all your thoughts with God. You will grow to view God as your loving Father and sovereign King, your best friend, your comforter, your rock. "The Lord is my rock, and my fortress, and my deliverer; my God, my strength, in whom I will trust; my buckler, and the horn of my salvation, and my high tower" (Psalms 18:2).

You are God's creation. God created you for His purpose. "Surrender your whole being to Him to be used for righteous purposes" (Romans 6:13).

Does God have a will for us? Yes! God wills for us to obey Him and follow His directions. God wills for us to have eternal life in His Kingdom. God gives us a way.

Scientific evidence

I have always greatly appreciated science. Many people I have known had trouble believing that the Bible is the truth. Some people claim there is no God. And of course there are numerous different "religions" or "beliefs" in the whole world. Can God's existence be proven scientifically? A man named Lee Strobel who used to not believe in God, has provided scientific evidence that God exists in his book and DVD *The Case for a Creator: A Six-Session Investigation of the Scientific Evidence That Points toward God* (2005). Ben Stein is a well-known actor, writer, and commentator on political, social and economic issues. He has publicly denounced the theory of evolution. In his documentary *Expelled: No Intelligence Allowed* (2008), he examines the criticisms that exist in today's scientific field towards people and journalists who have the perspective of Intelligent Design in science. There are websites such as http://www.doesgodexist.org that provides scientific evidence that God does exist and that the Bible is His Word. The conviction is that all men can logically, and rationally believe in God.

Can the existence and importance of Jesus Christ be scientifically proven? In the film *The Case for Christ* by Lee Strobal (2007), he retraces his spiritual journey from atheism to faith, examining several questions. How reliable is the New Testament? Does evidence exist for Jesus outside the Bible? Is there any reason to believe the resurrection was an actual historical event?

I can't provide all the scientific evidence that God exists and the Bible is the truth in this chapter. I can encourage you to research for yourself and examine the sources. I am not trying to force my beliefs on anyone. It is up to the individual what choices they make. I want you to know how I found meaning, purpose and joyfulness. You can search for yourself for the truth.

Recommended readings and resources

- The Holy Bible
- *Swordsearcher Bible Software* http://shop.nogreaterjoy.org/product_info.php/products_id/277; it includes helpful commentaries, dictionaries, greek and Hebrew aids, 19 Bibles in the Textus Receputus line and other books that aid in a person to understand the Bible.
- *By Divine Design* by Michael Pearl (2009)
- *The Purpose Driven Life: What on Earth am I Here for* by Rick Warren (2007)
- *Good and Evil* by Michael Pearl (2006)
- *30 Days to Understanding the Bible* by Max Anders (2005)
- www.nogreaterjoy.org for numerous audio CDs, books and DVDs to aid in your understanding of the Bible
- Fire Fighters for Christ www.firefighters.org for audio CDs to aid in principles based on the Bible
- *The Case for a Creator: A Six-Session Investigation of the Scientific Evidence That Points toward God* by Lee Strobel (2005). (Book and DVD)
- *Expelled: No Intelligence Allowed* by Ben Stein (2008). (DVD)
- *The Case for Christ* by Lee Strobal (2007). (DVD)
- http://www.doesgodexist.org

References

Pearl, M. (1998). *By Divine Design.* The Church at Cane Creek, 1000 Peal Road Pleasantville TN 37033. *The Holy Bible.* King James Version

Information summarized in this chapter came from information, understanding and experience acquired through prayer, experiences God provided to answer questions, listening to and reading numerous Bible commentaries and Bible study. The sources in which much of the information was acquired came from the recommended readings and resources.

Chapter 10

Solutions for Girls and Women

In this chapter I list and describe many life issues that girls and women face and I offer insight, encouragement, advice, solutions and suggestions. These life issues include: academics and education, peer pressure, growing up, body image, deciding on whether or not to join social cliques, disappointment of not meeting expectations, intense emotions, frustrating experiences and stress management, discerning who can be trusted, structuring time, choosing a career, dating, attending baby and bridal showers, marriage, sex, pregnancy, motherhood, money management, health and food, time management, self accountability, overcoming problems, death, character development and quality of life. The advantages and disadvantages of telling others that you have Asperger's are also discussed in this chapter.

Academics and education

Academics and education are two separate things. Academics are studies related to school or college such as reading, math, science or social studies. Many people with Asperger's have excesses and deficits when it comes to academics. This simply means that they may be extremely good at one subject while struggling in another. Some care deeply about their grades and do whatever it takes to make good grades. Others don't care about their grades at all, even if they have the potential to make good grades. I was good at math but struggled with reading, especially reading comprehension. When I look back at my school career, I do wish I had paid much more attention than I did. If you are aware that you don't pay much attention in school, try to give more effort and see what you have been missing. You may be surprised at how much you enjoy learning. If you are unable to pay attention because you just aren't interested, this is much harder. Try to reward yourself after class for paying attention. For example, if you like a certain treat or an activity like playing a computer game, say to yourself that only when you pay attention in school you can have your treat or special activity. Keep in mind this takes self discipline.

If you are really struggling in a subject, don't feel embarrassed to ask your teacher or tell your parent that you need extra help. Everybody needs help in some areas. Getting on-to-one help can be beneficial. I am happy that I asked one of my English teachers for help. She spent two hours showing me how to write an essay. The help she gave me helped me to write good essays in college. If you have a subject that you are really good at, allow yourself to enjoy your talent and think of ways to use that talent to help others or create and invent something.

Making good grades doesn't necessarily mean that you are becoming well educated. A well-educated person learns how to learn anything they want. Becoming educated means learning skills such as computer skills, sewing, money management, self accountability, people and social skills, how to help others, writing, cooking or gardening. Many life skills are not taught in school so it is important to learn what you can when you have the opportunity. Well-educated people know exactly how to find information they need and have a lifelong desire to continuously acquire knowledge. Learn about medicine and health. Learn how to be a good spouse and a good parent. Learn how to effectively manage money and time. Learn how to build and fix things. Learn how to solve problems. Learn how heal your body when it gets sick. Learn how to solve a plumbing problem when it happens. Learn how to cook nutritious meals. Learn how to effectively clean a house without using harmful chemicals. Learn how to plant and grow a garden of vegetables and fruits. Learn how to be self-sufficient. Learn anything and everything that interests you. You may be interested in sea life, the planets, computers, art, music, sewing or how things are made. And teach others who want to learn those things as well. There are libraries everywhere full of books. There is the Internet to search. There are bookstores and online bookstores. Finding information is now easier than ever. Learn how to truly improve quality of life. Remember, you are here on earth to prepare for eternal life. I believe out of all the books ever written, the Bible is your best educational source.

Peer pressure

Peer pressure is when other people try to get you to behave in a way that is acceptable to them. Peer pressure happens to all people, especially teens and young adults. However, girls with Asperger's often times desire to be accepted so they may be willing to do what is expected of them by peers in order to feel like they are fitting in. I'd rather not have people as friends if they would only accept me if I did what they wanted me to. It is not "cool" to go against your convictions and engage in immoral behavior just so you think you are accepted. If you have already been pressured by your peers to do something and you are still doing it, then stop. Focus on the people that love you as you are. If you are lonely then look around and carefully observe others. There is always someone else who doesn't seem to have a friend and they would love to have you as a friend. Don't do things that are wrong just so the others will accept you.

If you haven't already been pressured to do something you feel is wrong, prepare yourself for what you will do and say when it does happen. Imagine another peer coming up to you offering you a cigarette. What will you do and what will you say? You can simple say, "No thank you." If your peer continues to persuade you with words like "Come on, everybody is doing it and you will be like one of us." You can say something like, "not everybody is doing it and you don't have to do it either," then walk away.

Growing up

Growing up is hard for anyone to do, and even more so for girls with Asperger's. I remember when I was 11 and looking at pictures of myself as a little girl wishing I were little again. I hated the way my body was changing - with my hips getting so wide. I didn't want to do the things that preteens did, such as shaving my legs or underarms or starting my period.

I really didn't want to start wearing a bra. I didn't like it but I came to the point in time where I realized I had no choice in the matter. I was going to grow up and become a woman. I wish I wouldn't have allowed myself to be feeling so embarrassed. It is normal and natural. When I finally accepted this, things began to get much better.

By the time I was 16, I was really happy to get my drivers license. Growing up after that was not so bad. It could be fun. Instead of wishing for the past, I began to become eager to see what would come next in life. Graduation, college, career, dating, marriage and having children. Instead of being unhappy with growing and change, I began to do just the opposite, embrace every moment in life, time is precious, enjoy it and make the most out of it.

Concerns with the body

It's typical for girls and women alike to voice concerns for their body. I have heard so many complaints, such as "I'm so fat," "My ears stick out to far," "My nose is too long," "I wish my hair was straight instead of curly," "My hips stick out too far," "My breasts are too small," "My thighs are too large," or "My lips are too skinny." Girls are concerned with how they look, how they perceive themselves and how they think other people perceive them. There are many reasons for this, one of them being the advertisement of skinny models dolled up in layers of makeup and hairspray. Other reasons include thinking they should say those things because other girls expect them to say them, or maybe because they are truly unhappy with what they see in themselves. So many girls I have known are incredibly concerned with their body weight. Girls think that skinnier is prettier. I remember praying to God to make me naturally skinny so I wouldn't have to diet excessively like some girls did to be thin, because I enjoyed eating. Well, eating is normal and necessary and of course we are all going to enjoy it.

Things become a big problem when girls avoid eating altogether or cause themselves to vomit after they eat. They may lose weight, but they are not happy with themselves. Eighteen to 23 percent of girls with anorexia have Asperger's (Attwood, 2007). In reality, starving the body from food slows down the body's natural metabolism rate and can cause increased weight gain later in life. Making yourself throw up messes up the enamel on your teeth. Using real logic and real knowledge, you will find out that eating numerous small meals a day speeds up the metabolism (the process your body uses to digest food and use it for energy), and therefore you're more likely to have an ideal body weight later in life. You want to be healthy and happy with yourself. Learn about healthy eating. Eat all natural foods throughout the day, maintain a healthy metabolism, and get some exercise and feel good about yourself. There are just too many girls unhappy with their bodies and this doesn't have to be. You can choose not to be unhappy with your body.

Instead of focusing on what you don't like about your body, focus on what you do like. Do you like the color of your eyes? The color or texture of your hair? The softness of your skin? The pretty feet or toes you have? Your sweet smile and straight teeth? Don't obsess with what you don't like. Be happy and accept yourself. It's your choice.

Deciding whether or not to join social cliques mainstream

Carefully observe the other people your age. What are they doing? What do they talk about? Do you really want to be like them? Do they meet your expectations? Are they good enough for you? Do you enjoy being yourself? Please know that you don't have to be like everybody else.

When I was reading all the available, yet few, resources on girls and Asperger's, I came across a very interesting article written for girls with Asperger's in high school by a typical girl, Lisa Island (2006). Apparently in high school there are "unspoken teen social rules and expectations of peers." As I read the article, for the first time in my life, I was able to understand the "social code." I could have really used the information in that article when I was in high school. However, I am glad I made the choice during my senior to be myself, focus on the people who did like me and befriend the other kids who had few friends. If I had read this article in high school, I probably wouldn't have attempted to make friends with the foreign exchange students and the new students. Why? Apparently typical girls are very sensitive to their image of whom they talk to and sensitive to how others perceive them.

Making friends prior to upper middle school and high school takes a different method than making friends at younger ages. I made my best friends before high school and made many nice friends in college and after college. When I got to high school I came to the harsh realization that I just didn't know how to make any more friends. By the time I was a senior I made the connection that that was probably because all the other girls already had friends and they didn't need or want anymore. That assumption was absolutely false. Girls want to have many friends and the more friends they have, the more secure they feel. However, they are very insecure about how their current friends perceive them if they make friends with people outside their social clique. Here is what Lisa Island (2006) in her article "Advice on Friendship, Bulling and Fitting in" says about making friends in high school.

"Making a new friend is making more than just a single friend. Girls travel in packs and have a group mentality. Most typical girls have more than one friend, so a girl with Asperger's needs to be wary of fitting in with the group structure her new friend already belongs to. The easiest friendship to make would be making friends with a girl who does not have any other friendship commitments, but that is a more rare situation."

This explains to me why it was so difficult for me to make friends in high school. It is nice to have this clearly explained. Lisa Island continues on "Multiple Friends to Befriend."

"More often, a girl with Asperger's new friend will already belong to an existing social group, a clique that she will have to learn to navigate. Girls are insecure about losing friends and when a girl with Asperger's suddenly joins the clique, peers wonder how this will change their role in the group structure."

Maybe this explains why so many girls in high school ignore girls who seem different – not because they don't like a girl but because they are afraid they may lose their other friends if they are seen with a girl who is perceived as weird. Lisa Island said "peers do not want to be associated with 'the girl in the grandma glasses' or the 'wolf lover girl.' When other kids make fun of different kids, it is probably to do it in front of their friends and be more accepted by their clique; otherwise they probably wouldn't do it. Apparently, it really matters to teens what those in their clique think of them, and it seems they may even change themselves for peer acceptance. Why can't people just accept people as they are? Where did this social clique thing come from anyway?

This all seems so ridiculous to me now that I am out of college, married and have children, but if I were in high school reading this article, I probably would have taken it very seriously. I spent most of my time in high school trying to figure out the complex social code and never succeeded at it. I am glad I didn't succeed because I know that all those people I befriended who didn't have any friends were grateful for my friendship. If I had read this article years ago, I would have felt self conscious about talking with the other "different" kids with all the typical teens being so "insecure" about hanging out with people perceived as different. Maybe this is why it was so hard for me to fit in with other social groups because they all saw me as friends with the different kids. The more I think about it, the more it seems like the typical kids are the more insecure ones than the kids with Asperger's. Knowledge of the 'social code' causes insecurity. All people tend to care on some level what others think of them. Typical girls seem to care greatly, while I tended to care only somewhat. The main thing I cared about was what other people thought of me not having any friends at all. I didn't care who I was seen with, I just wanted to be seen with somebody.

Then there is the social hierarchy. Lisa Island explains that there is the popular/elite group whose teen members do the most admired activities such as football, cheerleading and whoever belongs to this popular group has what the other teens at school want. She explains that girls in this group follow the latest fashion, makeup trends and have easy social skills.

Lisa Island explains that below the popular group, there is the middle/mainstream group who are generally liked or just blend in with everyone else. Then there is the unique and unusual group who are involved in activities that other groups perceive as unpopular. Those in this group may be bullied.

Everybody has a choice and freedom to set goals. If you want to be in the popular group, then you will have to work your way up to it and learn how the popular kids behave, socialize and what activities they participate in. This sounds so crazy to me but Lisa Island mentions, "Typical peers have an extreme sensitivity to the popularity hierarchy and when a girl with Asperger's upsets the system by attempting to befriend beyond her limits of popularity, it is seen as inappropriate, as though she were upsetting a social law." Apparently, the social law is something typical teens just know, it is not written down or explained. Lisa Island did a great job of writing it down in a very organized easy to understand manner. Although I feel I disagree with this "social code," it is what it is.

When I was in high school I figured out that there were different cliques – such as the popular kids, the goody two shoes, the nerds etc. But I never made the connection that these cliques were in a hierarchy. Funny how the "popular" kids didn't want to talk to anybody else outside their "clique" and the reason being that they didn't want to be seen with unpopular kids. It seems to me that "popular" kids would have been the most secure, best role model and more likely to accept other people as friends if they were truly at the top of the hierarchy. Well, the Bible does say "And, behold, there are last which shall be first, and there are first which shall be last" (Luke 13:30).

So, there you have some understanding of the "social code." You can learn to do anything. You can learn to be a part of the mainstream and which social group you want to be in. You can also choose to be happy with the friends you do have and care less about what those in the cliques think of you. Do you really want to be in the popular group who forbids you to talk to other kids outside of the clique? You may learn to dress the way they want you to, wear make up the way they expect you to, style your hair to their standards and participate in the popular activities. You may get attention and a positive response; you may not. I don't know if the peers will accept you for who they think you are, or for who you really are. It is your choice. You can read Lisa Island's full article in the book *Asperger's and Girl's*. When you make your choice, think whether or not you will be happy with it or regret it 10 years from now, or even 20 or 30 years from now. What really matters in life?

Disappointment of not meeting expectations or pleasing others

I used to get so disappointed with myself when I made my parents or friends unhappy. I wanted so much for them to be pleased with me. Do you feel you are always trying to do what is expected of you? I sometimes felt guilty and embarrassed of myself for being 'different." I never talked about it with my parents or even my best friends. I was so ashamed. I had feelings that they knew I was different at times, but I thought if I didn't talk about it then there was a chance they didn't recognize it. Parents have pride in their children and when their children don't achieve what they expect, parents become disappointed. I was always scared that my parents might become disappointed in me. I felt so wonderful when I showed them my straight A report card or when I pitched a good ball game because I knew that they were proud.

Now that I look back on it, I shouldn't have felt so embarrassed. I should have talked to my mother about my social difficulties. She probably would have understood. She loved me because I was her daughter. Children can't always do what their parents expect them to do. I think it is good for children to not always meet their parents' expectations because parents need to know that kids can't be perfect and that they may have purposes in life they don't understand. When I changed my college major from chemical engineering to psychology my parents voiced their disapproval. But I just had to do psychology because I was so fascinated with children who had autism. After a few years, my parents said they were proud of my major and understood why I needed it.

Kids need to be able to talk to their parents about their difficulties. If you have social difficulties or any other issues, you should talk about them. I sure wish I did and I wish that I knew of someone that was experiencing the same things I was experiencing.

Intense emotions

Lights are too bright, noises are so loud it hurts, sudden touch feels irritating, smells are too strong, and emotions are too intense. Have you ever carefully observed other people in how they express their emotions? Some people are very expressive in that they cry at church, laugh hysterically during movies, or yell at their spouse at the grocery store. Some people don't show much emotion at all. Does this mean that these people don't feel emotions? Some people are very externalized and extraverted and others are very internalized and introverted. I have observed and analyzed all the children I have worked with express their emotions. I have noticed that boys express frustration and anger more physically than girls. Children who have very expressive personalities and are very loud and talkative express their emotions more clearly and visibly. Children who are quieter and like to play by themselves are quieter with their emotions. How do you express your emotions?

When I was a young child, I had an extraverted personality but when I became aware that I was different, I became an introvert. I am still an introvert and feel very uncomfortable expressing what I am feeling with others and especially in groups. I only feel comfortable showing happiness and sadness with my immediate family and my best friends. Even then, I sometimes don't want anybody else to know how I feel so I don't show it. When my dad died, I would not let myself cry in front of anyone. I only cried at night when everybody else was asleep or when I was in the car by myself. I feel embarrassed to cry in front of other people. I think it is okay if people want to keep their emotions from other certain people. But don't try to suppress the emotion to the point where it backfires and you loose control. Let yourself feel sad.

Sometimes the intensity of emotions can become too much. Let's say that emotions can be measured on a scale from one to 10. When I am happy I usually feel happiness of a 10 and when I am sad I feel sadness of a 10. When many emotions are experienced at once and they are all at a 10, this might be too much to bear for someone who doesn't understand what those emotions are. When I was a teenager I felt multiple emotions to an intense degree. I did not know what they were but I did know that I had to do something to get the intensity down or I would explode. There were times I would lock myself in the bathroom and poke my self up and down the arms with a safety pin. The physical pain from being pricked lessened the internal pain. I stopped doing this when I discovered running and exercising. If you hurt yourself, stop doing it and find another way to lessen your emotions.

I didn't talk about my feelings to anybody and I think that talking about them would have really helped me understand them. Looking back and remembering how I felt during those times, I label the emotions confusion, anger, disappointment, frustration, anxiousness and irritation. I was confused because I didn't understand why I couldn't fit in. I was angry because I didn't understand myself and knew that nobody else understood me either. I was disappointed in myself because I didn't think I was living up to the expectations of others. I was frustrated because my efforts were not working. I was anxious about everything and I was irritated at all the intensity of emotions and sensory disturbances. Put all of these emotions together at the same time with an intensity of a 10, what is a girl to do? There are solutions to every problem – right ones and wrong ones. Hurting myself was wrong; exercising was a better solution.

There are a list of basic emotions such as happiness, sadness, joyfulness, surprise, anger, disgust, excitement, embarrassment, fear, trust, guilt, disappointment, anticipation, shock, and awe. There are more complex emotions such as pride, contentment, ungratefulness, relief, irritation, jealousy, suffering, empathy, sympathy, regret, nervousness and anxiousness. Many children I have worked with experience emotions but don't know what they are. They need help in discovering what they are feeling so they can learn to verbalize their feelings, especially when they are the type that internalize their emotions. Many girls I have worked with would externalize their emotions as young children and begin to internalize them, as they grow older. People can assume that they are not feeling anything because they are not showing their emotions. However, it can be the exact opposite of what other people assume. These girls may feel the emotions to the highest degree, but have learned to hide them.

I have been accused of being emotionless and not caring at times where I express nothing when a tragedy is being discussed. Although I understand why they would make that assumption, they are wrong. I don't know how to appropriately show certain emotions so I keep them to myself. There have been many times in life where I tried to express my emotions in the same ways I observe other people express their emotions. I can do this sometimes but other times it feels very unnatural. Many times there are multiple emotions taking place at once and I don't know which one to express. How can you express joyfulness, fear and anticipation at the same time? Then there are times where there are intense feelings that don't even have a word to describe them. How are you supposed to show that? I believe many children with autism behave in puzzling ways when they feel very intense or when they feel unrecognizable emotions. There was one little girl I worked with who would cry and scream, "I want to be happy, where is happy," over and over when she was upset.

I think that as some girls with Asperger's grow up, they realize that they are different and they become very self-conscience about how they behave and develop fear in how to express themselves as well as feelings of embarrassment for doing so. Another problem is that there are typical methods to express certain emotions. For example, a happy person smiles or laughs, a sad person cries, a surprised person opens their mouth, an empathetic person listens and hugs, and an embarrassed person becomes quiet. I think sometimes that some girls with Asperger's have difficulty expressing their emotions in the way that they think everybody else expects them to. Instead of showing empathy by listening and hugging a friend, a girl with Asperger's may show empathy by offering a solution to their problem. I also believe that since people with Asperger's have difficulty interpreting social cues, they also have difficulty interpreting emotions in others. They also may have trouble recognizing a context that would cause them to feel an expected emotion.

I think it is important that everyone learn emotional stability. This may be more difficult for girls with Asperger's because their emotions feel so intense. Practice with dealing and coping with the bright lights, loud sounds and strong smells will help with learning emotional stability. Emotional stability is not suppressing emotions; it is behaving in a stable way when you feel emotion. If you feel angry to the highest level, should you throw breakable plates on the floor? Should you hurt yourself? Would it be better to go to the room and hit pillows or maybe even run a mile or two?

I have learned to appreciate my emotions and their intensity. I greatly enjoy experiencing intense feelings of joyfulness and contentment. For emotions that signal a problem such as fear, irritation, disappointment or anger, I analyze what the problem is and search for a solution. I search the Internet, read books and ask questions. I choose a solution and apply it. If the solution I chose does not work, I continue to apply solutions until one does work. For example, a few months after I had my second child I began to feel not only extremely joyful, but also irritated. I figured out that the feelings of irritation were coming from having to keep up with the housework and laundry. The solution I applied to this problem was to put everything that needs to be done on a weekly schedule. This solution effectively solved that problem and eliminated the feelings of irritation. You never have to continue tolerating an unpleasant emotion that signals a problem. Figure out the problem, search for a solution and apply it. Be joyful and enjoy the intensity of the good emotions.

Frustrating experiences and stress management

Everyone gets frustrated at times. However, it is the method a person uses to cope with feelings of frustration and stress that needs attention as well as the behavior a person does with their feelings. What do you do when you feel frustrated and stressed? I remember having difficult schoolwork as a child and would make the assumption that there was something wrong with the teacher for assigning such dumb homework. I would get so frustrated, my concentration would shut down, I would lose the ability to think and I became angry and began yelling at it. My mom would try to help me but I was already so distracted to attend to any of it. As I grew older I learned to better manage sudden bursts of stress. When I felt a sudden rise in stress, I had to stop what I was doing and get away from it. One time I can clearly remember, I got in a big argument with one of my best friends. I felt like I was going to go crazy with the way I felt. The room was spinning, my body painfully ached and I felt like I was going to jump out of my skin. In trying to escape this horrible feeling, I went outside and began running. I ran the roads of my neighborhood for about 45 minutes. When I got back home, I felt much better and more focused. After that, my strategy for relieving stress and pain was to exercise.

Different things can cause stress depending on what stage you are in life. Schoolwork, housework, relationships and finances will cause stress. Stress management is very important in order for you to stay focused.

Something that suddenly stresses me is when one of my family members gets sick. When my son was three, he suddenly began coughing this horrible sound and I just about fainted. I learned I had to prepare myself with the understanding that my children are going to get sick sometimes. The schedule is going to change so it is important to be prepared to tolerate the change. When a family member shows signs of becoming sick I get out all the herbs and make an herbal tea for the whole family to boost their immune systems and help fight the virus. I choose the "fight" response in the "fight or flight."

Managing stress is very possible and important for you and others around you and there are books written on it. But it is likely that what works for one person many not work for another person. It is important to decide for yourself that you are going to successfully manage your stress. You can choose not to behave in certain ways when you get stressed such as yelling at other people. It is best to make this choice before you get stressed. You know what usually stresses you out, so decide for yourself how you are going to behave. Maybe you can go outside for a walk or jog, go to another room, check your email, do 50 jumping jacks or sit-ups. Do anything that will help your body stabilize the stress hormones so you can get back focused. I think it important to include in this section, for better understanding, what stress is, why do people with Asperger's experience difficulty with managing stress and what research has been done.

Stress is something that can alter the homeostatic functions of certain physiological mechanisms of the body. Stress can increase blood pressure and heart rate, cause mood to fluctuate, change a person's perspective during certain situations, alter body temperature, and causes behavior changes. The secretion of stress hormones, from the adrenal medulla increases heart rate and blood in response to excitation and/or stress. The secretion of cortisol, a glucocorticoid, for the adrenal cortex also increases heart rate and blood pressure. Here is a simple description of the complicated stress response. Basically during the stress response, the corticotropin releasing factor (CRF) from the hypothalamus is released in the brain, which triggers the pituitary gland that releases adrenocorticotrophin ACTH into the blood stream. There is an immediate rise in cortisol levels secreted from the adrenal cortex. The pancreas then releases glucagen that goes to the pituitary gland and then secretes prolactin. In response to the prolactin, the brain secretes enkephalin and the pituitary responds by secreting vasopression that increases heart rate and raises blood pressure (Sapolsky, 1998). The body possesses an elaborate feedback system for controlling cortisol secretion and regulating the amount of cortisol in the bloodstream.

Why do people on the autism spectrum get frustrated easily and experience so much stress? There are published research studies that examine cortisol levels in children with autism and similar conditions.

- A study examining salivary cortisol levels in 20 18-year-old males with Asperger's Syndrome and 18 typical males found that cortisol spiked half an hour after waking in typical males but not in the Asperger's group. This difference may be related to characteristics of the resistance to change in people with Asperger's. It appears that the Asperger's group showed an impaired cortisol awakening response (Brosnan, 2009).
- Aihara and Hashimoto (1989) found that 11 out of 14 children with autism showed an abnormal secretion rhythm of GH, PRL, TSH, cortisol, LH and FSH in comparison to the two control groups of children with ADD and children with MR.
- Fernald and Grantham-McGregor (1998) found that stunted children had higher salivary cortisol concentrations, had higher heart rates during psychological testing, exhibited enhanced cardiovascular responsivity to a physical stressor, vocalized less, were more inhibited, and were less attentive.
- Jansen and colleagues (2003) found that children with autism showed an elevated cortisol response to psychosocial stress, in contrast to MCDD children who showed a reduced cortisol response. Both groups had higher cortisol response and heart rate than the typical children.
- Richdale and Prior (1992) found that there was both an abnormal cortisol circadian rhythm and a failure to suppress

cortisol secretion in children with autism. It was also found that children with autism had cortisol hypersecretion during the day during inclusion in school, which suggests an environmental stress response.

- Tordjman and his collegues (1997) measured the blood levels of the HPA-axis hormones beta-endorphin (BE), adrenocorticotropin hormone (ACTH), and cortisol in 48 autistic children, in 16 cognitively impaired children, and in 26 normal control children. Results revealed that levels of BE and ACTH were significantly higher in the children with autism than the other groups. The autistic group had significantly higher plasma levels of BE and ACTH, and indices of acute stress response.

Some researchers have speculated that there may be a dysfunction of the pineal-hypothalamic-pituitary-adrenal axis (HPA-axis) in the brains of children with autism. The HPA axis is the neuroendocrine system that responds to stress targeting the parts of the limbic system. Physical or psychological stress activates the HPA axis, leading to increased release of cortisol and other hormones. Hoshino and colleagues (1987) found that children with infantile autism showed an abnormal diurnal rhythm for saliva cortisol. These results suggest that the negative feedback mechanism of the HPA-axis may be disturbed in autistic children. There also may be more of a dysfunction in the HPA-axis in children with more severe autism than high functioning children (Hoshino, Ohno, Murata, Yokoyama, Kaneko & Kumashiro, 1984).Chamberlain and Herman (1990) presented a biochemical model for autism that a subgroup of autistic individuals may have a hypersecretion of pineal melatonin that produces a cascade of biochemical effects including a corresponding hyposecretion of pituitary proopiomelanocortin (POMC) peptides and a hypersecretion of hypothalamic opioid peptides and serotonin (5-HT). An increase in pineal melatonin may result in hypersecretion of 5-HT in hypothalamus and blood and the hypersecretion of melatonin may inhibit the release of hypothalamic corticotrophin-releasing hormone (CRH). Hyposecretion of CRH may result in decreased release of pituitary B-endorphin (B-E) and adrenocorticotrophin hormone (ACTH). This may decrease plasma concentrations of B-E, ACTH and cortisol in in individuals with autism.

Therefore, individuals with autism may have a dysfunction in the pineal-HPA-axis which, modulates POMC and 5-HT systems of the brain.

It helps to know that there may be a physiological problem within the typical stress response that can contribute to frustration and stress. With all this in mind, approach stress management boldly, find a good method that is good for you, fight and win, and obtain emotional stability.

Discerning who can be trusted

Discerning whom you can trust is a very important skill. You can do things to test or judge whether or not you can trust a person. Don't perceive a person to be what he or she is by the way they make you feel or by the way they treat you only. Carefully observe how that person treats other people. Are they just as nice to other people as they are to you? Pay attention to how that person talks about other people. Does that person speak badly about his or her other friends? If so, then it is likely that person will speak badly of you to their other friends.

I used to feel so important when new friends would share with me their "secrets" about other people. They would tell me all the bad things about their other friends, especially when the two friends were in an argument. I thought that surely this person really likes me if she tells me her secrets. After a while I began noticing that these supposedly friends were acting like best friends with the people they were speaking badly about. That didn't make sense. Then I began to wonder if these girls told others bad things about me. Gossip is common among girls. It makes people feel good to express their dislikes, disagreements and frustrations with other people in their lives, even if they really love these people they are talking badly about. I have even caught myself doing this before, but I have made the decision not to do it because I want people to trust me. I want to trust myself. Also "These six things doth the Lord hate: yea, seven are an abomination unto Him: A proud look, a lying tongue, and hands that shed innocent blood, a heart that deviseth wicked imaginations, feet that be swift in the running to mischief, a false witness that speaketh lies, and he that soweth discord among brethren" (Proverbs 6:16-19). Take careful notice of this seventh thing. "He that soweth discord among brethren."

This is an abomination to God! Speaking badly about other people can cause the people you speak with, to perceive bad things about the person you are talking about. I remember making harsh judgments on girls that gossiped, even if I didn't know them personally. Because this is wrong and also an abomination to God, I try to refrain from speaking badly about anyone. I don't want to influence another person's perspective of another person. Be cautious of trusting people who talk badly about other people with your secrets. They will most likely tell your secrets to other people.

It can be easy to let yourself trust someone because they make you feel important or special. It's common for boys in particular to try and get you to go places like to their homes when no one is a home. They may make you feel special, and you may want to please them. But don't risk it because boys usually have sex on their minds all the time.

Girls can be unkind to you by first pretending to be your best friends. Popular girls can purposely befriend a different girl in gaining their trust so that they can later humiliate them. I remember several times having conversations with girls at school in class where we sat by each other. They really seemed to be interested in me. Then when I would see them later at lunch or after school, they would completely ignore me even if I said "hi." Of course, all this makes sense now, they didn't want their other friends seeing them talk to me. I am glad I didn't let it bother me that much.

Another thing to look for in whether you can trust a friend is to pay attention to them saying things like "Katie told me not to tell anyone, but I am going to tell you, so please don't tell anyone else." If that friend is telling you someone else's secret, then they will likely tell yours.

Structuring time

I generate feelings of fear when I think I have nothing to do. I don't like having unstructured time or days without schedules. I know many children with autism and Asperger's need to always know what is coming next on the schedule. When I was a child, I would have a lot of free time at home. I made lists of things to do for when my time became idle. I could not tolerate feelings of boredom so I tried to never allow myself to get bored.

Whenever I didn't know what was coming next I frequently referred to my list. Some of the things on my lists included reading, writing a letter or poem, playing a game, playing the piano or drawing. This always helped me with free time. Even when I was in school and began to feel bored I would write a note, draw a picture or daydream. I even taught myself to write with my left hand.

When I got in high school, there was very little free time. There was school all day and multiple extra-curricular activities after school. I usually got home around eight p.m. on the weekdays - just in time for a late dinner followed by shower, homework and bed. I usually studied for tests early in the morning before school. On Saturdays, I typically had sports games or I spent time with my friends going to the mall or roller-skating. I loved my schedule to be this way - busy and structured.

I remained very busy in college with going to class, researching at the library, studying for exams between classes, teaching dance a few afternoons a week and working with children who had autism the rest of the time, even on weekends. I greatly enjoyed my time to be structured and filled with activities.

After having children, time became less structured and I became anxious. Babies wake up any time, there is no predictability, and it is difficult to schedule things around the baby's sleep schedule. My love for my baby helped with the anxiety. And after each child I had, I expected there to be interruptions in the schedule so that was not as such a big deal. However, structuring time was impossible on the days I was home. I developed methods to help with this such as having certain chores for certain days of the week and certain things to do in that day. It doesn't matter what time of day things get done as long as they get done that day. And if they don't all get done and there were chores left that the kids can't help with, I do them when everyone else goes to bed in order to stay on schedule.

If you feel like you are constantly trying to catch up with the time, be assured that you can create your own schedule to structure your time. First list all the things you have to do and all the things you want to do. Fill them all in on the calendar and refer to the calendar every day. Relax and don't worry about what you have to do. If it is not scheduled for that day, don't worry about it.

Choosing a Career

If you haven't already succeeded in a career, then you might have in mind what you might want to do. Many children with autism I have worked with have parents who are in the engineering and computer science careers, both men and women. If you do not have any ideas as of what you want to do, consider the field of autism. Because, on average, most girls desire a career helping people, you may want to do something that would contribute to improving the lives of others. I suggest for young women with Asperger's to consider helping children with autism because they have an insight others do not have which will give them advantage of better understanding the children and applying appropriate individual therapy techniques. Dr. Tony Attwood wrote in a letter,

"I have known a number of women with Asperger's syndrome who have decided to take their knowledge on Asperger's syndrome to a level where they are able to work with and support children who have a diagnosis of an autism spectrum disorder. A number of my colleagues have Asperger's syndrome and I think that they have a remarkable insight into Asperger's syndrome that can be exceptionally valuable for children with Asperger's syndrome as there can be degree of real empathy that those with Asperger's syndrome recognize and the suggestions made have greater authenticity and credibility."

There are many different ways you can help children with autism. You can become a special education teacher, a speech and language pathologist, and occupational therapist, a music therapist, an ABA (Applied Behavior Analysis) therapist, a behavior analyst, a clinical psychologist or a DAN (Defeat Autism Now) medical doctor. I had an incredible interest in autism and I loved to see the children make progress. I began as an ABA therapist and worked my way up to becoming a behavior analyst so I could also help the entire family as well as the child. Whatever career you decide will need a certain education path. For some, like being a teacher or music therapist a BA is required. Other occupations like speech and language pathologists and behavior analysts a MA is needed. Medical doctors and clinical psychologists will require a PhD. If you don't want to go to college at all, then consider being an ABA therapist.

You may want to be what I consider the most important career of a lifetime, a stay at home mother. I believe being a mother is by far the most important job on earth. Investing your time in your children is the best investment you can ever make. Although it may be the hardest job, it sure is the most rewarding. It may not pay money, but it pays in character development, joyfulness, and emotionally stability. Being a stay at home mom means learning all the jobs. You will be a nurse, a counselor, a behavior therapist, a teacher and a chef all at once. The things you can do when being a stay at home mom are unlimited. Although I am a "behavior analyst for children with autism" because of my educational credentials and experience with children who have autism, I am "mom" the majority of my time. I get to be a nurse, a teacher, an all-natural cook, an herbalist, a researcher, a writer, a photographer, a musician, an artist, a gardener, a naturopath, and a caretaker.

If you have no idea what you want to do, here is a summary of Liane Holliday Willey's suggestions in her book *Pretending to Be Normal* to:

1. Make a list of all the things you enjoy studying, talking about and actually doing.
2. Make a list of your skills and abilities.
3. Explore the possibility of turning one of those interests in to a career.

Research your career options, the sensory elements of the job's physical environment, the interpersonal expectations, the schedule, and the schooling and training necessary. You will need interview skills, and you can learn those by role play and learning non-verbal communication strategies. You can make a list of possible career choices. You can learn how to make your job a success with special accommodation requests (such as wearing ear plugs or sunglasses etc.). Always give your best effort, always let your employer know if you can't make it to work, never underestimate your own potential, do everything to improve and increase knowledge, be patient with other people, try to find employment that holds your interest, try not to quit a job without giving it some time and show appreciation.

Foreword by Liane Holliday Willey

Boys and dating

The rules for dating are very culturally sensitive. Some cultures embrace arranged marriages. In some places, the bride doesn't meet her groom until the wedding day. Some require that the boy and girl get to know each other by participating in family activities only and when they decide if they want to get married, they do so within a week or so. Many societies are more lenient and allow their teens to date alone but have rules. For example, no dating until the child reaches a certain age and when you go on a date, it is required to return by a specific time. Dating begins at different ages in different cultures.

Many people think that falling in love or feeling that you are 'in love' with a person is what you need to make the choice whether or not to date someone, continue to date someone or get married. Although the media advertises this, this is not necessarily true. I was "in love" with a boy and accepted his marriage proposal. But with careful thought and prediction of the future based on his character, I decided it best not to marry him. I understand that no man is perfect. I wanted a man who would be a wonderful father to my children and this boy probably would not have been a decent father. I allowed intelligence to overpower emotions. Before getting married to my husband, I examined carefully how he treated other people, other children and his family members. I was very happy with what I saw. He treats our children and me the way I had predicted.

It is very important to be able to judge a person's character and decide on if you want to be with that person the rest of your life. When I was a teenager, I was disappointed in all the divorces I was seeing and all the unhappy marriages. I was determined to have a happy marriage and seek the solutions to make it work. Feeling like you are "in-love" with a boy is a very nice feeling to have that can be extremely powerful. But you must use logic and intelligence when it comes to dating. Pay attention to how the boy treats his friends, his family and what his characteristics are. Pay attention to all the other married couples who got married because they felt like they were "in-love" with each other. The current divorce rate is 40 to 50 percent (Stanly, 2003). This rate has nearly doubled since the 1930s. This means that out of every 10 marriages, four or five of them end divorce. Divorce can be one of the most stressful events in a person's life.

It is important for girls with Asperger's to date according to the type of boy they would want to be with all the time, maybe for the rest of their lives. Date boys they feel comfortable with and can someone she be herself. Don't try to make yourself someone you are not just to get a boy to like you. You can't be fake forever. I remember having a crush on a boy in high school that wouldn't have anything to do with me. I decided that I was going to win him over so I participated in the activities he did, wore extra make-up and wore tight blue jeans. It was exhausting doing these things that I didn't like. I hated make-up and tight jeans. He showed a little interest in me but that is when I observed that he flirted with many of the other girls. Although I loved the attention I received from him, I knew I couldn't continue changing myself to win his heart.

Dating is not always easy and can be awkward at times. There are things you can do and things you can avoid to make it easier. Below is a list of points to consider.

Points to consider:

- Sometimes you may have intense feelings for a boy but he may not feel the same way about you.
- Sometimes a boy you are dating will break up with you and this may break your heart. Although it may seem like the end of the world, allow intellect to help you cope.
- You might break the heart of another boy who really likes you. It is very important that you clearly communicate to him that you need to break it off. Don't just stop talking to him assuming that he will finally get the hint.
- You may be vulnerable to the wild boys who have excellent social skills who want sex. They may tell you things and make you feel accepted and special so you will feel like you are in love with them and possibly lose your virginity. If you do give them sex, they are likely to break up with you soon after because he met his goal and is ready for a new one.
- Don't avoid a boy who is interested in you just because he is not popular and you are afraid of what other people will think of you if they see you with him. He might be a true gentleman. I have noticed popular boys to be more

conceited and selfish while many unpopular, quiet boys are more considerate of others.
- You don't find your one true love by being fake. You find him by living your life and being the best version of yourself that you can (Myers, 2006).
- When you are looking to meet new people, dance clubs and parties may not be the best places to go. They are "sensory nightmares" (Myers, 2006). Also being in situations where people are judged solely on outer appearances and social finesses is not good. A local park, fitness center, library, museum or church may be ideal places for girls with Asperger's to meet boys.
- Don't let any friends or any family members pressure you about dating boys that they prefer you to date. You want to be happy with the potential husband you spend your time with.
- When getting to know a boy, you can use learned friendship skills to have conversations. There is give and take. You don't want to talk excessively for 45 minutes about yourself with eagerness for the boy to get to know you. Ask him questions and let him talk about himself and pay attention to what he says so that you can get to know him. Males like to talk about themselves and they like to be admired.
- Consider tips for conversation.
- Pay attention to the things a boy is interested in. A relationship where there are shared interests, similar philosophies and values are more likely to succeed and make better marriages.
- Maintain good hygiene and dress appropriately when interacting with boys. Don't overdo it by putting on too much perfume, wearing too much makeup or wearing a skirt that is too short.
- Be optimistic, ask questions and answer questions honestly.

Marriage

What is the purpose of dating? The answer to this question will be different for many people. I believe it is getting to know someone to see if he is a good candidate for marriage. You have a choice whether or not to get married and have children.

If you would like to get married, understand that you will live the rest of your life with your husband. This may be the most important choice of your lifetime. It will affect your quality of life and it will also affect the character of your children. Pay attention to the character in a potential husband. If he treats you wonderfully and you have feelings for him, this is not the only reason to marry. Pay attention to how he treats other people. This is the way you and your children will be treated at home. Pay attention to how he reacts in stressful situations and how he solves problems. Does he lose his temper easily? Is he lazy or is he hardworking? Is he responsible? Is he considerate, honest, loyal, self controlled, thankful and authentic? Is he faithful to God? Will this man be a good influence on your children; love your children and train them up as they should go? Does this man even want children and if so, then how many? Will this man be a good provider for the family? "Charm is deceitful and beauty is passing, but a woman who fears the Lord, she shall be praised" (Proverbs 31:30. You will have to use intelligence and good judgment when deciding on a person to marry.

If you get married, be a good wife. "Who can find a virtuous woman? For her price is far above rubies" (Proverbs 31:10). Tell your husband before you get married that you have Asperger's and help him understand what it is and how you personally embrace the characteristics. He will most likely appreciate you for your special talents and gifts. Follow God's directions on how to be a good spouse and you will have a heavenly marriage. Don't hold feelings of pride because you think you are too good to be and act the way God created you to be. Love and cherish your husband. Smile and be joyful towards your husband. Don't allow your heart to feel bitterness. Do fun things with your husband. Your husband should be your best friend. When your husband makes a mistake (he will make many of them), don't hold grudges. Accept that your husband will not be perfect but delight in your husband's good character. "Accept one another, then, just as Christ accepted you, in order to bring praise to God" (Romans 15:7). When you get married to a man, you are rejecting all other men for the rest of your life. It is important that you model a good relationship for your children to see. You want them to want what you have in a marriage when it is time for them to marry.

All marriages will encounter problems. There are hundreds of well-written books on making a marriage better. I have read numerous of these books, but it can sometimes be difficult to put apply the advice in real life. There are books where it takes both the man and the woman to participate in the activities. When I began reading books that teach women how to be good wives, my marriage became amazing. The little changes in my behavior caused changes in my husband's behavior. You want a wonderful, joyful, happy and successful marriage. This is very possible!

Not all girls on the autism spectrum want to get married. They may find their meaning in life through other things like career. For example, Temple Grandin (2006) who has high functioning autism says,

I have been reasonably happy even though I am totally celibate. Celibacy avoided a lot of complicated social situations. Sometimes I realize I am missing experiences that other people have, but I keep myself super busy doing many interesting things. My lifestyle is not for everyone with Asperger's. It was easier for me because the brain circuits that made my friend Carol swoon over the Beatles are just not hooked up in me. Others on the spectrum want to get married and be emotionally related. It all depends which circuits get connected.

Getting married is your choice. You can determine what will make your life meaningful. If you greatly desire to raise children, then marriage is a must.

Sex

Most schools have some sort of sex education and teach about sexually transmitted diseases. If you have questions don't hesitate to ask your parents or to find books on the subject. Television shows, movies, magazines and other media sources teach that if you feel like you're "in love" with the person then it is okay to have sex as long as you use protection. This is incorrect information. Don't have sex with anybody before you get married. The first time you have sex should be on your wedding night with your husband. This is what sex was designed to be for. It doesn't have to be complicated. God designed sex for one woman and one man. Make the decision now that you will not have sex until you are married. It will be so worth it if you do. Don't allow yourself to get in a situation where you are alone with a man and he has the opportunity to try to get you to have sex. If you are not married and have already had sex, then you can stop and wait until you marry. It is your choice. If you are married and are having troubles in your marriage with sex, there are many books that can help you with the particular problem you are having.

Pregnancy

If you desire to have children, pregnancy can be a wonderful experience. It can also be a difficult experience if you experience morning sickness, especially during the first few months. The nausea and vomiting usually goes away by the fourth month of pregnancy. It is a delightful experience to feel the baby moving inside. Be sure not to eat tuna fish (good source of mercury), have dental amalgams (50% percent mercury) put in your teeth or take a vaccine with thimerosal (mercury preservative) in it. Ask your friends and family members for references on a good doctor. When you decide on a doctor, be sure to go to every scheduled visit. Hearing the baby's heart beat for the first time is a breathtaking experience. And seeing the baby on the ultrasound may cause you to perceive time to momentarily stop.

There is a common problem that girls with Asperger's will face during pregnancy. The heightened sensory experience you already have will be further heightened during pregnancy. When I was pregnant with my children, smells were much stronger, lights appeared brighter, noises were more distracting and I couldn't stand to be touched at all. The worst were the smells. The smell of deodorant was unbearable for me. I couldn't tolerate the smell of shampoo, dish soap, toothpaste, lotion or perfume. I had trouble cleaning the kitchen and bathrooms because I couldn't stand the smell of any cleaners. I used baking soda to clean and sometimes would make a very diluted formula of rubbing alcohol and water. I couldn't tolerate the smell of certain foods such as salad dressings or garlic. It was best just to eliminate them altogether during pregnancy. The increase in my senses diminished after childbirth, and my senses went back to the way they were.

Motherhood

Having and raising children is the most precious blessing of a lifetime (in my opinion). Be a good parent. Use your talents and gifts in your parenting. Spend time with your children, read to them everyday, play with them and teach them how to do everything. Teach them responsibility and how to work. When they are one they can clean up their toys, and when they are two they can help put dirty laundry in the washing machine. They can also sort silverware and clean the floor and cabinets with a rag and soapy water. The older they grow, the more they can do. Teach them moral character. Be a good model for them. Model correct behavior and teach self-control. Teach them about the Bible and Jesus. Teach them how to share Jesus with others.

Your children are yours and it is your responsibility to teach and raise them. You are never too busy for your children. They always come first and they are the most important part of your life. Love them, laugh with them, color with them, play Playdoh, cook with them, take nature walks with them and teach them how to be good spouses and good parents. Pretend play with them, swim with them, build sand castles, have tea parties, jump on the trampoline, play tag and play charades. Enjoy your children. Smile and laugh all the time. The way you teach them, model behavior for them, spend time with them will contribute to their character when they grow up and how they raise their own children. "Train up a child in the way he should go: and when he is old, he will not depart from it" (Proverbs 22:6).

It is possible that your children will have some of the characteristics of Asperger's. You know what characteristics to look for but don't get discouraged if they have a few of the characteristics. You have the advantage of knowing how to help them with any social problems or sensory issues. My kids have some of the characteristics but to a very mild degree. I took careful measures to prevent them from developing the severe expression of autism (discussed in last chapter). You can do the same. There is a truth and God will reveal it to you. Simply seek and ask Him.

Attending baby showers and bridal showers

Baby and bridal showers are frequent and common social parties for all women. It seems there is always someone in the family or a friend that is about to have a baby or getting married. Girls like to celebrate these special occasions by having parties. I have always generated a great deal of anxiety about going to these parties because I knew there would be a lot of girls and a lot of loud socializing. I could very easily choose not to go, however, my loyalty to my friend or my family member the shower is for gives me desire to go. My heart still beats rapidly as I walk up to the house where the party is, but once I am there and greet my friend and eat refreshments, everything is fine. Although I may leave the event a little early, it's important that I made a presence. If I don't know anyone else at the party, I look around at the other girls and observe what they are doing. I find a girl who is not talking with anyone and say, "Hi, I'm Kristi, the bride is my cousin, how do you know the bride?" This usually generates a little conversation. This makes me feel like people aren't judging me for not talking to anyone and it probably makes the other person feel good too that they have someone to talk to.

Money Management

Managing money is one of people's biggest problems in this world. Credit cards are not good. Name brand items aren't necessary. You can buy a pair of store brand jeans for a fifth of the price of name brand; better yet you can buy a pair of name brand jeans at a yard sale for a dollar or two. Don't feel the need to impress other people with expensive materialistic things. Spend your money wisely; don't waste it. Buy used cars instead of brand new ones. Pray for wisdom. You will need money for your needs but don't get fixated on money or love money. "Keep you lives from the love of money and be content with what you have, because God has said, "Never will I leave you, never will I forsake you" (Hebrews 13:5). "How much better to get wisdom than gold, to chose understanding rather than silver" (Proverbs 16:16).

I am not here to tell you exactly how to spend your hard-earned money. There are experts for that such as Dave Ramsey, a financial expert and author of *Financial Peace*. However, you need to know that if you waste your money then you will have less of it. Getting into debt is not a good idea and can cause a lot of short-term and long-term stress. If you want something really badly, then you can save your money for it. Create a budget, and include all expenses and monetary goals. Keep track of what you buy and add it up at the end of each month to see exactly where your money is going. You might be surprised to find that most of your money is being spent on going out to eat.

Health and food

Many people with Asperger's have food allergies and are sensitive to extra food additives. Eliminating food allergies, as well as preservatives, artificial dyes and processed foods will make you feel better. After I gave up wheat and began eating all natural foods, I felt like I was living in a different body. The pain and inflammation in my back and abdomen went away. However, at times of great stress the inflammation would come back. I try to get enough exercise to reduce the stress.

Be careful to fully trust modern day medical doctors. They mainly use conventional treatments such as antibiotics, cough suppressants made with artificial dyes and ingredients and painkillers. Emergency care is great only in times of emergencies. Learn about all the illnesses and how to treat them naturally. It is not good for the body to take unnecessary antibiotics because these kill the good bacteria in the body as well as the bad. If you have to take an antibiotic, consider taking a probiotic (good bacteria your body needs). This will help repair damage done to the body by the antibiotic. Learn about herbs and natural medicine.

Eat right in order to have a good immune system and avoid painful and terminal illnesses. Learn all about the herbs, why they are used and how to use them. For example, Yarrow is good for fevers, colds and flu. Echinacea boosts immune system. When you have a cough, make a concentrated tea of peppermint leaf, thyme, eucalyptus, Echinacea, licorice root and ginger root to loosen the mucus and promote faster healing. Cayenne pepper is good for almost anything. Read about it. Learn to look up things you want to learn. There is so much knowledge available. Many doctors are now learning natural remedies.

Take care of your body in order to avoid and prevent terminal illnesses such as cancer, diabetes, arthritis and digestive disorders. Your immune system is like an army. If properly nourished and well trained, an invader virus and bacteria will be conquered. Pay attention to what you put inside you body. Be careful of what you buy to eat in the grocery stores. Read the ingredients labels before you buy new things. Avoid foods processed with hydrogenated oils. Choose water and juice rather than soda. Make sure the juice you buy is 100 percent juice and does not have added ingredients such as high fructose corn syrup. Be careful not to eat products with bleached wheat flour. Research and learn what bleached white flour can do to the body. It causes constipation, irritable bowel syndrome and other ailments. Try to eat something raw everyday whether it is a raw vegetable, fruit or raw nuts. Raw plants have live enzymes essential for the body's cells. Eat fresh and natural. Eat organic when possible. Research everything you can. Pray for the truth. Grow your own food if you can. Buy raw honey instead of processed honey. Get your essential fatty acids (Omega 3,6,9) by taking flax seed oil, cod liver oil and eating raw walnuts. Educate others who desire to learn. It is so much easier to live in a healthy body than an unhealthy one.

Time management

Time has to be managed very carefully because you can't ever get it back. You don't want to be 70 years old and look back on your life with many regrets. Spend your time wisely and don't waste it. You have a very short time in this life to learn all you can and develop character. Do what is meaningful. Ask God for recognition of what is meaningful. Pay attention to what is important. You can choose to watch four hours of television every night before bed or you can read books and learn, help others or develop relationships with family and friends. How you spend your time is your choice.

Self accountability

You are going to make mistakes. Don't blame other people for your mistakes. Take responsibility for your actions. Admit you are wrong when you are and try not to tell other people they are wrong. Don't judge other people when they are not self accountable. Be a good model for them to see. Everybody makes mistakes so remember that when you make a mistake. Don't be harsh on yourself, just admit you were wrong, learn from it and move on. No big deal. Learn from your mistakes so you don't repeat them. When you do something wrong or make a mistake, ask yourself, "What could I have done instead?" Next time you will be prepared in a situation similar. Don't dwell on your mistakes; learn from your mistakes. Embrace life as a learning experience.

Overcoming life's problems

You will be faced with an array of problems throughout life. It is important to create good problem solving skills. Also, if you foresee a problem in the future, it is possible to take preventative action so that it won't happen. When a problem is present, think of all possible solutions and decide on the best one. Put the solution to action. If the solution you chose doesn't solve the problem, then determine other possible solutions, and put them to action. Problems will not go away by themselves. You will likely come across some problems in areas of finance, marriage, child raising, your job and relationships. Seek for the truth and find knowledge. Whenever I come across a problem, I search for books and ask wise people for advice.

When a loved ones dies

Experiencing death of a loved one in this life is inevitable. My dad died when he was 67 and it was the most tragic thing I have experienced. It can be very painful to lose someone you love. Death is a part of living. We have no control over this. "The wages of sin is death, but the gift of God is eternal life through Jesus Christ" (Romans 6:23). Remember "Therefore we are always confident and know that as long as we are at home in the body we are away from the Lord. We live by Faith, not by sight. We are confident, I say, and would prefer to be away from the body and at home with the Lord" (2 Cor. 5:6-8). Jesus says, "Do not let your hearts be troubled. Trust in God, trust also in me. In my Father's house are many rooms; if it were not so, I would have told you. I am going there to prepare a place for you. And if I go and prepare a place for you, I will come back and take you to be with me that you may be where I am. You know the way to the place where I am going" (John 14: 1-4). Keep God's eternal program in your mind all the time. Having God's purpose in mind helps with the coping of the death of a loved one.

Character development

There are so many good and bad character traits. Ask God for help on choosing and applying the right traits. Choose love over hate. Choose obedience to God rather than disobedience. Choose being considerate rather than rude. Choose being honest rather than lying. You will have many choices in life. Below are some battles that you may experience personally.

- Contentment vs. unhappiness
- Gentleness vs. mean
- Gratitude vs. unthankfulness
- Humbleness vs. pride
- Persistence on what is right
- Responsibility vs. laziness
- Authenticity vs. fake
- Compassionate vs. uncaring
- Courage vs. cowardness
- Discernment vs. denial
- Faith vs. distrust
- Optimism vs. pessimism
- Purity vs. impure
- Generosity vs. greedy
- Trust in God vs. trust in man
- A love of God's Word vs. a love of the devil's world

Quality of Life

Life is all about making choices. Everyday you are making choices that will affect your quality of life. Choose what is best for your brain, soul, spirit and body. You will be presented with some very difficult choices all throughout life. Say no to alcohol, cigarettes, cocaine, marijuana, and other drugs that will alter your senses. Say no to people pressuring you to do things that are wrong. Those horror movies and morally degrading movies are not good for you and do not honor God. Pray for wisdom, knowledge and understanding. Pray for the truth and discernment. Smile and be joyful. Focus on what you have rather than what you don't have. Follow God's directions in the Bible and you will have the best quality of life. Be a good example for others to follow. Teach the truth to those willing to learn. Don't let your struggles with Asperger's characteristics get in your way. Be determined to solve any problem and have a wonderful, successful, joyful quality of life.

Should you Tell People you have Asperger's?

Different people with Asperger's will have different advice on whether or not to tell people you have it and who to tell. What I think is that since Asperger's is a spectrum from mild to severe, the individual should weigh the advantages and disadvantages of disclosing personal information before telling specific people in their lives. I believe that those with a milder expression should consider not disclosing to most people. Those with a more severe expression of Asperger's may want to and need to tell some people, but not all people in their lives.

Reasons for not telling:

- Many people in the community do not fully understand what Asperger's really is and people tend to be afraid of what they don't understand.
- If you tell them, they may become distant.
- If you do tell someone, you are likely going to remind yourself that the person knows and wonder if that person

is thinking about you have Asperger's every time you see or talk to that person.
- People may not believe you. People with Asperger's struggle on the inside and may be able to cover up those struggles. Others cannot see those struggles and sensory sensitivities.
- People may perceive you as disabled and not include you in groups and social events.
- Some people already have a perception of what Asperger's is and if you tell them you have it, they will assume you have all the things that match their perceptions of it.
- Since many girls are sensitive about how other people perceive them and who they hang out with, they may not want to become known as the girl who "hangs out with the girl who has Asperger's."
- You might later wish you didn't tell someone after all.

Reasons for telling:

- Some people who once assumed you were weird and different will have an explanation of why you are that way. They may be more willing to accept you.
- When people learn of what Asperger's is, they may look into it further by learning more about it. Because of the increased rate in autism spectrum conditions, Asperger's will become a common condition and people who know about it may be more accepting.
- People who frequently make fun of you may decrease their teasing after they know why you are the way you are.
- To increase awareness, understanding and acceptance of Asperger's in society.
- The possible satisfaction in knowing that other people will have an explanation of why you are the way you are.
- The possible satisfaction in knowing that you may be better understood than before.
- People may know someone else on the autism spectrum, they may be able to refer you to them and you will have experience and information to help them.

Depending on your place on the spectrum will depend on how you analyze who, when and how to tell. Make a list of people in your life such as your boyfriend/spouse, family members, best friends, friends, acquaintances, teachers/professors or coaches and analyze the pros and cons of telling each person.

When I first discovered I had Asperger's I didn't tell anyone other than my husband and parents. I did have a desire to tell those who had made fun of me being different as a kid as an explanation to why I was different. But I assumed they probably never had heard of Asperger's so I thought it would be best not to tell. There came a time I realized I needed to tell one of my coworkers as she had complained to another coworker about having problems with me not being able to read social cues. A couple of years later, one of the parents of the children I worked with asked me if I had Asperger's so I was truthful. There have only been two people who have asked me if I have Asperger's, and I honestly tell them I do. They know enough about it to be able to see the characteristics. Then I assume there may be other people who can recognize in people but don't say anything.

I have met many people who I see many of the characteristics in but I don't say anything about it. Except one time. I was receiving training from a photographer and I noticed that his high intellect, intense interest, focus and knowledge on cameras, exact eye for detail and some personal information he shared with me about his life, that I assumed he had Asperger's. One day he said he always wondered why he was so weird, and I told him he probably had Asperger's. He said he had never heard of Asperger's so I told him to do an Internet search on it. He did, and when we had our next lesson, he said with a big smile, "I do have Asperger's, and it is such a relief to know why I am the way I am."

I do think there are people who should know, especially a person's spouse. This is the person you will live the rest of your life with, and it is important they understand you. I think it is okay to tell your children, if you have them, because some of them are likely to have some of the characteristics as well. You can teach them what Asperger's is, and they will grow up knowing about it and they probably won't think it is a big deal. Children love their parents and look up to them. Telling other family members such as in-laws, aunts, uncles and cousins is up to you. You weigh the reasons for telling and reasons for not telling and decide for yourself if it is necessary to tell. It probably is not necessary to tell strangers, distant family or acquaintances. If you have children or want to have children, it is probably not necessary to tell people in your children's lives such as their friends and their friend's parents, their teachers and coaches. If you have a more severe expression of Asperger's or need to express your strengths and weaknesses so your boss can use your talents to benefit the workplace, you may want to tell him or her. If you are the authority in the workplace, then it is up to you whether or not tell your employees. But you don't want your employees to think of you as inferior and possibly find ways to take advantage of you.

If you do tell people, be sure to give them a very brief description of it such as that "it is a neurological difference that causes me to perceive things differently than most people." And briefly suggest that if they are interested in learning more they can ask you questions or get a better understanding by reading some of the resources such as Tony Attowood's book *The Complete Guide to Asperger's Syndrome*.

Suggested readings and resources

Asperger Support

- http://www.aspfi.org/
- http://www.aspergersyndrome.org
- http://www.grasp.org
- http://autism.about.com/od/aspergerssyndrome/a/adultdxas.htm

Peer pressure

- *How to Say No and Keep Your Friends: Peer Pressure Reversal for Teens and Preteens* by Sharon Scott (1997)

Teen social code and adolescence

- "Girl to Girl: Advice on Friendship, Bullying, and Fitting in" by Lisa Island (2006) in the book *Asperger's and Girls*
- *Freaks, Geeks & Asperger Syndrome: A User Guide to Adolescence* by Luke Jackson (2002)

Stress management

- *The Stress Management Handbook* Lori Leyden-Rubenstein (1999)
- *Asperger Syndrome and Anxiety: A Guide to Successful Stress Management* by Nick Dubin and Valerie Gaus (2009)

Growing up

- *Preparing for Life: The Complete Guide for Transitioning to Adulthood for Those with Autism and Asperger's Syndrome* by Jed Baker (2006)

Career

- *Developing Talents: Careers For Individuals With Asperger Syndrome And High-functioning Autism- Updated, Expanded Edition* by Temple Grandin and Kate Duffy (2008)
- *Finding Square Holes: Discover Who You Really Are and Find the Perfect Career* by Anita Houghton (2005)
- *Career Match: Connecting Who You Are with What You'll Love to Do* by Shoya Zichy and Ann Bidou (2007)
- *Asperger Syndrome Employment Workbook: An Employment Workbook for Adults With Asperger Syndrome* by Roger N. Meyer and Tony Attwood (2001)

Dating

- *A Smart Girls Guide to Boys: Surviving Crushes, Staying True to Yourself & Other Stuff* by Nancy Holyoke and Bonnie Timmons (2001)
- "Aspie Do's and Don'ts: Dating, Relationships, and Marriage" by Jennifer McIlwee (2006) Myers in the book *Asperger's and Girls*.
- *Aspergers in Love: Couple Relationships and Family Affairs* by Maxine C. Aston (2003)

Being a good wife

- *The Excellent Wife: A Biblical Perspective* by Martha Peace (2001)
- *Created to Be His Help Meet: Discover How God Can Make Your Marriage Glorious* by Debi Pearl (2004)

Sex

- *Intimate Issues: Twenty-One Questions Christian Women Ask About Sex* by Linda Dillow and Lorraine Pintus (2009)
- *Holy Sex – Song of Solomon* by Michael Pearl (2002)

Being a good parent

- *To Train up a Child* by Michael and Debi Pearl (1994)
- *Shepherding a Child's Heart* by Tedd Trip (1995)
- *Revolutionary Parenting: What the Research Shows Really Works* by George Barna (2007)

Money Management

- *Financial Peace Revisited* by Dave Ramsey (2003)
- *Financial Basics: Money-Management Guide for Students* by Susan Knox (2004)

Character

- *Building Moral Intelligence: The Seven Essential Virtues that Teach Kids to Do the Right Thing* by Michele and Ed.D. Borba (2002)
- *Emotional Intelligence: 10th Anniversary Edition; Why It Can Matter More Than IQ* by Daniel Goleman (2006)
- *What Do You Stand For? For Teens: A Guide To Building Character* by Barbara A. Lewis and Pamela Espeland (2005)
- *Laying Down the Rails: A Charlotte Mason Habits Handbook* by Sonya Shayfer (2007)

Health and the immune system

- *Healthy Eating for Life for Women* by Physicians Committee for Responsible Medicine and Physicians Committee for Responsible Medicine (2002)
- *Lessons from The Miracle Doctors: A Step-by-Step Guide to Optimum Health and Relief from Catastrophic Illness* by Jon Barron (2008)
- *Supperimmunity for Kids: What to Feed Your Children to Keep Them Healthy Now, and Prevent Disease in Their Future* Leo Galland and Dian Dincin Buchman (1989)

- *Smart Medicine for a Healthier Child by* Janet Zand, Robert Rountree, and Rachel Walton (2003)
- *The ABC Herbal: A Simplified Guide to Natural Healthcare for Children by* Steven H. Horne (1995)

Disclosure

- *Ask and Tell: Self-Advocacy and Disclosure for People on the Autism Spectrum* by Ruth Elaine Joyner Hane, Kassiane Sibley, Stephen M. Shore, Roger N. Meyer, Phil Schwartz and Liane Holliday Willey (2004)

References

Aihara, R. & Hashimoto, T. (1989). Neuroendocrinologic studies on autism. *Number To Hattatsu, 21,*154-162.

Attwood, T. (2007). *The Complete Guide to Asperger's Syndrome.* London, UK: Jessica Kingsley Publishers.

Brosnan (2009). Reviewed by Miranda Hill and Louse Chang. Asperger's Syndrome:Stress Hormone a clue. Asperger's Syndrome Patients May Not Get Typical Morning Spike in Stress Hormone Cortisol, Study Shows *Psychoneuroendocrinology. Reviewed December 22nd, 2009.* http://www.webmd.com/brain/autism/news/20090402/aspergers-syndrome-stress-hormone-a-clue

Chamberlain, R.S. & Herman, B.H. (1990). A novel biochemical model linking dysfunctions in brain melatonin, proopiomelanocortin peptides, and serotonin in autism. *Biological Psychiatry 28*, 773-793.

Fernald, L.C. & Grantham-McGregor, S.M. (1998). Stress response in school-age children who have been growth retarded since early childhood. *American Journal of Clinical Nutrition, 68,* 691-8.

Grandin, Temple. (2006). For Me, a Good Career Gave Life Meaning. *Girls and Asperger's.* Future Horizons, Inc.

Hoshino, Y., Ohno, Y., Murata, S., Yokoyama, F., Kaneko, M. & Kumashiro, H. (1984). Dexamethasone suppression test in autistic children. *Folia Psychiatric Neurology Japanese, 38,* 445-9.

Hoshino, Y., Yokoyama, F., Watanabe, M., Murata, S., Kaneko, M. & Kumashiro, H. (1987). The diurnal variation and response to dexamethasone suppression test of salivacortisol level in autistic children. *Japanese Journal of PsychiatryNeurology 41,* 227-35.

Island, Lisa. (2006). Girl to Girl: Advice on Friendship, Bullying, and Fitting in. *Asperger's and Girl's.* Future Horizons, Inc, Texas.

Jansen, L.M., Gispen-de, Wied, C.C., Van der Gaag, R.J. & Van Engeland, H. (2003). Differentiation between autism and multiple complex developmental disorder in response to psychosocial stress. *Neuropsychopharmacology, 28,* 582-590.

Jansen, L.M., Gispen-de Wied, C.C., Van der Gaag, R.J., Ten Hove, F., Willemsen-Swinkels, S.W.,

Harteveld, E. & Van Engeland, H. (2000). Unresponsiveness to psychosocial stress in a subgroup of autistic-like children, multiple complex developmental disorder. *Psychoneuroendocrinology, 25,* 753-64.

Myers, J. M. (2006). Aspie Do's and Don'ts: Dating, Relationships, and Marriage. *Asperger's and Girls,* Future Horizons, Inc.

Richdale, A.L. & Prior, M.R. (1992). Urinary cortisol circadian rhythm in a group of high-functioning children with autism. *Journal of Autism and Other Developmental Disorders 22,* 433-447.

Sapolsky, R.M. (1998). *Why Zebras Don't get Ulcers: An Updated Guide to Stres,Stress-related Diseases and Coping.* W.H. Freeman and Company.

Stanly, S. M. (2003). What Really is the Divorce Rate? State of the Art Tools for an Extraordinary marriage. Retrieved October 26th, 2009. http://www.prepinc.com/main/Docs/what_really_div_rate.html.

Tordjman, S., Anderson, G.M., McBride, P.A., Hertzig, M.E., Snow, M.E., Hall, L.M., Thompson, S.M.,

Ferrari, P. & Cohen, D.J. (1997). Plasma beta-endorphin, adrenocorticotropin hormone, and cortisol in autism. *Journal of Child Psychiatry, 38,* 705-715.

Willey, L.H. (1999). *Pretending to be Normal: Living with Asperger's Syndrome.* Jessica Kingsley Publishers.

CHAPTER 11

Insight for Caregivers and Teachers

If I could go back in time as a child, with what I know now, and communicate to my parent or teacher what I really needed from them, the things discussed in this chapter are what I would request. It is likely that you may not be aware of what your daughter experiences. Have you assumed she was shy or bashful? Have you assumed she was a complainer? Have you assumed she was a "drama queen?" Have you assumed she was a problem child? Have you assumed she was "out of sync?" What your child needs is understanding, support, love, acceptance, teaching and direction.

My parents delighted in my interests and laughed with me instead of at me. Although my parents thought I was oversensitive and did recognize I had social difficulties, they did not make fun of me or show their disapproval of my personality. If they had, I may have been drawn into a lost world of depression unable to find my way out. I did not have other siblings for them to compare me to. My parent's acceptance of me gave my life meaning and hope.

Because Asperger's syndrome means different things to different people and at different ages, and because most girls don't realize they are different until the middle school years, the content discussed in this chapter is mainly for parents and teachers of girls in their middle school years on up. For the parent or teacher who has a girl with Asperger's, this chapter will give you a perspective on how to support the girl. If you feel guilty or in any way feel bad that your girl has Asperger's or for how you have responded to her in the past, don't worry about it anymore. It is not your fault. You didn't have the information you needed to understand Asperger's. I don't blame my parents for anything at all, and I don't want my mom feeling bad. For the girl with Asperger's who has or wants to have children, this chapter will be refreshing in how to support your children.

Understanding

There is nothing that would have helped me more than understanding. Although I felt accepted by my parents, I knew they did not understand me. I didn't even understand myself. Kids my age constantly telling me I was weird, different, crazy, difficult, annoying, foolish, a nuisance and a problem made me feel like an absolute failure. It is bad enough to get this from peers, but to get it from a parent or teacher would be too much. Take the time to understand your daughter's point of view, her way of perceiving things, her world. Tell her that you understand her and that you accept her the way she is. Focus on her talents instead of her weaknesses. Tell her that she doesn't have to feel embarrassed or ashamed and that she can come to you to talk about any problem. Provide understanding and support and provide solutions to problems when asked. Help her understand herself.

Don't tell her to, "Do what the other kids are doing." Don't ask her, "Why can't you just be like everybody else?" And certainly don't ask her, "What is wrong with you?" Don't humiliate her by using sarcasm with her in groups and gatherings. Don't ridicule her for not having many friends. Don't criticize her interests. Don't assume she is being rude when she is being direct. Don't make fun of her for not understanding sarcasm or figurative speech. Don't feel like your girl has to be "normal" in order to be successful.

Do assure her that she is an important part of your life. Do compliment her on her strengths. Help her with her weaknesses and realize that her sensory sensitivities are real. Provide support and assist her in learning to cope with sensitivities. Help her learn figurative speech so she can better understand others. Make sure she is loved and feels loved and become interested in what she is interested in. Speak clearly to her, encourage her efforts, become her friend and teacher and give her confidence at all times.

There are probably times that you do not understand your girl's behavior. I have learned that difficult behavior usually occurs as a result of feelings of frustration and stress. Help your girl to find ways to decrease stress, be able to predict when a situation is about to become stressful and communicate the need for a break. Your help, support and understanding will be a tremendous asset to her life.

Mainstream?

When I ask parents what they want for their child on the spectrum, almost every parent says, "to be in inclusion and be like the other kids." They want their children to be included in a typical classroom environment. This is understandable. And they also want their children to be "normal." This is not understandable. What is normal anyway? I hear so many parents telling their kids "try to make friends today" and "do what the other kids do." From my experience, parents seem to be more concerned with perceptions of other people peering in on their children instead of becoming advocates of their children. Children are being pushed and pressured to become people they are not. Square peg children are being forced into a round hole. This causes a great deal of anxiety and struggle for both the parents and the children. Parents should be the people whose children feel comfortable around, trust and approach with problems.

Pay careful attention to the children that are in contact with your daughter. What are they doing? Are the other children displaying negative actions, including having a bad attitude or drinking alcohol? If so, do you really want your child to be this way? Do you really want your daughter to be exactly like them? Do you really want your child to live the exact standardized life that society has created for them? Some girls with Asperger's who constantly feel out of place will make themselves appear to be a part of the mainstream to feel accepted and included. Some of them may fall into the trap of peer pressure and get into trouble with the intentions of being accepted. Not all of them are going to stand against peer pressure. Do you really want your daughter to do what everyone else is doing?

Girls with Asperger's can learn how to make friends and to participate in groups, but their participation may not feel natural to them. They can be given a choice whether or not they want to join the mainstream. If they choose not to, they should be understood. They can use their ability to imitate to reach any social goal but they may not want to. Don't be disappointed in them for choosing to be who they are. Is it really all that important to be popular anyway? What really matters in life?

School and Academics

School is not just the place for learning. School is a complex network of social hierarchies and situations. Attending school is very difficult for most people with Asperger's. I didn't develop a love for learning until after I graduated from school. By pairing learning with social anxiety, the result will be anxiety with learning. Have you ever noticed your girl to come home from school and explode with frustration and anger? Or have you ever noticed her come home and shut the door in your face wanting to be left alone? After experiencing anxiety and stress all day while holding in intense emotions while at the same time trying to pretend to be like everyone else, a girl needs downtime. Don't make her do her homework as soon as she gets home. Give her time to recooperate. Suggest that she do some of her favorite activities.

It is very important for parents to know how to prepare young girls with Asperger's for what they will experience in school. Tell your girl what school is all about and what she will experience in school. Teach her about all the social hierarchies and the unspoken social code. Inform her that she can come to you with any problem for any situation. When she does come to you for help or to just vent a problem, listen to her and don't be judgmental. Try to understand her point of view. Don't make fun of her because she doesn't have as many friends as everybody else. Don't make her feel bad for not being popular. Give her tips and pointers on how to reach her goals reasonably. Help her get a few close friends and encourage her to invite them over frequently. Make your home fun and welcoming for your girls friends. Provide activities and good food, but don't interfere too much.

According to Jennifer Myers (2006), many parents have asked questions including, "How can I make my child socially adept?" or "How can I get her to want to be sociable like the other kids?" The answer is that you can't, and more importantly, you should not. Girls with Asperger's need more time to recover from social interactions than typical girls, and they must work harder in social situations than typical girls.

Pay careful attention to how your daughter is learning. Does your child learn better by seeing, hearing or doing? Most people with Asperger's prefer visual learning. If she is struggling with an academic area, use visual cues to help her learn. Draw pictures for her and teach her to do the same. Help her improve her auditory processing by pairing visuals with words. Teach her things by using things that interest her. It is much easier to pay attention to something that is interesting. For example, if she is struggling with algebra, make up word problems with her favorite things. If she loves *Star Wars*, say something like, "If Darth Vador has 25 light sabors and Luke Skywalker has 49, then how many more light sabors does Darth Vador need to have the same as Luke?" If your girl is really struggling in an area, spend one-on-one time teaching her one step at a time or consider getting her a one-on-one tutor. It is much easier for a person with Asperger's to learn with no other people around. This way, she can ask questions she needs and there are less sensory distracters to tune out.

Some people with Asperger's are very well organized and some are just the opposite. If your girl is not well organized and doesn't seem to keep up with her books, homework or assignments, help her create a system such as a weekly or monthly or daily calendar or a visual schedule. Most people with Asperger's appreciate being able to see what is going to happen in advance. For those who need extra help with staying on task, a written daily schedule would be beneficial.

Dating

According to Jennifer Myers (2006) in her article *Aspie Do's and Don'ts: Dating, Relationships, and Marriage* "Girls with Asperger's should be encouraged from an early age to look at dating and marriage realistically, factually and logically." "A girl who has an accepting family will not be bound to the societal rules of who to date. A girl who is pushed to be the sociable, "normal" girl what she really can't be will learn a lot of rules that are contrary to who she is and will cause her great pain as her "rule bound" Aspie nature ties her up in others' expectations."

There are all kids of rules for dating but the fact is that girls with Asperger's don't need to necessarily date by the rules, but to date the kind of person she would want to spend a lot of time with. Don't encourage your daughter to present herself as someone she is not in order to win a boy's heart. Give real information about what marriage is like. Talk to your daughter about the difference between "feeling in love" and reality. She may feel like she is in love with a boy, but help her be able to see into the future if she spends her whole life with him. Will he be a good father? Does he show self-control when in challenging situations? How does he treat his other family members? Does he insist on having his way all the time? There are so many questions to ask. Give your girl knowledge and perspective.

Do you want your daughter to be like what society teaches through advertisement and the media? Tell her at the youngest age possible that sex is only for marriage. Teach her how to say no to all those boys who try to manipulate her to get into her pants. Set rules for dating.

Adolescence

Perhaps the most difficult time in a girl's life is the stage of puberty. During puberty, there are many physical, hormonal, emotional and mental changes happening. It is important to prepare your girl ahead of time with what changes she will experience. Change can be difficult, especially for girls with Asperger's. One of the families I have worked with had an excellent idea on preparing their daughter for starting her period. Her mom told her that when she started they would throw a "chick party." When the girl first started, she was excited and happy because she would get to stay up all night doing "girl" things.

Be able to carefully observe where your child is on the spectrum and word your teaching accordingly. Your child will need to learn modesty and maintain good hygiene. Some children will need very simple descriptions. However some will not want to feel like you are talking to them like they are a baby. Some girls, very logical thinkers, will need and probably want very technical teachings with details, pictures and books. The book *Girl's Growing up on the Autism Spectrum* by Shana Nichols, Gina Moravcik and Samara Tetenbaum is a good source of information and help. The events in a teenager's life can be very confusing and this book covers many issues faced by girls with an autism spectrum condition.

Preparing her for the real world

Parents, it is your job to prepare your child for the real world. There are so many things that are not taught in schools. Make sure your child is paying attention. You can teach her money management, time management, self-accountability, moral intelligence, emotional stability, how to be a good mother, how to be a good wife, how to manage a home, how to research and learn anything of interest and how to succeed in life. Teach the moral habits of integrity, obedience and self-control. Teach cleanliness, order, purity, patience, respect and generosity. Teach conversation, social skills, pragmatics, attention, effort, observation, concentration and reflection. There are so many skills that your daughter may be interested in learning such as calligraphy, art, gardening, sewing, beading, computer skills, photography, pottery, robotics, scrapbooking and woodworking. If you don't know how to do any of these things and she is interested in learning, there is a growing number of self-help and how to do videos and books. Teach consequences to behaviors such as drug abuse and premarital sex.

What is your girl going to do after graduation? I have witnessed a grown girl become extremely depressed and frequently cry after graduating high school because she said she didn't know how to do anything else, but to go to school. I can relate to that. School is not going to prepare your girl for real life. Give her a focus, an outlook and choices of what to do when she graduates. Does she want to go to college? Does she want to get married? Does she want to be a Mother one day? What are her interests that could lead into a career or how to make a living? Prepare her for responsibility. Prepare her for hard work. Prepare her for self-accountability. Give her the knowledge she needs for good money and time management. Teach her about taxes and insurance companies. Teach her life skills such as record keeping, cooking healthy, CPR, yard care and home care. Teach her to think outside the box.

Suggested Readings

- *The Complete Guide to Asperger's Syndrome* by Tony Attwood (2008)
- *The Myriad Gifts of Asperger's Syndrome* by John Ortiz (2008)
- *Can I Tell You About Asperger Syndrome: A Guide for Friends and Family* by Jude Welton, Jane Telford, and Elizabeth Newson (2003)
- *Misdiagnosis And Dual Diagnoses Of Gifted Children And Adults: ADHD, Bipolar, OCD, Asperger's, Depression, And Other Disorders* by James T. Webb, Edward R. Amend, Nadia E. Webb, and Jean Goerss (2005)
- *Your Life is Not a Label: A Guide to Living Fully with Autism and Asperger's Syndrome* by Jerry Newport and Ron Bass (2001)
- *Asperger's and Girls* featuring Tony Attwood and Temple Grandin (2006)
- *Congratulations! It's Asperger Syndrome* Jen Birch (2003)
- *Pretending to be Normal by* Liane Holiday-Willey (1999)
- *Thinking in Pictures* by Temple Grandin (1995)
- *Life Behind Glass. A Personal Account of Autism Spectrum Disorder* by Wendy Lawson (2003)
- *Nobody Nowhere: The Remarkable Autobiography of an Autistic Girl* by Donna Williams (1992)
- *Women From Another Planet?: Our Lives in the Universe of Autism* by Jean Miller (2003)
- *The OASIS Guide to Asperger Syndrome: Completely Revised and Updated: Advice, Support, Insight, and Inspiration* by

Patricia Romanowski Bashe, Barbara L. Kirby, Simon Baron-Cohen, and Tony Attwood (2005)
- *Girls Growing Up on the Autism Spectrum* by Shana Nichols, Gina Moravcik and Samara Tetenbaum (2009)

References

Myers, J. M. (2006). *Aspie Do's and Don'ts: Dating, Relationships, and Marriage. Asperger's and Girls. Future Horizons.*

Chapter 12

Understanding and preventing autism

I describe my long and extensive journey of research into understanding what autism really is, methods to recover it and methods to preventing it. I think there is enough published research with factors that can be put together that would lead to the prevention of autism in those with a genetic predisposition. Girls with Asperger's should know this information so they can learn about preventive measures since their children may be more likely to have a genetic predisposition to developing autism.

I describe the growing rates of autism and related conditions, list the behavioral conditions, briefly state the most common therapies, list common medical conditions, brain findings and treatments and discuss what causes the medical conditions and treatments. I examine why both common behavioral and medical treatments help some children but not all, summarize research regarding the factors that cause autism, discuss vaccines and what causes some children to have reactions to the vaccines but not others, give reasons why other conditions such as ADHD, Asthma and allergies are related to autism and describe other risk factors contributing to the cause of autism. I define mercury and what it does, and I describe methylation and glutathione and discuss how testosterone plays a role in autism. I put the available pieces of the mystery of autism together for a clearer picture of what it is, how to treat it and how to prevent it.

I offer a list of suggestions to recognize factors of a genetic predisposition. Other suggestions are offered on how to support the immune system. I share my story of how I believe that my children had a genetic predisposition but methods were taken to prevent them from developing autism.

Growing rates of autism

The chief of the Center for Disease Control and Prevention, Dr. Marshalyn Yeargin-Allsopp, states that "It is extremely difficult to accurately estimate the number of children who have an ASD" because "medical records often do not provide such information, and identification is often made by schools or education specialists." There have been numerous studies in numerous populations identifying the number of known children with an ASD (Autism spectrum disorder). Therefore, there are estimates of the rates of autism.

- In the 1960s, the rate for autism was approximately 4 or 5 in 10,000
- In 1980, 4500 new cases each year reported in the USA alone
- In 1999, the rate for autism was about 1 in 500
- In 2001, the rate for autism was said to be about 1 in 250
- In 2003, the rate of autism was said to be about 1 in 170
- In 2007, the rate for autism was said to be 1 in 150
- In 2009, the rate for autism was said to be 1 in 100 (Centers for Disease Control, 2009)

Between the 12-year period 1992 to 2004, there has been a 1,055 percent increase in autism (Autism conferences of America, 2004). Using this same rate, approximately 10 in every 100 children, or one in every 10 children will have an ASD by the year 2020. Going 12 years further into the year 2032, 22 in every 100 or one out of every 4 or 5 children will have an ASD. Hopefully the world, the government and doctors will know enough, will care for the children enough, and there will be enough research proving that autism can be prevented. I would like to see the rates of autism decline as true autism awareness increases.

Autism spectrum conditions are reported to occur in all racial, ethnic, and socioeconomic groups. Studies have shown that among identical twins, if one child has an ASD, then the other will be affected about 60 to 96 percent of the time. In non-identical twins, if one child has an ASD, then the other is affected about 0 to 24 percent of the time. Parents who have a child with an ASD have a two to eight percent chance of having a second child who is also affected (Boyle, Van Naarden Braun & Yeargin-Allsopp, 2005).

Autism is not the only childhood epidemic that has been rising. Over the past 20 years, ADHD has increased by 400 percent, Asthma has increased by 300 percent, and allergies have increased by 400 percent (Bock & Stauth, 2008). Approximately 13 percent of children have a developmental disability, ranging from mild such as speech and language impairments to serious developmental disabilities, such as intellectual disabilities, cerebral palsy, and autism (Boulet, Boyle & Schieve, 2009). What is going on here?

There is a truth that needs to be found. Recent research is being directed to the truth, however, for many higher authorities, dollar signs are getting in the way of doing anything about it. So, it is extremely important that parents, family members, doctors and other professionals take action and read all the research and pray for discernment on which is the truth so that they can help their precious children and prevent further children from developing the condition. Let's do an examination of what research is available putting the pieces of the research together for a clearer picture of what autism really is and methods to preventing it.

Behavioral conditions in children with autism

Children with autism display a bewildering array of behavioral deficits and excesses in attention, cognition, speech, language, affective, and social functioning, communication and imaginative play along with behavioral excesses including noncompliance, self-stimulation and tantrums. Examples of self-stimulation behaviors include hand flapping, staring at the hands, twirling in circles, verbal repetitiveness, teeth grinding, tissue rubbing and rocking from side to side or back and forth. The duration and type of self-stimulation behaviors vary among children. Some other associated features of autism include abnormal posture and motor behavior, odd responses to sensory input such as loud noises, bright lights, or certain ways of touch, abnormality in eating, drinking and sleeping, abnormalities of mood and self injurious behavior. Most of the children I have worked with have these conditions in common: preference for sameness (crying or tantruming when something is missing or the when the routine is different); difficulty in transitions (crying or tantruming when an adult stops and activity and begins a new one), particular stimming behaviors such as spinning or humming but they are specific in individual children (one child will spin objects, another child will constantly hum, another child will flap hands); sensory sensitivities (holding ears, squinting, flinching, quivering). Something has to be **causing** these behavioral deficits and excesses. For now, let's look at the treatments for these behavioral deficits and excesses before we get to causes.

Behavioral treatments that have helped some Children with autism but not all

Before any medical attention was given to autism, many behavioral treatments had been created and applied. Applied Behavior Analysis (ABA) is a scientifically validated branch of behavioral psychology that first began with Ivar Lovas in the 1960s with children with autism. The ABA method is to modify behavior by decreasing undesirable behavior while increasing more desirable behavior that requires consistency. The objective of intervention is to teach the child these skills that will facilitate his cognitive and behavioral development and help him achieve the greatest degree of independence and the highest quality of life by helping him reach his greatest potential. The intervention not only affects the child, but the whole family as well.

Discrete Trial Training (DTT) is a specific method of teaching utilizing the methods of ABA to maximize learning. It is a teaching technique or process used to develop many skills, including cognitive, communication, play, social and self-help skills. Pivotal Response Training (PRT) also using the methods of ABA was developed primarily by Drs. Bob and Lynn Koegel that targets pivotal developmental areas while teaching. This method is more child-lead than teacher directed. There are many other treatments that have been used that are not scientifically validated such as TEACH, floor time and facilitated communication. Other treatments that many parents seek in additional to behavioral treatments are Occupational Therapy, Speech Therapy, sensory integration therapy and music therapy.

Medical conditions in children with autism

As I worked with more and more children and listened to their parents speak to me about their children's health, doctor visits and results from blood tests, I noticed there were some very direct similarities in their medical issues. These included:

- -Yeast overgrowth
- -Heavy Metals toxicity
- -Food Allergies
- -Frequent infections
- -Leaky Gut syndrome
- -Bowel problems – diarrhea and constipation
- -Low muscle tone – undernourished muscle tissue

To this day I don't think I have ever worked with a child that when tested didn't have yeast or at least one heavy metal at toxic levels (mercury being most common followed by lead, arsenic, aluminum and cadmium) and food allergies. Books were being written on remedies for autism based on these medical conditions. Puzzle pieces were being identified as to what autism was, but there was still no clear picture.

The brain in autism

- Nash & Bonesteel found an intriguing abnormality in the cerebellum (which regulates sensory information and coordination) of both children and adults with autism. An important class of cells called Purkinje are were far more smaller and more tightly packed together in a number of

- people with autism than typical people. The cerebellum uses these cells to receive information from the outside world, compute the meaning and prepare other areas of the brain to respond appropriately (Nash & Bonesteel, 2002).
- Bauman and Kemper (2003) also implied that anatomic features are consistently abnormal in including reduced numbers of Purkinje cells in the cerebellum as well as small tightly packed neurons in the entorhinal cortex (important memory center) and in the middle of the amygdala (emotional processing). Bauman also examined postmortem tissue from the brains of nearly 30 autistic individuals who died between the ages of 5 and 74 and found abnormalities in the limbic system, an area that includes the amygdala.
- There is evidence of children with autism having differences in the sizes of certain brain structures. This larger brain volume is not present at birth, but appears during the first few years (Frith, 2003).
- Courchesne and collegues (2001) found abnormal regulation of brain growth in autism that results in early overgrowth of the brain followed by abnormally slowed growth.
- Neuroimaging studies by Courchesne and his colleagues (2001) found neuron-packed gray matter of the cerebral cortex and white matter, which contains the fibrous connections projecting to and from the cerebral cortex and other areas of the brain, including the cerebellum. This abnormal brain growth in children with autism is not uniformly distributed.
- Gaffney, Tsai, Kuperman and Minchin (1987) found that the cerebellums of patients with autism were proportionally smaller and the fourth ventricles were proportionally larger. This suggests that there are biological changes in cerebellum of autistic children.
- Treffery and his colleagues found that autistic savant syndrome to be identified as having damage to the left side of the brain (Treffery, Darold, Wallace & Gregory, 2002).
- Twenty percent of children with autism have damaged mitochondria or a mitochondrial disorder. Mitochondria are the energy producing section of our cells converting food and oxygen into energy for use by the body (Kirby, 2008)

- Children with autism have damaged Myelin Sheath and Exposed Nerves. (Kennedy & Kirby, 2009). Myelin Sheath in the brain is the insulator, which protects nerves from electrical impulses while simultaneously causing those impulses to travel faster.

The medical symptoms and brain findings I have described are contributing to the cause of the behavior deficits and excesses seen in children with autism. But what is causing these medical symptoms and the structural damage in the brain? Something has to be **causing** these symptoms and brain findings. But for now, let's look at the treatments being applied for these medical conditions before we get to causes.

Common Medical treatments that have helped some Children with autism but not all

- **Special Diets for Leaky Gut syndrome.** This special diet is applied by eliminating all foods containing gluten and casein from a child's diet. Wheat, barley, oats and rye all contain gluten and anything made from cow's milk contains casein. Research on this began in 1995 by Lucarelli and his collegues. Lucarelli suggested children with autism could not fully digest these complex proteins because they were leaking into their blood stream from intestines, crossing the blood brain barrier and acting like an opioid drug in the brain causing behavioral problems and learning difficulties. Other diets include the oxcelate diet and the special carbohydrate diet.
- **Vit. B6 and magnesium.** Bernard Rimland (2003) researched B6 and magnesium in children with autism and found that B6 provided positive results in his studies, 12 out of 16 children with autism showed considerable behavioral improvements when given 100-600 mg of B6 per day. Several parents of children I have worked with informed me of giving their child high doses of vitamin B6 and magnesium which, some thought, contributed to increase in expressive language.
- **DMG.** N-Dimethylglycine (DMG) is a metabolic enhancer making the process of metabolism (breaking down or

building up of compounds in the body) quicker and more efficient. Bernard Rimland also studied this and found that 80 percent of parents reported better speech, eating and willingness when their children took DMG. Many parents of children I have worked with mentioned giving DMG to their children,

- **Secretin.** In 1996, a boy with severe autism, Parker Beck, who was suffering from continual vomiting and diarrhea, was brought to the University of Maryland for investigation, which included the administration of secretin. After he got home, Parker's digestive problems improved markedly, and so did his autistic symptoms. Parker's mother became an enthusiastic proponent of secretin as a possible cure for autism. There have been seven clinical trials on secretin and six have shown it to be ineffective.
- **Super Nu Thera.** Super Nu-Thera® developed by Kirkman is a multiple vitamin/mineral supplement featuring B-6, and magnesium also containing the rest of the B-vitamins, vitamin C, the oil soluble vitamins (E, A, and D) as well as the minerals zinc, manganese and selenium. A lot of the children I have seen have tried Super Nu Thera ' some with posititve results such as increase in attention and some with negative such as an increase in stimming behaviors.
- **Probiotics.** Probiotics are supplements containing potentially beneficial live bacteria. The use of antibiotics kills both the good and bad bacteria, therefore making the intestinal environment a good place for yeast to grow. Probiotics are given to increase the good bacteria and to help with yeast overgrowth. Many parents of children with autism have reported great improvements in their children's behavior and The Autism Clinic recommends a special, ultra-high potency probiotic supplement specially formulated for children with autism.
- **Cod Liver Oil.** Cod liver oil is a nutritional supplement derived from the liver of cod fish. It has high levels of omega 3 fatty acids, EPA, DHA, vitamin A and D. A few parents have mentioned to me they think Cod liver oil is the cure for autism they were so amazed at the progress of their

children when beginning this supplement. Other parents, however, remarked not seeing any change in their children.
- **Vit. B12 shot or nasal spray.** Vitamin B12 is an essential vitamin for healthy brain function. It is important in helping to manufacture the myelin sheath - a protective layer surrounding nerves in the brain – and it also helps the brain to produce neurotransmitters, which are vital for communication within the brain. Many parents express an improvement in social communication in their children. Most of the research on B12 has been anecdotal, meaning conclusions are based on what parents say instead of experimental evaluations.
- **Nystatin or Dyflucan.** Nystatin and Dyflucan are Anti fungals given to kill candida yeast in the intestines; some children I have worked with would suddenly begin talking after about a month on Nystatin; some would decrease stimming and increase attention. Others showed no change. Parents who tried Nystatin and saw a great improvement in their children would claim that Nystatin is the cure for autism.
- **Chelation therapy.** Chelation is the administration of chelating agents to remove heavy metals from the body. DMSA, DMPS and EDTA are common chelators. Chelation can be administered orally, intraveniously, as a suppositoy and on the skin. Chelation has been widely used to treat autism, maybe up to 8% of children with autis(Turner, 2009). Although there is currently no scientific support for chelation as a therapy for autism, many parents I have worked with exclaim womderful results with chelation theray while others report a regression.
- **Drugs.** According to Hunsinger and his colleagues (2000) there has not been a single medication shown to consistently alter the symptoms or the course of autism in the majority of children. The present pharmacotherapy may help but does not provide a cure. Specific psycho stimulants, antidepressants and anti-anxiety drugs have been used and studied with mixed results. Parents report an improvement, no change or a regression.

Foreword by Liane Holliday Willey

Over the course of my experience with children with autism, parents would report to me what medical treatments they were giving their children. Some seemed to help some children while some didn't. I wanted to learn more so I read as many books I could find on the subject. I began seeing that autism wasn't a "behavioral disorder" as once believed, but it was more of a "medical condition."

Some books written as the view of autism shifts from a behavioral disorder perspective to a medical perspective

- **Unraveling the Mystery of Autism and Pervasive Developmental Disorder: A Mother's Story of Research & Recovery** by Karyn Seroussi with a foreward by Bernard Rimland gives scientific evidence pointing to the connections between autism and diet. The author believes that the inability to digest certain proteins was contributing to her son's autism, which was related to his reaction to MMR vaccine. After Seroussi eliminated foods containing casein and gluten proteins from her son's diet, he made such dramatic improvement that, by age four, she claims he was typically functioning. She does caution that not every child with autism may respond to a diet change.
- **Children with Starving Brains: A Medical Treatment Guide for Autism Spectrum Disorder** by Jaquelyn McCandless implies that genetic predisposition activated by "triggers" such as pesticides and heavy metals in vaccines can lead to immune system impairment, gut dysfunction, and pathogen invasion such as yeast and viruses in many children. It gives a step-by-step treatment guide based on the notion that ASD and common conditions such as ADHD is a complex biomedical illness resulting in significant brain malnutrition.
- **Changing the Course of Autism: A Scientific Approach for Parents and Physicians** by Bryan Jepson. This book shows how autism can be treated as a medical disease, rather than a behavioral disorder.
- **Nourishing Hope for Autism: Nutrition Intervention for Healing Our Children** by Julie Matthews. Matthews, an

autism nutrition specialist, provides scientific understanding of why diet helps heal children with autism. It teaches the critical connection between the nutrients that go into the digestive system and the impact they have on the child's brain.
- **My Cure for Autism** by P Dwivedi gives natural remedies for candida yeast infections and parasites and how to detoxify the bodies of children with autism.
- **Autism and Its Medical Management: A Guide for Parents and Professionals** by Michael G., M.D. Chez teaches how to use the research on the medical knowledge of autism to understand autism and the subtypes of autism and that autism should be treated individually.

Why do treatments for autism (both behavioral treatments and medical treatments) help some children but not all children with autism?

There does not seem to be a single "cure-for-all" treatment for autism. There are lots of treatments. Some treatments are beneficial, and others offer no improvement. And some treatments are also more scientifically validated than others. Anecdotal reports by parents, behaviorists, teachers and doctors should be highly valued. But the reports are so different in degree it is difficult to give specific recommendations for any one individual with autism. Not only do children with autism display a different array of behavioral deficits and excesses but they also have various biological deficits and excesses. As the observable characteristics of autism are a spectrum, the biological characteristics of autism are a spectrum as well.

Dr. Kenneth Bock (2007), a DAN doctor, wrote a book called *Healing the New Childhood Epidemics; Autism, ADHD, Asthma and Allergies, The Groundbreaking Program for the 4-A Disorders*. In this book, Dr. Bock seems to put together many pieces of the puzzle to get a first look at the picture of what autism is. The reason no single treatment works for all children is that each child has different biochemical deficits and excesses inside his or her body. For example, some children have very low vitamin A while other have extremely too high vitamin A. I think that this might be why Super Nu Thera works for some but not all. Some children have very low levels of zinc and copper while others do not. Some children have toxic levels of mercury only while others have toxic levels of mercury, lead and arsenic. Some have allergies to wheat while others have allergies to wheat, milk, soy, corn, peanuts, eggs or more. There are ways to determine what biological deficits and excesses a child has with lots of laboratory testing. This will give doctors and parents a clue in which treatments will better benefit their child. So what causes the different biochemical deficits and excesses and the brain deficits and excesses?

The current research regarding the attributes contributing to The cause of autism

There is a list of things thought to contribute to the cause of autism, but let's begin with vaccines since it has been the most popular topic in the autism field. I estimate that about nine out of every 10 families I have worked with would begin with the same story. "He was developing fine and he was even talking until he got that vaccine..." There is a great deal of controversy, and quite a bit of research as well as many of books and articles written on the subject of vaccines. It is important to understand that there is not 100% sufficient testing of vaccines. I think it important to learn more about vaccines.

What is in vaccines?

- Aluminum
- Egg protein
- MSG
- Sulfites
- Benzethonium chloride
- Ethylene glycol (used in antifreeze)
- Formaldehyde (carcinogen)
- Gelatin
- Glutamate
- Neomycin
- Phenol
- Streptomycin
- Thimerosal (ethyl mercury)

Not all of the listed ingredients are in every single vaccine. But each vaccine contains many of these ingredients many of which are toxic to the body. There are three types of vaccines; live (weakened live virus); dead; and DNA genetically engineered vaccines. The viruses used in vaccines are grown in aborted human fetuses, monkey kidneys and chick embryos. Vaccines recommended by the federal government given to children beginning the day after birth are the Hep. B, DTP, Hib, Polio, MMR and Varicella. Children are given 33 doses of 10 vaccines by the time they are five years old (Cave, 2001).

There are numerous published writings regarding vaccines and autism, many which conclude there is a connection between autism and vaccines and some that conclude there is no scientific link. Most parents with children who have autism have reported that their children regressed into autism after certain vaccines. The Thinktwice Global Vaccine institute receives numerous reports of a link between the MMR vaccine and autism. "Exactly 14 days after my son's MMR vaccination, he had a measles and mumps type reaction. He has now been diagnosed as autistic. He also has leaky gut syndrome and asthma. My son was in PERFECT health up until the day of his reaction. He lost all powers of speech on that day and has never regained them." In another report, "After my son's MMR shot at 12 months, his development and personality changed. He would stare off and not notice anything, not even the waving of my hand in front of his face. His personality became nothing – he lost all words and still has none. It is so hard so see my only son lose his personality and life to a shot" (Miller, 2004). Jenny McCarthy, who has a son with autism, published a book *Mother Warriors* with summaries of her interviews with mothers who shared their stories about their children's autism and what they did to help their children recover. All the stories are similar in that parents saw a tremendous change in their children after vaccines. I myself have listened to the similar vaccine stories from almost all the families of children with autism I have worked with.

There are over 4,900 court cases filed by parents who believe vaccines caused their children's autism (Kirby, 2008). There is debate on what ingredient in the vaccines caused autism. Did the mercury preservative thimerosal cause autism? Did the weakened viruses cause the autism? Did the other toxic ingredients in vaccines cause autism? Is it the combination of all the ingredients that brought about the autism? Studies show that as the number of required vaccines increased, the number of children with autism skyrocketed (Miller, 2003).

Vaccines are linked to other conditions as well as autism

Vaccines contain DNA and RNA – carriers of genetic material. Viral RNA enters DNA. This can be in body for years and be responsible for autoimmune disorders such as asthma, diabetes, food allergies and rheumatoid arthritis. There is currently a tragic trend towards deteriorating health in children and adults that is well substantiated by scientific reports. Conditions that are rapidly on the rise are allergic diseases, asthma, eczema, autoimmune diseases and childhood behavioral conditions. Because of the increased need for antibiotics for ear infections and respiratory infections, the immune system is becoming impaired. There are also many syndromes of chemical sensitivity and chronic fatigue disabling millions of young people. There is evidence that vaccination programs may stunt the normal development of the immune system and that there may be a direct relationship between vaccinations and the modern epidemics (Buttram, 2003).

People in general are unaware of the true number of persons, mostly children, who have been permanently damaged or killed by one or more of the vaccines. About 30,000 reports of adverse reactions to vaccines are made to the FDA EVERY YEAR (VAERS). But this number only includes emergency hospitalizations, irreversible injuries, and deaths. These numbers are underestimated because the FDA estimates that 90 percent of doctors don't even report reactions (Thinktwice).

More factors on vaccines

- Vaccines do not guarantee 100% immunity. The vast majority of measles occur in people who have already been immunized. In 1988, 69% of children in the US who got measles were already vaccinated. In 1989, 89% of children in the US who got measles had been vaccinated. It 1995, 56% of measles cases in the US occurred in those who had

received the measles vaccine. During a pertussis outbreak in Ohio, 82% of children who got it had already been vaccinated. When flu strains in the environment match the flue strains in vaccine, the vaccine is only 35% effective and when flu strains in the environment do not match the strains in the flu vaccines, the vaccines is 0% effective (Miller, 2004).
- If vaccines do give immunity, they have not shown to provide lifelong immunity because there has been a shift of the diseases in older age groups. No vaccine has been proven to be safe (Miller, 2004).
- There is a link between early contaminated polio vaccines and the origin of HIV and AIDS and some types of cancers (SV-40 virus) because of the virus being grown in a monkey kidney. In Stephanie Cave's book *What Your Doctor May Not tell you about Children's Vaccinations*, it says, "Experts estimate that between 1954 and 1963, 30 to100 million Americans and 100 more million throughout the world were exposed to the SV-40 virus through ill-conceived polio vaccines. The SV-40 virus can be spread sexually and to the fetus. This can lead to cancer. The AIDs virus was introduced to the human population through this vaccine due to growing polio virus in monkey blood and then injecting it into human blood" (Cave, 2001).
- There are virtually no incidences of autism among the Amish who do not vaccinate their children (Olmsted, 2005).
- There are no recorded cases of autism in the group of 35,000 home-schooled children centered in the Chicago who are not vaccinated for religious reasons (Vaccine Reality).

Are vaccines really safe? Are vaccines even effective? I recommend you read and research for yourself. There are safer vaccine schedules recommended and offered by some doctors and lists of things you can do to boost a child's immune system prior to getting a vaccine. Stephanie Cave provides a safer vaccine schedule in her book *What Your Doctor May No Tell You About Children's Vaccinations*. Can you become exempted from having to get vaccines? Every state allows at least 1 exemption whether it is medical, philosophical or religious. I highly recommend you read more on the subject of vaccine safety for your self. When you do your search find out who the author of the material you examine is. For example, in the book *Autism's False Prophets: Bad Science, Risky Medicine, and the Search for a Cure,* Paul Offit tries to explain how vaccines are not related to autism. But the author invented a vaccine for rotavirus and is associated with Merck pharmaceuticals.

So if vaccines cause autism, then why don't all Children who are vaccinated get autism?

I am not saying vaccines are the sole cause of autism. Research is pointing out that vaccines **contribute to the cause** of autism and other maladies. Dr. Bock (2007) says, "When all of these maladies are combined, in both their mild and virulent forms, they are present in almost half of all American children." Bock believes there are four main reasons for the increase in autism and related conditions.

1. Toxins proliferated
2. Nutrition deteriorated
3. Vaccines increased
4. Ability to Detoxify dwindled

I believe that these factors listed are causing the medical symptoms discussed earlier in children's bodies, which are causing the behavioral deficits and excesses.

So, why are the other half of children that do not develop symptoms of the autism spectrum, have ADHD, allergies, asthma or other conditions when exposed to these factors? What causes some children to have reactions to the vaccines while others do not?

Here are the factors that are believed to influence susceptibility:

- Genetic predisposition
- Illness during a vaccination
- Acceleration of the vaccination schedule beyond the norm, to compensate for missed vaccinations
- Taking an antibiotic at the time of vaccination

- Exposure to other environmental toxins, in combination with the vaccination toxins
- Exposure to toxins in utero
- Nutritional deficits, or excesses
- Exposure to other viruses and bacteria
- Presence of other health insults, including candida problems and allergies
- A family history of autoimmunity and allergies

Dr. Bock believes that children who suffer the most destructive forms of these assaults are in an unlucky nexus of genetics and environment. As most DAN Doctors say "Genetics load the gun, and environment pulls the trigger." However, Bock also says that even the children who have a genetic vulnerability would probably still be able to remain healthy, if they were not exposed to **mercury** (Bock, 2007).

Let's talk about Mercury

Mercury is an element that does not break down. It occurs naturally and is found in oceans, rocks and soils. It becomes airborne when rocks erode, volcanoes erupt and soil decomposes. It then circulates in the atmosphere and is redistributed throughout the environment. Large amounts of mercury also become airborne when coal, oil or natural gas is burned as fuel or mercury-containing garbage is incinerated. Once in the air, mercury can fall to the ground with rain and snow, landing on soils or water bodies, causing contamination. Lakes and rivers are also contaminated when there is a direct discharge of mercury-laden industrial waste or municipal sewage. Once present in these water bodies, mercury accumulates in fish and may ultimately reach the dinner table. Today, mercury is released to the environment from many sources. It is still used in household and commercial products, as well as industrial processes. Coal-fired power plants, incinerators, some manufacturing plants, hospitals, dental offices, schools and even homes have all been found to release mercury. In the home, mercury can be found in fluorescent lights, thermostats, thermometers, and even some children's toys. At school, mercury may be in science and chemistry classrooms, the nurse's office and electrical systems. Mercury is an environmental problem around the world. States with many lakes are especially aware of this because one of the most serious ways people are exposed to mercury is through eating contaminated fish (multiple online dictionaries).

How toxic is Mercury?

- It is scientifically proven that mercury is the most poisonous naturally occurring, non-radioactive, substance on our planet. It damages the central nervous system, endocrine system, brain, kidneys and other organs. Long-term exposure results in brain damage and death.
- Mercury is particularly toxic to fetuses and infants. Women who have been exposed to mercury in pregnancy have sometimes given birth to children with serious birth defects.
- Mercury exposure in young children can have severe neurological consequences, preventing nerve sheaths from forming properly. Mercury inhibits the formation of myelin, the building block protein that forms these sheaths (multiple online dictionaries).
- Dental Amalgams consist of at least 50% mercury. Andrew Cutler put together a book *Amalgam Illness: Diagnosis and treatment, what you can do to get better, how your doctor can help*. Mercury from your metal fillings is causing a long list of bodily disturbances.
- Multiple studies show the amount of mercury present in blood, urine and saliva is positively correlated with the number of dental fillings and that chewing and brushing releases the mercury at a faster rate (FDA Amalgam Health Effects Review; Kingman & Brown, 1998; Mortada & Sobh, 2002; Kraub & M.Deyhle, 1997; Monaci et al. 2002; Bjorkman et al. 1997; Motorkina, 1997).
- The amount of mercury present in breast milk is positively correlated with the number of dental fillings in the mother's mouth (The Dental Wellness Institute).
- About 15 percent of newborns have been exposed to toxic levels of mercury in utero and certain types of fish are the culprits. Sixteen percent of American Women had toxic blood mercury levels. Forty-four states advise women of child-bearing age to limit eating many types of fish (Hawthorne, 2004).

- Mercury in prenatal experience. I have heard a lot of anecdotal case stories from the families I have worked with and also read in books from women who have children with autism make remarks such as they got a flu shot shortly before or during pregnancy. The flu shot contains thimerosal, a mercury preservative. I have heard many mothers say they had dental work done while pregnant. In researching this I found from Generation Rescue that many mothers who have children with high mercury also have high mercury levels. Mercury in the mother's body is passed to the baby during pregnancy. Primary contributors to babies being exposed to mercury in utero: vaccines during pregnancy or immediately before pregnancy; Dental Mercury amalgams; Fish consumption before and during pregnancy.
- In the book *Diagnosis: Mercury: Money, Politics, and Poison,* Jane Hightower demonstrates how important it is to understand mercury's wide-ranging health effects and the urgent need to set stricter limits on the amount of this neurotoxin emitted from coal-fired power plants, that contaminates the fish we eat.

Mercury poisoning symptoms in family members of Children with autism

I have noticed that many children who have autism that I have worked with have a parent who appears to have symptoms of mercury poisoning. They may have a parent with an autoimmune disorder such as diabetes, rheumatoid arthritis and fibromyalgia. I have also noticed a parent with having a high intelligence, having a career in engineering or computer science. Heart attacks, cancer and dementia or Alzheimer's seems to be something common in families who have children with autism. One third of children with autism have a close relative who had an early heart attack (Bock, 2007). I have also noticed that many of the parents of the children I have worked with also have a lot of Asperger's characteristics. Mercury is related to sensory dysfunction, which is very common in people on the autism spectrum. Autism seems to have some kind of link to intelligence. These parents seem to have very high IQs and when I ask them, they admit they are gifted or have had a very easy time in physics, math and chemistry. They also suffer from some kind of health problem which research shows that these health problems may be a result of high levels of mercury. Many of the health problems include chronic fatigue syndrome, autoimmune conditions, allergies, asthma, insomnia, skin rashes, muscle tremors, weight problems such as loss of weight or weight gain, irritable bowel syndrome, Parkinson's disease, panic attacks, anxiety, depression, obsessive compulsiveness, different types of arthritis, fibromyalgia, gastritis, anorexia, bulimia and yeast syndrome (Cutler, 1999).

Mercury and intelligence

Because of my own experience with mercury and my increased intelligence after being exposed; my dad, who had health problems, was an engineer with an IQ of 140; and many of the children I worked with are extremely intelligent and so are their parents, I wonder if mercury exposure has anything to do with increasing one's IQ. I also wonder why so many children with autism have an IQ below 70 while so many others have an IQ above 130.

My theory is that because mercury damages brain neurons, other parts of the brain have to compensate or become more active. Developmental research shows that when children are young, their brains are pruning (neurons are dying) themselves and that this necessary pruning can result in higher intelligence later in life. If the brain is prevented from adequately pruning itself, then there are too many neurons and connections which may make it harder to process information later on (Hirsh—Pasek & Golinkoff, 2003).

In the two long-term studies of children exposed to methyl mercury from breast milk, children exposed to mercury from the breast milk scored higher on developmental tests than formula-fed children. Grandjean and colleagues (1995) found that babies who were exposed to methyl mercury from their mothers' milk had **higher** developmental scores than formula-fed babies. This study suggested "if methyl mercury exposure from human milk had any adverse effect on milestone development in these infants, the effect was compensated for or overruled by advantages associated with nursing." In another study Jensen (2005) found "marginally better neuropsychological performance" in seven year olds who had been exposed to methyl mercury via breast milk.

Mild mitochondrial dysfunction reportedly has been associated with intelligence, because it can increase activity of the brain's NMDA receptors. A large number of receptors can produce increased intelligence (Kirby, 2008). It is estimated that about 10% of children with an autism spectrum condition have an identifiable genetic, neurologic or metabolic disorder, such as fragile X, Down syndrome, Angelman syndrome, San Filippo syndrome, phenylketonuria, Cohen syndrome, and Smith-Lemli-Opitz syndrome. As we learn more about genetics, the number of children with an an autism spectrum condition and an identifiable genetic condition will likely increase (Cohen et al., 2005).

But what about those children who have autism who never talk and have a very low IQ? There is research about mercury causing developmental delays leaving most to assume that "there is no doubt that mercury causes developmental delays" (Bystrianyk, 2008). A study published by CDC in 2007, found that 33 to 59 percent of the children who had an autism spectrum condition also had an intellectual disability (intelligence quotient <=70) (Rice, 2007).

Mercury inhibits the body from being able to excrete other toxins such as lead and arsenic, so when a person who has had damage to their detoxification system, and is exposed to lead or other toxins, those toxins are likely to stay in the body and do damage. Numerous studies have been done showing that lead causes a decline in IQ. Many of the children I have worked with who have had testing for heavy metals, have toxic levels of many metals such as lead, arsenic, aluminum and cadmium. These children with toxic loads of multiple metals appear to have more of the severe expression of autism and have problems in many areas of development. Then there are the children who are exceptional at math, problem solving and reading but they have a problem with socializing and communicating effectively. These children's parents have reported to me that mercury was the only metal that showed up as toxic in their blood tests. I never cease to be amazed when I see a three-year-old child with autism sit down and read a book, even the dictionary. And it is mind-blowing when a child will tell you to the decimal place the answer to a complex math problem within seconds. Perhaps some parts of their brains have compensated for damage that has been done to other parts.

We already know that children with autism have different brain structures than the typical brain. Are the brains of highly intellectual people different than those with average intelligence? Einstein, assumed by many experts to have had Asperger's, is very well known as a genius and when he died his brain was autopsied. Einstein's brain had a higher ratio of glial cells to neurons than normal brains and wider in the area concerned with math and special thinking with Sylvain fissure was almost absent in that brain area (Michael, 2007).

Here are a couple websites to view a video of how mercury can damage brain neurons and cause neuron degeneration.

- http://www.youtube.com/watch?v=XU8nSn5Ezd8
- http://video.google.com/videoplay?docid=-2743601445411193926&q=ucalgary+mercury&hl=en#

Here is a video showing mercury vapor from a dental amalgam

- http://www.youtube.com/watch?v=9ylnQ-T7oiA

More research done on autism Metallothionein dysfunction

There is research showing that autism is associated with dysfunction of multiple chemical imbalances and problems with the methylation process and other abnormalities. Schwartz, 2004 describes that Metallothionein, amino acids proteins is responsible for:

1. Regulate zinc and copper levels in blood.
2. Detoxify Mercury and other harmful metals.
3. Regulate the development and function of the Immune System.
4. Regulate the development and pruning of brain neurons.
5. Prevent yeast overgrowth in the GI tract.

6. Produce enzymes that break down casein and gluten (DPP IV).
7. Respond appropriately to intestinal inflammation.
8. Produce stomach acid.
9. Regulate taste and texture discrimination on the tongue
10. Normalize hippocampal function and behavior control
11. Normalize the development of emotional memory and socialization.

Factors that can disable metallothionein

1. Severe zinc depletion
2. Abnormalities in the Glutathione Antioxidant System
3. A deficiency in cysteine
4. Malfunction of metal regulating elements.
5. Genetic inherited modifications in the structure of the metallothionein proteins (i.e.: mutations). It is likely that autism propensity is not determined by a single genetic defect, but rather by several genetic variances.
6. Toxic metals like Mercury, lead and cadmium. Even excess copper, an essential element, has been shown to temporarily disable the Metallothionein proteins.
7. Pyrrole chemistry disorders
8. Impaired functioning of an antioxidant enzyme called super oxide dismutase (SOD).
9. Free radicals, emotional stress, infection and inflammation may also deplete metallothioneins.

Prenatal testosterone

Simon Baron Cohen (2009), director of autism research center at Cambridge University in the UK has done a lot of research examining the relationship between pre-natal testosterone and social skills. His findings indicate that the higher the prenatal testosterone, the more observable autistic traits. This may explain why autism affects many more boys than girls.

Relationship between Mercury, Testosterone and Glutiathione

In doing a Google search on testosterone, mercury and glutathione this is what I found.

- Testosterone significantly potentiates mercury toxicity. Testosterone greatly enhances the destructive power of mercury.
- Glutathione is an antioxidant that protects cells from toxins.
- Testosterone also inhibits the body's ability to make glutathione.
- David and Marl Geier (2006) found that all children with autism had significantly low levels of glutathione.
- When mercury enters the body, it binds to glutathione.
- Mercury increases testosterone levels while dramatically lowering glutathione levels.
- Yeast, found in almost every child with autism also lowers glutathione.
- Food allergies, found in almost every child with autism, lowers glutathione.
- Mercury can cause yeast syndrome and food allergies.
- The testosterone molecule is also the perfect shape so that when it is combined with mercury the mercury will be tightly bound to the testosterone, making it very difficult to remove from the body with chelators. This may explain why so many children who undergo chelation do not have positive results.
- Dysfunction with Methylation is related to low levels of glutathione

The Geiers theorized that if they were able to temporarily turn off testosterone production with Lupron, they might be able to release these trapped stores of mercury. The Geiers claim to have treated more than 200 patients with Lupron until the testosterone levels normalized, then DMSA to chelate mercury. According to David Geier, there have been incredible changes, "almost like a light switch" as these children make rapid improvements. Treatment of children with autism by Lupron seems to have some unique characteristics. Usually, one injection of Lupron is enough to normalize testosterone levels, but when children with autism were administered Lupron, their testosterone levels often went up. It seemed as if their bodies were loaded with testosterone and as the body's natural production of testosterone was temporarily interrupted it came pouring out of the body's hidden stores. A modified Lupron protocol was created, with testing of testosterone levels guiding more frequent administration of the drug until testosterone levels were normalized. The Geiers have found that the best results are achieved when patients are given a slow-release shot, and a daily injection (Heckenlively, 2008).

What is autism?

Putting the research together, the pieces of the puzzle are coming together for a clearer picture of the mystery of autism. Although the entire autism puzzle is not fully completed, it is clear that not one single thing causes autism. Things that load the gun include: genetic predisposition, mercury exposure, testosterone, allergies, antibiotics, infections, yeast, other heavy metals, problems with methylation, and low levels of glutathione. What can cause the gun to fire? Vaccines. What is autism? Autism results from a blow to the immune system. Once the immune system is damaged, other toxins, viruses and bacteria that enter the body will most likely stay there and do further damage such as to the brain, nervous and endocrine system. The body may develop problems in the intestines with yeast and bacteria, which can lead to leaky gut syndrome, which can lead to increasing food allergies, which can lead to increase in immune deficiency, which can contribute to autistic behavior. What causes the different variations in autism? Maybe a different number of toxins and heavy metals with different amounts, home environment, the number and the degree of food allergies and stages of yeast (there are 4 stages). What causes the different degrees of autism depends on just how much damage has been done to the immune system, brain, nervous and endocrine system.

Toxins everywhere

Hundreds of common household items including children's toys, backpacks, car seats, and even pet products are tainted with lead, arsenic, mercury, cadmium, chromium and other toxins (McCormick, 2009; Healthy Stuff).

- Healthystuff.org tested more than 400 dog and cat products, including chew toys, tennis balls, collars, leashes, and beds and found that more that 45 percent contained detectable levels of one or more hazardous chemicals. Ninety percent of the pet products tested were made in China. They tested pet tennis balls and sporting tennis balls and found that 50 percent of the tennis balls tested had lead.
- Fifty eight percent of the car seats tested contained one or more hazardous chemicals, including PVC, BFRs, and heavy metals. Thirty-one percent contained BFRs. These chemicals can cause adverse health affects on babies and young children.
- More than 60 common back-to-school supplies, including backpacks, pencil cases, binders, and lunchboxes were tested. Tests revealed that 68% contained one or more chemicals of concern. Specifically, 56% were made out of PVC and 22% contained detectable levels of lead.
- More than 100 plastic women's handbags were tested. Lead was found in more than 75%.
- One third of toys tested had high levels of at least one of the following toxins including lead, chlorine, cadmium, arsenic, mercury and bromine.
- To learn more about the toxin content in specific toys and household products visit www.healthystuff.org
- Toxins in the womb. In a WTC study, researchers tested pregnant women from Washington, California, and Oregon and found that every woman tested had BPA, which is a hormone disrupting chemical used to make certain plastics, in plastic water bottles and linings for canned foods. BPA is linked to cancer, early puberty, obesity, reproductive problems and diabetes. The women had at least two Teflon chemicals in their blood. Every woman was found to have mercury in her blood. Every woman had at least four phthalates, which are found in shower curtains, shampoo, soap and other consumer products (Washington TOXICS Coalition).

Prevention

Can autism be prevented? If the blow to the immune system can be prevented, then it makes sense that autism can be prevented.

Factors to look for that may increase the chances of a child developing autism

- Family member with Asperger's or Autism
- Parent or close relative with autoimmune condition
- Parent with high intellect, engineering or computer science
- Parent with symptoms of mercury poisoning
- Mother who has several mercury dental amalgams
- Mother who had a flu vaccine while pregnant
- Mother who consumed a lot of fish while pregnant
- A family member who has had a reaction to vaccines

Methods to protecting the immune system

- Pregnant women should not eat fish. Fish, especially the larger fish like tuna and shark is contaminated with mercury.
- Pregnant women should not have amalgams fillings put in or removed.
- Pregnant women should avoid drinking hot drinks and chewing gum (causing mercury from amalgam fillings to leak out).
- Pregnant women should not get flu vaccines because they contain thimerosal (mercury preservative).
- Pregnant women should avoid drinking from plastic products containing BPA.
- Pregnant women should be aware of the household products containing toxic chemicals.
- Do not give cow's milk or wheat to babies or young children. Casein and gluten seem to contribute to a child's autism.
- If vaccination is absolutely necessary, use a safer vaccine schedule (Stephanie Cave).

- If vaccination is absolutely necessary, make sure child does not have any signs of sickness or infection. Boost child's immune system prior to vaccination by giving them vitamin C, A, and E, selenium and other immune boosters such as Echinacea.
- If there seems to be a genetic predisposition to autism, be extremely cautious of vaccines. Learn all you can do to support the immune system (see suggested readings). Learn all you can about vaccines, their safety and efficacy (see suggested readings.
- Decrease exposure to other toxins.
- Don't cook on cookware made from aluminum and Teflon.
- Don't allow children to play with toys that are painted and made in China (most paint in China contains lead).
- Don't allow babies to put painted toys in their mouths.
- Don't allow children to have or play with jewelry.
- Be aware of possible toxins in other toys and household products.
- Don't eat foods with preservatives, artificial ingredients, or artificial colors.
- Do not eat anything artificial, expecially artificial sweeteners such as Aspartame.
- Eat fresh and organic foods.
- Get a reverse osmosis water filter to filter out heavy metals, bacteria and other toxins out of drinking water.
- Wash hands after handling and playing on treated wood.
- ALWAYS wash hands before eating.

Steps to Autism

Below are two methods of the basic steps that I believe that can lead to the onset of autism.

One method

Prenatal Testosterone and other toxins=> Prenatal and/or Environmental Mercury Exposure => Glutathione Dysfuntion => Yeast overgrowth => Food allergies and sensitivities => Stress on immune system => Infections => Antibiotics => Increase in yeast overgrowth => Increase in food allergies => Poor immune system => Vaccines => TOTAL BLOW TO THE IMMUNE SYSTEM => AUTISM

Another method

Pre-natal Mercury exposure => Increase in testosterone => Glutathione dysfunction => Inability to excrete other toxins that enter the body (lead, arsenic, aluminum, more mercury...) => Toxins do damage to immune system and specific parts of the body including the brain and intestines => Infections => Antibiotics =>Yeast overgrowth => Food allergies => Poor immune system functioning => Vaccines => TOTAL BLOW TO THE IMMUNE SYSTEM => AUTISM

My children prevented from autism

My first child, a boy, was extremely active in the womb, always kicking, punching and squirming. He was a very intense baby, didn't sleep well, and always wanted to be bounced and rocked. My husband and I had to take turns every night rocking and bouncing him to keep him from crying. He was very sound sensitive and would jerk his little newborn body whenever a loud noise came, and even at the sound of a plastic bag being rattled his body looked like it convulsed. Note the clues from infancy.

He met all of his milestones early. I have recorded all of his first words and milestones. He was holding his head up at one month old. He sat up a week before turning five months old and he walked at 10 months. He even had remarkable fine motor skills, using a perfect pincer grasp at six months old noticing the tiniest little strings on the floor carefully and precisely picking them up. He had 14 words he regularly spoke by 12 months of age. By 18 months, he had 70 words and could count to five and recite some of the alphabet. By the time he was 27 months old he was asking why and where questions. By the time he was four years old he could do math on a first grade level. My son is very systematic and logical in his thinking. Several people have commented to me they think he is gifted.

I notice a few characteristics of Asperger's such as the literal perception, extreme logical thinking and sound and touch sensitivity. Sometimes when he hears something unpleasant he will squint his eyes and quiver. He has always had an extreme fascination in robots. He has always enjoyed taking everything apart that he can find. He has an intense curiosity about how things work. When he learned how to walk at 10 months he emptied every drawer and cabinet in the house.

He is an excessive question asker – constantly asking questions all day long. Although he has a few characteristics of Asperger's, he has an incredible ability to make friends. I am always intrigued, impressed and astonished by how much he loves people, and how easy it is for him to befriend anyone of any age and in any group size. He doesn't think about it, he just joins in and fits in. The other kids seem to really like him. He delights in people. My son has also always loved to pretend play, pretending to be a robot or something else and always wanting someone else to pretend play with him as well. My son wakes up in the mornings describing every detail of all the dreams he had with such enthusiasm and will go on and on about his dreams. I find his dreams to be very fascinating.

Before I got pregnant with him, I frequently ate tuna fish. I probably ate five cans of tuna fish per week while in college. I craved tuna fish and it was easy to carry along with me to the university. When I found out that there was a warning for pregnant women to avoid eating tuna fish because of the high levels of mercury, I stopped eating it. This led me to do research on mercury and I found out the mercury was related to autism. The more I read, the more everything began to make sense to me about my childhood, my Dad who had Asperger's, Parkinson's disease, fungal infections and terrible allergies, my being exposed to mercury in the broken thermometer, eating fish on a regular basis, and that measles shot before my life turned upside down resulting in a brain change and health problems including hypoglycemia, endometriosis, hyperthyroidism, and Asperger's.

Since I had so many parents of children with autism telling me that they believed vaccines caused their children's autism, I read as many books on the topic I could find. I prayed for the truth and for guidance on whether or not to vaccinate my son. My husband and I decided not to vaccinate our son. I felt that he had the genetic predisposition to have a reaction to the vaccine since I had a reaction to a measles shot when I was 10. I felt that there were already large amounts of mercury in my body and that I needed to learn everything I could to support my baby's immune system.

Since my son was an infant, he easily got carsick. I related to that because I easily got carsick as well. My son and I both are not able to tolerate swinging or spinning without getting sick. I did not allow him to have casein or gluten products until he was 18 months old. When he was almost two, I noticed a rash on his lower belly. A coworker, who also has a son with autism who had a severe reaction to his vaccines, told me that it looked like yeast. I gave my son probiotics and put antifungal cream on his skin. The rash went away. I decided to order a few home-testing kits that tested for heavy metals in urine. My son tested very high for mercury. I tested very high for mercury.

I noticed my-two-year old son, was frequently sneezing, coughing and had a constant stuffy nose. He always had rough skin and eczema on his belly and legs. I took wheat out of his diet and most of the eczema went away. I noticed a pattern that whenever he ate ice cream, like at a birthday party or for a rare special treat, the next day he would run a low grade fever and cry because his legs hurt. When he was four years old, I took him to a DAN doctor to have his blood tested for allergies. When the doctor was evaluating him, I told the doctor about my symptoms of mercury poisoning as well as my son's allergies and yeast problems. With this in mind, I asked the doctor if he thought my son would have developed autism if I had gotten him vaccinated. He answered, "Most likely." His blood tests revealed one food allergy and 17 food sensitivities. What would have happened to his immune system if I allowed him to be injected with a vaccine made of eggs, along with all the other toxic ingredients in the vaccine and the virus itself, and fed him cow's milk or his other allergic foods? His immune system may have been blown. He also had his toenails studied because they had always looked defective. The toenail tested positive for yeast.

I do everything I can to support my sons immune system. I give him daily doses of vitamin C, probiotic, cod liver oil and flax seed oil. When he gets sick I make a concentrated tea of specific herbs and have him take a tablespoon of it every ten minutes. I have a record of every instance he has been sick, how long it lasted, what the symptoms were and what I did for it. Before I discovered herbal remedies, I allowed him to take an antibiotic one time for an upper-respiratory infection. While on the antibiotic, I noticed big red patches on his bottom with white stuff. This was a terrible yeast rash. Wow, I can't believe how much yeast grew on him after a couple days of antibiotics. I learned how to prevent ear infections and respiratory infections by continual support of the immune system because I didn't want him to have to need antibiotics again. And he hasn't needed since then.

Referring to the steps to autism method one, my son went through every step until the vaccine part. I strongly feel that if I had my son vaccinated, he would have developed the severe expression of autism. One time when his yeast was really bad he began to stim running back and fourth flapping. I treated that yeast with all the natural products such as oregano oil and grapefruit seed extract plus probiotics and the rash went away. I suspected my son had genetic predisposition to develop autism because of my and my Dad's Aspergers and the prenatal exposure to mercury, which I think may have contributed to his allergies and yeast.

When I was pregnant with my second child, she didn't squirm, kick and punch my insides the way my son did. I thought it was because she was a girl and girls were much gentler than boys. Well, I think fetal behavior is a great predictor of a child's personality and temperament. My son is a very intense and dramatic person while my daughter is a very calm and quiet person.

When my first daughter was born she was very quiet, peaceful and a good sleeper. She met her milestones on time or a little above average. She had 12 words by 12 months of age and 40 words by 18 months. She was able to speak in simple sentences by 24 months. Her motor skills development such as holding her head up (2 months) and crawling (8 months) and walking (12 months) occurred at average age. She was able to pedal and steer a tricycle at 20 months of age. People have described her as being very graceful and extremely coordinated. My son on the other hand, has been described as somewhat clumsy. My daughter did not receive any vaccines.

When she had just turned two, I found her sucking on a small battery that came out of a children's toothbrush. She had terrible diarrhea for several months afterwards. Batteries contain many different toxins are very high in cadmium. When I tested her urine, the test revealed very high levels of cadmium. My daughter has a few characteristics of Asperger's. She is drastically sensory sensitive to fabrics. One day, I required her to wear socks because it was cold outside. I knew she didn't like socks, but I thought better for her to wear them than to have freezing cold feet. Well, she cried hysterically the entire time we were outside screaming "IT HURTS, MY SOCK HURTS!" When I was a kid, I remember how aggravating my socks were so I haven't made her wear them anymore. She also refuses to wear any clothing that feels "too tight."

My daughter has some difficulty making friends. When we are in social situations and there are other children, she will either stand away while watching them or she will go off and play by herself. She has always been uncomfortable around people in general. When she was an infant she would not tolerate anybody looking at her or holding her other than me, her Dad and her Nana. Most people perceive her to be extremely shy and bashful. There are two little girls that are a few years older than her that took a liking to her. Then my daughter became fixated on them and those two girls are all my daughter wants to talk about. This is something I did when I was a little kid – that is fixate on particular people and talk about them excessively.

Although my daughter is uncomfortable in social situations and around other kids, she plays rather well with her older brother and younger sister. She has an incredible memory and will frequently mention things that happened a year or more ago in her life. My daughter is an excellent problem solver and enjoys doing puzzles and shape sorters. She is very good at understanding cause and effect and making inferences and predicting outcomes. She has always had a strong interest in babies and when she sees one in public she gets so happy shrieking "MOMMY MOMMY, THERE'S A BABY!!!!" She frequently asks me when I am going to have another baby. Whenever we see a newborn she tells me that she wants a baby like that. She also has a great interest in animals of all kinds. She is very good with animals and handles them very well, especially baby animals such as rabbits, kittens and puppies. It amazes me how the animals take a liking to her. I do a lot of role-play to help her learn social skills.

There was a point in time when she wouldn't even look at another person, not even her aunt, cousins or grandmother. With role-play and social stories she will say hi to most people who say hi to her and thank you when someone gives her a compliment. There have been times when I would ask her if she wanted to play with the other kids and she would respond "I don't know how" or "help me." I tell her I understand how she feels but it is possible to learn how if she wanted to. I try to get her playing next to other children and then help her find out about the other children by asking them questions. She has learned to imitate her older brother's social skills in some situations, but I can tell it doesn't come natural to her.

My daughter has an excellent immune system and does not seem to have any allergies. She has never had any infection and when she gets a cold, it is very minor and she completely recovers very quickly. I wonder how her immune system would be if I hadn't followed through with all the research on keeping an immune system in good shape or if she were vaccinated. She has had several yeast rashes since she was born. I do everything I can to keep her immune system healthy including giving her daily vitamin C, all natural multi-vitamin, vitamin D on rainy or cloudy days when she doesn't get any sun light, probiotic and cod liver old and/or flax seed oil. I have taught her about eating healthy, especially organic vegetables and fruits.

My third baby is only one year old as I write this. She has not met her language milestones like her older two siblings, she had five words when she turned 12 months old. She began walking when she was almost 14 months old. Research shows that children who have older siblings usually tend to speak at a later age. She is a very affectionate child, loves to be hugged and cuddled. She absolutely adores books and is frequently bringing me a book to read to her. How can I not stop what I am doing to sit on the floor with her in my lap to read her a book she brought me? I love my kids.

My third child was exposed to higher levels of mercury, I think, because one of my dental fillings broke when I was pregnant with her and another one broke when she was a couple months old. I did extensive research on this and found the studies done on infants exposed to higher levels of mercury in the breast milk scored higher on developmental exams later in life than bottled fed babies. I decided to continue breast-feeding her and wait to get my dental amalgams fixed. She developed eczema on her arms shortly after she began eating baby food. I did a food elimination diet trying to determine what she was allergic to. I wasn't able to get the eczema to go away so I decided to try eliminating all non-organic foods from her diet. Three days on a strict organic diet, her eczema completely disappeared. There really is a difference in organic food compared to non-organic food. After she as a year old I went to a mercury free dentist to have all my dental amalgams safely removed and replaced with a non-mercury composite fillings. Then I did a three month body detox including colon cleanse, parasite cleanse, kidney cleanse, natural chelation, and liver and gallbladder cleanse. I wanted to do this cleanse before getting pregnant again with our fourth child.

I don't really think any of my kids have Asperger's syndrome although they may have more characteristics than typical kids. In order to have it or not, I believe a person would have a certain number to a certain degree. My kids are still young, so time will also tell if they have it or not. I don't really think the label is that important in most cases, it is a word to be able to communicate to other people what the problem is. Since I home school my kids, I don't think an evaluation is necessary. I try my best to keep my children away from toxins. But it seems that research is showing just about everything is toxic. I try not to flip out whenever I read another research study showing another product is harmful for human health.

Hope

Since many people with Asperger's do have symptoms of mercury poisoning – whether the mercury caused the Asperger's or the Asperger's contributed to the poor mercury detoxification, they can learn methods of supporting their immune systems, taking the right supplements, watch what they eat and decrease the amount of toxins they are exposed to in order to feel better. The book *Amalgam Illness, diagnosis and treatment, what you can do to get better, how your doctor can help* by Andrew Cutler is an amazingly informative book on how to treat mercury poisoning symptoms. *Lessons from the Miracle Doctors* by John Barron is a wonderful source for learning to detox the body and decrease the amount of toxins you are exposed to.

Children with autism can make remarkable progress with different types of therapies and biomedical interventions. A parent with a child who has autism should find a DAN doctor to get comprehensive testing to see exactly what biological deficits and excesses, food and environmental allergies, test for yeast and allow the DAN doctor to help re-balance the child's body. At the same time, the child can receive ABA therapy for help with improving cognition, language skills and social skills. Continue to read and search, gain as much knowledge as you can. Search the library and the Internet. Research is being published everyday. Children with autism need a very stable life with structured routines. There is hope. Children can be prevented from developing the severe expression of autism and the ones who have already developed it can be recovered to the best of their potential. Tell everybody you know.

"We each have our own way of living in the world, together we are like a symphony. Some are the melody, some are the rhythm, and some are the harmony. It all blends together, we are like a symphony, and each part is crucial. We all contribute to the song of life." ...Sondra Williams

Suggested Readings
Understanding autism and treatment

- *Healing the New Childhood Epidemics: Autism, Adhd, Asthma, and Allergies. The Groundbreaking Program for the 4-A Disorders* by Kenneth Bock and Cameron Stauth (2007)
- *My Cure for Autism: A Real Answer* by P. Dwividi (2008)
- *A Child's Journey out of Autism: One Family's Story of Living in Hope and Finding a Cure* by Leeann Whiffen (2009)
- *Healing and Preventing Autism: A complete Guide* by Jenny McCarthy and Dr. Jerry Kartzinel (2009)
- *Mother Warriors: A Nation of Parents Healing Autism Against All Odds* by Jenny McCarthy (2009)

- *He's Not Autistic But...: How We Pulled Our Son From the Mouth of the Abyss* by Tenna Merchant (2007)
- *Unraveling the Mystery of Autism and Pervasive Developmental Disorder: A Mother's Story of Research & Recovery* by Karyn Seroussi with a foreword by Bernard Rimland (2002)
- *Children with Starving Brains: A Medical Treatment Guide for Autism Spectrum Disorder* by Jaquelyn McCandless Teresa Binstock, and Jack Zimmerman (2009)
- *Changing the Course of Autism: A Scientific Approach for Parents and Physicians* by Bryan Jepson Katie Wright, and Jane Johnson (2007)
- *Nourishing Hope for Autism: Nutrition Intervention for Healing Our Children* by Julie Matthews (2008)
- *Autism and Its Medical Management: A Guide for Parents and Professionals* by Michael G., M.D. Chez (2009)

Vaccines

- *Vaccines: Are they really safe and Effective?* By Neil Z. Miller (2004)
- *What Your Doctor May not tell you about Childhood Vaccines* by Stephanie Cave with Deborah Mitchell (2001)
- *Vaccines, Autism and Childhood Disorders: Crucial Data that could save your child's life* by Neil Z. Miller forwarded by Bernard Rimland (2003)
- *Evidence of Harm: Mercury in Vaccines and the Autism Epidemic: A Medical Controversy* by David Kirby (2006)
- *When Your Doctor is Wrong, Hepatitis B Vaccine and Autism* by Judy Converse (2002)
- *A Shot in the Dark* by H. Coulter (1991)
- *Vaccine Safety Manual for Concerned Families and Health Practitioners: Guide to Immunization Risks and Protection* by Neil Z. Miller and Russell, M.D. Blaylock (2008)
- *The Virus and the Vaccine: Contaminated Vaccine, Deadly Cancers, and Government Neglect* by Debbie Bookchin and Jim Schumacher (2005)

- *Vaccinations: A Thoughtful Parent's Guide: How to Make Safe, Sensible Decisions about the Risks, Benefits, and Alternatives* by Aviva Jill Romm (2001)
- *Raising a Vaccine Free Child* by Wendy Lydall (2009)
- www.thinktwice.com

Immune System Support

- *Superimmunity for Kids: What to Feed your children to keep them healthy now – and prevent disease in their future* by Leo Galland with Dian Cincin Buchman (1988)
- *The ABC Herbal: A Simplified Guide to Natural Health Care for Children* by Steven H. Horne (2005)
- *How to Raise a Healthy Child in Spite of Your Doctor* Robert S. Mendelsohn (1987)
- *The Immune System Cure: Optimize Your Immune System in 30 Days-The Natural Way!* by Lorna Vanderheaghe (2000)

Detox

- *Lessons from the Miracle Doctors: A Step by Step Guide to Optimun Health and Relief from Catastrophic Illness* by Jon Barron (2008)
- *Amalgam Illness diagnosis and treatment: What you can do to get better How your doctor can help* by Andrew Hall Cutler (1999).

Mercury websites

- http://www.toxicmercuryamalgam.com/index.htm - The Dangers of Mercury
- http://www.ec.gc.ca/MERCURY/SM/EN/sm-mcp.cfm?SELECT=SM
- http://www.youtube.com/watch?v=XU8nSn5Ezd8
- http://video.google.com/videoplay?docid=-2743601445411193926&q=ucalgary+mercury&hl=en#
- http://www.youtube.com/watch?v=9ylnQ-T7oiA

References

Autism Conferences of America (2004). Rate of Autism. Retrieved November 7th, 2009. http://www.autism-conferences.com/services.html

Bauman, ML. & Kemper, TL. (2003). The neuropathology of the autism spectrum disorders: what have we learned? *Novartis Foundation Symposium, 251*, 112-122.

Baron-Cohen, S., Auyeung, B. Ashwin,. E., Knickmeyer, .R., Taylor, k. & Hackett, G. (2009). Fetal Testosterone and Autistic Traits. Br J Psychology Feb;100(Pt 1):1-22. Epub 2008 Jun 10. http://www.ncbi.nlm.nih.gov/pubmed/18547459

Boulet, S.L, Coyle, C.A. & Schieve L.A. (2009). Health Care Use and Health and Functional Impact of Developmental Disabilities Among US Children, 1997-2005. Arch Pediatr Adolesc Med. January:163(1)19-26.

Boyle C, Van Naarden Braun K, Yeargin-Allsopp M. The Prevalence and the Genetic Epidemiology of Developmental Disabilities. In: Genetics of Developmental Disabilities. Merlin Butler and John Meany eds. 2005.

Bystrianyk, R. (2008). Learning and Developmental Disabilities linked to Environmental Toxins. Health Sentinal. Retrieved November 10th, 2009. http://www.healthsentinel.com/joomla/index.php?option=com_content&view=article&id=2442:learning-and-developmental-disabilities-linked-to-environmental-toxins&catid=5:original&Itemid=24

Cave, S. & Mitchell, D. (2001). What Your Doctor May Not Tell You About Children's Vaccinations. Warner Books.

Centers for Disease Control and Prevention. (2009). Autism Spectrum Disorders (ASDS). Data and Statistics. CDC Statement on Autism Data. Center for Disease Control and Prevention. Your online source for credible health information. Retrieved November 7ᵗʰ, 2009. http://www.cdc.gov/ncbddd/autism/data.html

Cohen, D., Pichard, N., Tordjman, S., Baumann, C., Burglen, L., Excoffier, E., Lazar, G., Mazet, P., Pinquier, C., Verloes, A., Héron, D. (2005) Specific genetic disorders and autism: clinical contribution towards their identification Journal of Autism and Developmental Disorders. Feb;35(1):103-16.Retrieved November 7ᵗʰ, 2009. http://www.ncbi.nlm.nih.gov/pubmed/15796126

Courchesne, E., Karns, C.M., Davis, H.R., Ziccardi, R.,Carper, R.A., Tigue, Z.D., Chisum, H.J., Moses, P., Pierce, K., Lord, C., Lincoln, A.J., Pizzo, S., Schreibman L., Haas, R.H., Akshoomoff, N.A., Courchesne, R.Y. (2001) Unusual brain growth patterns in early life in patients with autistic disorder: An MRI study. Neurology 57:245–254.

Cutler, A. H. (1999). Amalgam Issness diagnosis and treatment. What you can do to get better. How yourdoctor can help. Sammanish, WA.

Bock, K. & Staugth (2008). Healing the New Childhood Epidemics. Autism, ADHD, Asthma and Allergies. The Groundbreaking Program for the 4-A Disorders.Ballantine books. P 18.-19, 56-57

Buttram, H. E. (2003). Forward II in Vaccines: Are they really safe and effective by Neil Miller. New Atleantean Press. P. 8

FDA Amalgam Health Effects Review DAMS, Inc. Retrieved November 10ᵗʰ, 2009. http://www.flcv.com/fdarev.html

Frith,C. (2003). What do imaging studies tell us about the neural basis of autism? Novartis Foundation Symptoms, 251, 149-166.

Gaffney, G.R., Tsai, L.Y., Kuperman, S. & Minchin, S. (1987). Cerebella structure in autism. *American Journal of Discovery Child, 141*, 1330-1332.

Geier, M. & Geier, D. (2006). Dr. Mard Geier & Dr. David Geier discuss mercury & testosterone in autism: part 3. Retrieved November 10th, 2009. http://video.google.com/videoplay?docid=-2862868836336117925#

Grandjean, P. Weihe, P. & White, R.F. (1995). Milestone Development in infants exposed to Methylmercury from Human Milk. Journal of Toxicology Clinical Toxicology. 1992;30(1):49-61. http://www.ncbi.nlm.nih.gov/pubmed/7603642?dopt=Abstract

Hawthorne., M (2004). New Mercury Warning for Pregnant Women, 1 in 7 newborns may be affected!. Chicago Tribune. International Indian Treaty Council. Retrieved November 10th, 2009. http://www.treatycouncil.org/new_page_5211421311.htm

Healthy Stuff.org Researching Toxic Chemicals in Everyday Products

Heckenlively, K. (2008). Mercury, Testosterone and Autism – A really Big Idea! Age of Autism. Retrieved November 10th, 2009. http://www.ageofautism.com/2008/04/mea-culpa-mea-m.html

Hirsh-Pasek, K. & Golinkoff R.M. (2003). Einstein Never Used Flash Cards: How our Children Really Learn and why They Need to Play More and Memorize Less. Rodal, Inc

Hunsinger, D.M., Nguyen, T., Zebraski, S.E., Raffa, R.B. (2000). Is there a basis for novel pharmacotherapy of autism? *Life Science, 67,* 1667-1682.

Jensen, T.K., Grandjean, P., Jorgensen, E.B., White, R.F., Debes, F., Weihe, P. (2005). Effects of breast feeding on neuropsychological development in a community with methylmercury exposure from seafood. J Expo Anal Environ Epidemiol. 2005 Jan 26. http://www.nature.com/jes/journal/v15/n5/abs/7500420a.html

Kennedy, R.F. & Kirby, D. (2009). Vaccine Court: Autism Debate Continues. The Huffington Post. Retrieved November 8th, 2009. http://www.huffingtonpost.com/robert-f-kennedy-jr-and-david-kirby/vaccine-court-autism-deba_b_169673.html?view=print

Kirby, D. (2008). The Next Big Autism Bomb: Are 1 in 50 kids potentially at risk? The Huffington Post. Retrieved November 8th, 2009. http://www.huffingtonpost.com/david-kirby/the-next-big-autism-bomb-b_93627.html

Kirby, D. (2008). Government Concedes Vaccine-autism case in Federal Court. Now What? The Huggington Post. Febuary 25th, 2008. Retrieved November 10th, 2009. http://www.huffingtonpost.com/david-kirby/government-concedes-vacci_b_88323.html

Lucarelli, S., Frediani, T., Zingoni, A.M., Ferruzzi, F., Giardini, O., Quintieri, F., Barbato, M., D'Eufemia, P. & Cardi, E. (1995). Food allergy and infantile autism. *Panminerva Medicine, 37,* 137-141.

McCormick, L. W. (2009). Report Finds Toxins Common in Products for Children, Pets. Comsumer Affairs News. Retrieved December 19th, 2009. http://www.consumeraffairs.com/news04/2009/09/toxins.html

Michael (2007). The Strange Case of Einsein's Brain. Nomadic Nation. Retrieved November 10th, 2009. http://www.nomadicnation.com/articles/science/the-strange-case-of-einsteins-brain/

Miller, N. (2003). Vccines, Autism and Childhood Disorders: Crucial Data that could save your child's life. New Atlantean Press.

Miller, N. (2004). Vaccines: Are they really safe and effective? New Atlantean Press. P. 29, 42, 86, 94.

Nash, M.J. & Bonesteel, A. (2002). The secrets of autism. *Time, 159.*

Olmstead, D. (2005). No Autism for Unvaccinated Amish? The Age of Autism: A pretty Big Secret. Infowars.com. Retrieved November 10th, 2009. http://www.infowars.com/articles/science/autism_none_for_unvaccinated_amish.htm

Rice, C. (2007). Prevalence of Autism Spectrum Disorders --- Autism and Developmental Disabilities Monitoring Network, 14 Sites, United States, 2002. Autism and Developmental Disabilities Monitoring Network Surveillance Year 2002 Principal Investigators February 9, 2007 / 56(SS01);12-28 Retrieved November 7th, 2009. http://www.cdc.gov/mmwr/preview/mmwrhtml/ss5601a2.htm

Rimland, B. (2003). Vitamin B6 and Magnesium in the Treatment of Autism. In S.E. Edelson and R. Bernard (Eds.), *Treating Autism* (pp 25-28). San Diego CA: Autism Research Institute.

Schwartz, A. (2004). Causes, Etiology and Biochemical Abnormalities in autism. The Nutrition Notebook. Retrieved November 10th, 2009. http://www.springboard4health.com/notebook/health_autism2.html

The Dental Wellness Institute. Mercury Detoxification, Chronic Mercury Poisoning and Amalgam Fillings. References Articles with Abstracts. Retrieved November 10th, 2009. http://www.dentalwellness4u.com/products/refdoc.html

Thinktwice: Global Vaccine Institute. Immunization Ploys. Are Parents being Manipulated? 30 Tactics used by the medical profession to hoodwink the public. Retrieved November 10th, 2009. http://www.thinktwice.com/ploys.htm

Treffery, Darold, A., Wallace &Gregory, L. (2002). Islands of genius. Scientific American, 286, 76-86.

Turner, J. & Odle, T. (2009). Chelation Therapy. Answers.com. Retrieved November 8th, 2009. http://www.answers.com/topic/chelation-therapy

Vaccine Adverse Event Reporting (VAERS). Vaccine Adverse Event Reporting System. Centers for Disease Control and Prevention, online source for credible Health Information. Retrieved November 10th, 2009. http://www.cdc.gov/vaccinesafety/Activities/vaers.html

Vaccine Reality. Safe or Effective Children that aren't vaccinated don't get Autism. Retrieved November 10th, 2009. http://www.taxtyranny.ca/images/HTML/Vaccines/153Vaccines.html

Washingtons TOXIC Coalition. Groundbreaking Study Finds Babies Exposed To Chemicals Before They Are Born. Chemicals found in plastics, non-stick products, sports water bottles, and beverage cans detected in bodies of pregnant women. November 16th, 2009. Retrieved December 19th, 2009. http://www.watoxics.org/news/pressroom/press-releases/groundbreaking-study-finds-babies-exposed-to-chemicals-before-they-are-born

Yeargin-Allsopp. M. (2007). Press Release. CDC Online Newsroom. CDC Releases New Data on Autism Spectrum Disorders (ASDs) from Multiple Communities in the United State. Centers for Disease Control and Prevention. Your online source for credible health information. Retrieved November 7th, 2009. http://www.cdc.gov/media/pressrel/2007/r070208.htm